THE
TOASTMASTER'S
HANDBOOK

THE
TOASTMASTER'S
HANDBOOK

by

Herbert V. Prochnow

A. Thomas & Co.

BLACKPOOL

Original English edition published by Prentice Hall Inc., 70 Fifth Ave, New York, N.Y. Copyright 1949 in United States of America by Prentice Hall Inc.

Second printing, June 1949
Third printing, July 1949
Fourth printing, September 1949
Fifth printing, December 1949
Sixth printing, April 1950
Seventh printing, January 1951
Eighth printing, February 1951
Ninth printing, January 1952
First British edition, July 1953

PRINTED IN GREAT BRITAIN BY
MORRISON AND GIBB LIMITED, LONDON AND EDINBURGH

PREFACE

EVERY month many thousands of luncheons, dinners, conventions, discussion groups and other types of meetings are held in this country. Some one person, whether he is called the chairman, president or toastmaster, is responsible for every meeting, and particularly for the program.

This book aims to bring to the person in charge of a meeting a great wealth of helpful material to assure the success of his work and the capable discharge of his important responsibilities. For the responsibilities of the chairman or toastmaster are extremely important. Consider the thousands of community organizations; church groups; chambers of commerce; Rotary, Kiwanis, Lions and Optimists Clubs; parent-teachers associations; conventions; and many other groups which hold meetings attended by millions of persons every year. Many individuals attend forty or fifty luncheon discussions alone each year. The number of hours spent in these meetings approaches fantastic figures. If the plans for the meetings are slipshod and careless, the waste of time in these vast audiences is certain to be as great as it is inexcusable.

The author believes that nothing should be left undone by the chairman or toastmaster which will assure those attending that they will be well rewarded for the time spent at any meeting. Time is one of the most precious assets each of us possesses. It is the responsibility of the chairman or toastmaster to see that not one minute of it is wasted. That requires preparation. To paraphrase Emerson: There is no such thing as competent performance without complete preparation. There is nothing better than a well-prepared and planned "impromptu" introduction! Pytheas said of the orations of the great Demosthenes, "His impromptus smell of the lamp."

The chapters of this book are arranged to provide a wide variety of practical material suitable for use on many occasions. Chapters 1,

2 and 3 deal with the responsibilities and techniques of the toast-master, and they present a concise and frank statement of the fundamental duties of the toastmaster. Chapter 4 gives dozens of illustrations of all kinds of actual introductions used by many exceptionally able chairmen. The reader also will find in this chapter illustrations of remarks made in beginning a discussion period, presenting gifts, and introducing a mayor to a convention; a mayor's welcoming speech; invocations; and statements suitable for various types of occasions. The precise techniques used by some of the most capable chairmen are fully illustrated and provide a great deal of valuable and useful material.

Chapter 5 gives a large number of examples of actual responses to introductions which have been made by well-known speakers. Chapter 6 contains scores of interesting stories which have been used by speakers, many of whom are distinguished and nationally known Americans. It is possible to use these stories effectively in introductions and speeches.

Chapter 7 includes over four hundred epigrams which will help to give fire and sparkle to introductions. It is believed that Chapter 8 is especially unique and may be the source of much worthwhile material for the toastmaster. For example, the toastmaster may be called upon to introduce a musician, businessman, teacher or doctor. In this chapter there are hundreds of quotations relating to these and many other professions and occupations, as well as quotations covering different occasions such as luncheons, dinners and wedding anniversaries. Finally, in Chapter 9 has been included an extensive collection of carefully selected humorous stories which the toastmaster may use to suit his varied needs.

It is believed this book presents a great deal of material never before included and so presented in any book for toastmasters. It is obviously a handbook not only for toastmasters, but also for all public speakers, ministers, attorneys, teachers, salesmen, and others who have opportunities to use a practical, helpful reference work of this character. The general reader will likewise find entertaining stories in a number of chapters.

H. V. P.

CONTENTS

1. Responsibilities of the Toastmaster   3

2. Techniques of the Toastmaster   18

3. Ten Fundamentals for the Toastmaster   34

4. Illustrations of Actual Introductions   35

5. Illustrations of How Speakers Respond to Toastmasters   117

6. Interesting Stories from Introductions and Speeches   135

7. Epigrams and Witticisms   184

8. Quotations for Many Different Occasions   208

9. Humorous Stories for All Occasions   293

THE
TOASTMASTER'S
HANDBOOK

A ¥

CHAPTER I

RESPONSIBILITIES OF THE TOASTMASTER

In 1891, I. H. Browley said that—

"These dinner speeches tire me; they are tedious, flat and stale;
From a hundred thousand tables comes a melancholy wail,
As a hundred thousand banqueters sit up in evening dress
And salute each moldy chestnut with a signal of distress."

It is the specific responsibility of the toastmaster to see that the speeches are not tedious, flat and stale and that there is no reason for a melancholy wail from a hundred thousand banqueters. A thoroughly competent toastmaster assumes charge of everything from the arrangement of the program to the ventilation of the room.

Plan the Complete Program

Sometimes the chairman of a meeting has complete charge of the program and assigns to the toastmaster simply the responsibility of introducing the speaker. However, for purposes of this book, and in order to make the discussion comprehensive and thorough, we shall assume that one person, whether he has the title of chairman, president, master of ceremonies, or toastmaster, has complete charge of every detail of the program. The responsibilities may be divided among several persons but this discussion will cover all of them.

Someone has said that if you sit in one of the great sidewalk cafes of Paris long enough, everyone in the world will pass your table. It may also be said that if you will take an active part in your community in the parent-teachers association, church work, the Rotary, Kiwanis, Lions, Toastmasters, Optimists, university club, trade and professional associations, the association of commerce, the country club, the woman's club, Red Cross, Boy Scouts, or any one of a thousand worthwhile community activities, you will be called upon to plan a program, introduce speakers, and conduct a meeting. Each one of us finds that sooner or later—for better or for worse—he is called upon to serve as chairman or toastmaster of a meeting.

In Shakespeare's *Midsummer Night's Dream* Quince says to Snug, who was given the lion's part in the play, "You may do it extempore, for it is nothing but roaring." And roaring may be all right for an audience which is satisfied with noise. But what audience is satisfied simply with noise, and who wants simply to be a lion? The person who conducts a program may do it extemporaneously. He may handle the meeting in an off-the-cuff manner, hoping that everything will go well. However, managing a program for an intelligent audience in this way is to invite disaster.

Moreover, any chairman who will bring together one hundred persons, for example, for a luncheon for an hour and a half and fail to prepare for that hour and a half by checking every detail—the luncheon, the speaker, the introduction, the comfort of the audience and the speaker—has simply robbed, the word is robbed, one hundred persons of one hundred and fifty hours of time. There is a colossal waste of time in luncheons, dinners, conventions and meetings of all kinds because of inefficient and incompetent management, and because of inadequate preparation by program chairmen and program committees. Ten hours of thorough, hard work by a program chairman may make ten hundred worthwhile hours for an audience of 1,000 men, each of whom gives one hour of precious time. A person who wastes the time of others robs them of a portion of life itself.

Cicero said regarding Antonius, "All his speeches were, in appearance, the unpremeditated effusion of an honest heart; and yet, in reality, they were preconceived with so much skill that the judges were not so well prepared as they should have been to withstand the force of them!" In the same manner a program may proceed so smoothly and efficiently that it appears wholly extemporaneous; and yet, in reality, it has been prepared with so much skill that the audience is almost unaware of the reasons for its effectiveness.

Subjects for the Program

The chairman must assume responsibility for the complete program. Nothing short of this is adequate. One of the first requirements is to determine the nature of the subjects which the organization wishes discussed. This will necessarily depend largely upon the particular interests of those composing the group. Business, economic, social and political conditions may all be factors influencing the choice of subjects for discussion.

Members of organizations are often asked to express their opinions verbally or in answer to written questionnaires regarding the types of programs they desire, such as travel and illustrated lectures, political discussions, scientific addresses and humorous speeches. They are also asked to submit names of possible speakers, preferably persons they have heard. In some cases there will be a wide range of possible acceptable subjects. Some speakers also will be permitted to select their own subjects within broad fields, such as medicine, law, banking, accounting, journalism and engineering.

How and Where to Secure Good Speakers

A far more difficult problem in planning the program is the question of how and where to secure good speakers. Members of any organization will ordinarily have friendships extending over a relatively wide area which will enable them to suggest good speakers about whom they have heard others comment or actually have heard themselves. Newspaper accounts of speeches which have been given before other groups will provide clues of possible speakers. Individuals who have achieved some particular distinction in a community or who have returned from trips abroad are prospective speakers.

Sometimes it is desirable also to write to distinguished persons asking them if they contemplate visiting in or near your city in the months immediately ahead. Anyone who expects to make such a visit may be willing to give an address at that time. Large business concerns may have men who visit certain cities or states with regularity and have a worthwhile message they are willing to present. When

United States Senator Roe and Representative Doe come back to your state between sessions of Congress, they may welcome an opportunity to speak to your club. When a local doctor returns from the convention of the American Medical Association, he may be induced to talk on the latest studies on heart disease or arthritis.

Professor Brown is a distinguished scientist on the faculty of Keene University His old home is in your city, and he visits there once each year. The chances are that he would be flattered by an invitation to speak in his old home town. The governor of the state and prominent state officials are definite possibilities for programs.

The opportunities for uncovering unusual speaking talent and for learning about situations that will make excellent speakers available are unlimited. The wide-awake program chairman will use them.

Current subjects of widespread public interest will automatically suggest the names of persons competent in those fields or already in the public eye because of their discussions of these subjects. Local judges, ministers, attorneys, businessmen and educators are all possibilities. Finding top-notch speakers is largely a matter of alertness, imagination and aggressiveness on the part of the chairman.

A Time Schedule for the Meeting

After obtaining the speaker the chairman should work out a schedule of the meeting in detail, indicating exactly how it will be conducted. No chairman should take the chance of conducting a meeting with nothing more than a hazy conception of the time each part of the program will require. He may have a luncheon program for the Mudville Club scheduled from 12:15 noon to 1:45 P.M. He hopes the luncheon will be over at 1:05 P.M. so he can have five minutes for announcements and the introduction of guests, five minutes to introduce the speaker and thirty minutes—the period from 1:15 P.M. to 1:45 P.M.—for the speaker. But the chairman has failed to inform the hotel of his schedule and the luncheon itself takes until 1.15 P.M. Moreover, he has failed to check carefully the time required for announcements and the introduction of guests, with the result that fifteen more minutes elapse. At 1:30 P.M. he makes his introduction of the speaker which is completed at 1:35 P.M. leaving the speaker ten minutes instead of thirty minutes. While this is going on the audience becomes aware of the situation, as most of those in attendance have appointments and responsibilities in their businesses and professions shortly after 1:45 P.M. There is an air of restlessness in the audience and some persons whose appointments are particularly pressing leave rather than tc get up and go during the speech. In the meantime, beginning about 1:15 P.M., the speaker senses the situation and starts mentally cutting his speech. First, he takes out a humorous story or two. Time keeps running against him, so he cuts out an interesting illustration. Then another. He wishes to make three points in his address. At 1:25 P.M. he knows that is impossible. Out goes one point. At 1:30 P.M. out goes the second point. At 1:35 P.M. he is a nervous wreck in a cold sweat. How in the world did he ever agree to address this audience anyhow? He has a kind of sickly inner laugh when he remembers how the program chairman urged him by letter to accept. "He would be the principal feature. They all wanted to hear him," the chairman said. The speaker accepted, worked twelve hours to prepare the speech and traveled sixty miles to make it.

Now he hears the chairman apologizing to the audience for the "unavoidable" reduction in the time for the address, but "we are certain our distinguished speaker will give us something worthwhile in the time remaining." And so he gets up and presents a disjointed and rambling speech that lacks almost everything he had planned to give it. There is no joy in the Mudville Club—mighty Casey has struck out.

How many speakers have had precisely the foregoing experience? Scheduled to speak thirty minutes at a luncheon, they are given ten minutes. A speaker agrees to address a dinner meeting. The dinner starts forty-five minutes late; the treasurer's report, the minutes of the last meeting and a discussion of the annual ladies' night take forty minutes; the high school glee club sings an hour instead of thirty minutes. When everyone is ready to go home, the address of the evening is announced. It does not make sense, and yet that is the manner in which hundreds of meetings are conducted. Sometimes a member of a club will bring a previously unannounced guest from

Korea, China or Timbuktu, who is asked to say just a word. The guest traces the history of his country, its present problems and future promise for twenty-five minutes while the invited speaker and audience sit by helplessly. It doesn't make any difference whether the invited speaker is important or not important. There is no way to get back the time which was rightfully his and of which he has been robbed. To paraphrase a quotation from *The New England Primer* in 1688,

> The uninvited guest cuts down all,
> Both great and small.

There is practically no way for an invited guest to insist on his rights during a program that is obviously being badly managed. As Nicholas Murray Butler said, "One of the embarrassments of being a gentleman is that you are not permitted to be violent in asserting your rights." The chairman might well follow Bacon's advice, "Be sure to leave other men their turns to speak."

The person who wishes to conduct a meeting with efficiency and in a manner to win the praise of the audience and those who participate in the program will prepare a simple memorandum for himself carefully scheduling the time to be given each part of the program. Sometimes the time schedule for a meeting is even given in the printed program for the benefit of the entire audience and the program participants. For example, the Rotary Club of Chicago often uses a schedule similar to the following in its printed program:

> 12:30—Silent Invocation
> 12:31—"The Star-Spangled Banner" led by Harry
> L. Ruggles
> 12:33-1:10—Luncheon and Fellowship
> 1:10—Announcements and Introductions
> 1:27—Introduction of the Speaker
> 1:30—Address by The Honorable Dwight H.
> Green, Governor of the State of Illinois,
> on "Cooperation Between Citizen and Gov-
> ernment."
> 2:00—Adjourn

Courtesies Shown the Speaker

No program chairman should expect a speaker to prepare a speech conscientiously and take the time necessary to attend a meeting to deliver it without showing the speaker even the most ordinary courtesies. A well-known businessman told the author, "Many clubs and business associations will importune you strongly to come to their communities perhaps fifty, one hundred or five hundred miles away to give an address. You dislike greatly to take the time and effort evenings after your work in the office to prepare it. But you finally agree to do it. Your audience expects a masterpiece. You do your best to deliver it. The audience is on its way out of the room before the chairman gives a ten word sentence of brief appreciation. No one took care of your hotel reservation. Sometimes you even buy your own luncheon or dinner ticket. The only time you get a word of appreciation is a year or two later when the program again requires a businessman as a speaker. Then they call you long-distance to extend the invitation and express appreciation for your address given months ago."

This businessman may have been too critical of program chairmen as a group, but there is no good excuse for a program chairman or committee overlooking any of the little courtesies that really reward a speaker, particularly the speaker who comes to a club without accepting any remuneration whatsoever.

In the first place a good hotel room should be reserved for the speaker if he is to stay overnight. Even if he is in the city only during the day, a hotel room reserved for him for the day is a splendid way to give him the proper attention and perhaps the short rest he deserves. He may find it helpful to go over his notes or manuscript alone before the program. If the speaker has work he wishes to do or desires privacy, respect his wishes.

It is a mark of real courtesy if a member of the organization which the speaker is to address meets him at the train and takes him to the hotel. It may also be possible to take him on a short drive around the city or have a meal with him. The author remembers some unusual and unexpected courtesies shown him in Salt Lake City where he was to address the annual convention of the Utah Bankers Association. Shortly after his arrival at the Hotel Utah a beautiful basket of fruit was delivered to his room through the kindness of one of the officials of a local bank. At noon the president of another bank invited the speaker to luncheon. The local bankers and the Utah Bankers Association showed a thoughtfulness for the speaker which was almost embarrassing in the many ways in which it found expression. Courtesy is a language everyone understands.

Publicity for the Speaker and the Meeting

Prior to the meeting the proper person in the organization, perhaps the program chairman, will have obtained information and perhaps a glossy photograph of the speaker for use by local newspapers for advance publicity. Copies of the speech or excerpts from it may also be obtained and sent to the newspapers for release at the time the speech is delivered. Advance copies of a speech make it easier for a reporter to make a good summary of the speech, and they give the speaker greater assurance that he will be accurately quoted.

Copies of newspaper clippings announcing the speaker, as well as news items printed about his speech itself, will be welcomed by him. The speaker may never have an opportunity to see the local newspaper and thoughtfulness in sending publicity material of interest to him will be greatly appreciated.

The president or program chairman of the organization holding the meeting may wish to write the speaker expressing gratitude for his address and commending it. If the speech shows conscientious preparation and contains a worthwhile message, he may write in addition to the speaker's superior. For example, let us assume that Professor Jones makes an excellent address before the annual convention of the state bar association. The best way to express gratitude is to write the president of the university in which Professor Jones teaches, perhaps sending a copy of the letter to Professor Jones. It is not imperative that a copy of the letter be sent to Professor Jones, as the president of the university will certainly tell the professor about it. Professor Jones being a modest, conscientious person will prepare an able address, but will never tell his superior, the president, about the success of the meeting. In the business world too, almost invariably the best reward for speakers is a strong word of commendation to their superiors. Top officials of most businesses welcome letters indicating that members of their organizations have earned the appreciation and good will of audiences.

In some instances organizations furnish a modest gift for the speaker, such as a book, a box of candy, or some local product. One credit men's association in Indiana sent the wife of a speaker a large bouquet of roses on the Christmas following a speech that had been given in November. A large corporation in Chicago selling electrical appliances gave an economist whose speech had greatly impressed them an attractive table radio. Gifts of this kind are rare instances of thoughtfulness and courtesy, but they do show what some organizations do for good speakers. A bit of appreciation—a spoken word, a letter, a small gift—may be the means of showing speakers who do conscientious, hard work on their addresses that audiences are really grateful for superior achievement.

Rotary International has given careful consideration to this whole matter of expressing appreciation to speakers and has distributed the suggestions which follow to each one of its more than 6,000 clubs:

An Obligation Due Speakers

Is your club considerate of its out-of-town speakers?

Among other courtesies extended to the club program speaker—such as meeting him at the station, introducing him to club members, giving him all of his agreed-upon time to speak, thanking him for his talk—does the president or chairman remember to offer to reimburse the out-of-town speaker for expenses he may have incurred in making the trip to your community?

The latter is not only a courtesy, but an obligation that is due the invited speaker. It can be handled in a way that need cause no embarrassment to anyone.

Recently, when a Rotarian accepted an invitation to address a certain Rotary club 75 miles distant, he was met at the train and conducted to the meeting-place. After the meeting the guest was quietly handed an envelope containing a thank-you note and money adequate to cover his expenses. Such procedure is routine in this club.

Even though the speaker may live only a few miles away, it may take four or five hours out of his day to deliver a 25-minute talk to your club. This he may be glad to do without any honorarium, but the club does have an obligation to make sure that he is reimbursed for all out-of-pocket expenses.

The guest may good-naturedly refuse to accept anything, but the club secretary or other officer should tactfully persuade him to accept—and thus the club will feel free to call again upon him, or some other member of his club, for a talk.

Before the Meeting Starts

Some time in advance inform the speaker of the exact time and place of the meeting, and make arrangements to meet him beforehand. For example, you may tell him that the program will start at the Community Hall at eight o'clock, and you or someone you designate will call for him at his hotel at 7:40 P.M. Sometimes the speaker and the guests at the speaker's table are asked to assemble in a special room near the meeting place in order to become acquainted and to march in to the speaker's table in some definite order. In that event tell each person, in writing as a rule, about the arrangements.

It is good policy to have the speaker and the guests at the speaker's table meet each other prior to the beginning of the meeting. Sometimes it is possible also to introduce the speaker to other members of the audience before the meeting.

If some special seating arrangement is planned for the speaker's table, each guest should be informed in advance of his place. At any event, the speaker should always be advised of his place at the table.

Members of the Audience Are Guests

A toastmaster who aims at perfection in the discharge of his duties considers that the members of the audience are his guests. From the time the first person arrives until the last one leaves a competent toastmaster will do everything possible for the best interests of his guests.

A Program That Is Too Long

Sooner or later, and generally sooner, every chairman finds himself with a program that is too long. The program may have too many speakers. It may have too much entertainment, or there may be too much business to be conducted. As that eminent philosopher, the radio comedian, Jimmy Durante, has said, "Everybody wants to get into the act." This is too often true.

The problem should be considered from two viewpoints: (1) how to prevent this situation from arising; and (2) what to do if it has arisen.

The program chairman must never lose sight of the simple fact that he will be held responsible for a program that is too long. It is his job, ruthlessly if necessary, to insist on a program that can be presented properly within the necessary time limits. Under no condition should he permit himself to be a party to plans that result in too long a program—a program that is distinctly unfair to the participants and a headache to the audience. To paraphrase Gertrude Stein: A chairman, is a chairman, is a chairman. Whatever meaning Gertrude Stein would have attached to this statement, it certainly meant that a chairman was meant to be chairman, exactly that.

Just plain sense will tell the chairman how much time he can allot for the program. If the program includes dinner, for example, and is scheduled to begin at 6:30 P.M. and be over at 9:00 P.M., there are exactly 150 minutes available. If the dinner requires 75 minutes, then 75 minutes remain for announcements, introductions of guests at the speaker's table, business matters, introduction of the speakers, their speeches and entertainment. Deduct 5 minutes for announcements, 5 minutes for the introduction of guests, 10 minutes for business matters, and 15 minutes for entertainment—then 40 minutes remain. Five minutes may be needed to introduce a speaker and 5 minutes may well be set up for some delay in the program, or in case some parts of it run over a minute or two. Approximately 30 minutes remain for a speaker. There is no method by which 30 minutes can be divided to include two speeches of 25 minutes each. Thirty minutes will also not include one 45-minute speech. It is the job of the chairman to hold the non-essentials to an absolute minimum and reserve every possible minute for his entertainment and speaker, particularly the latter, if the speaker is considered the main part of the program.

Once the schedule is fixed, every part of the program must conform to it and nothing should be added which throws the program and the time schedule clear out of balance. Inserting twice as much entertainment as the time will permit, arranging for two speakers when the time will only permit one, or arranging for three speakers when the time will only permit two—these are all cases of incompetent program management. If the toastmaster is to err on the number of speakers, it is better to err on the side of having too few on the program. It has been said that intelligent people express themselves briefly and say at once whatever is to be said. Likewise, intelligent chairmen build programs which are not too long and which move with dispatch.

Order of the Speeches

If there are several speakers on a program, it is probably best as a rule to have the principal speaker last, assuming that one speaker is considered the main speaker. If this speaker is scheduled earlier, some members of an audience may walk out after this speech and not hear a very good speaker who is less well known.

Where a convention, for example, is particularly desirous of having its delegates hear the message of a particular speaker, he may be given a place on the program at a time when the convention has its peak attendance at the sessions.

Once in a while there is a speaker who wishes unusual privileges. He may ask to speak ahead of others so he can leave for a train. This may be a very good reason for giving him a special position on the program. However, this does not entitle a speaker to take more time than has been set aside for his speech, thereby reducing the time available for others.

A speaker may also ask to be moved ahead or after other speakers in order to get what he believes is a preferential position on the program. It is the responsibility of the chairman to be fair and completely impartial in dealing with responsibilities of this character.

Time Allotted Each Speaker

Earlier in this chapter we have indicated how important it is to conduct a meeting on schedule. Each speaker should be advised in advance exactly how much time will be given to him. This information can be included in the original invitation. When the day for the meeting comes, he can be shown the schedule for the meeting so he understands clearly the time set aside for him. The speaker is justified in expecting the chairman to adhere conscientiously to the schedule throughout the program. A time schedule is not something to which the speaker is to be held rigidly at all events while the chairman does as he pleases, even taking time of the speaker.

Publicity for the Meeting

Reference has already been made to the possibility of obtaining glossy photographs of the speaker and copies of his speech, or excerpts from it, for the press. In addition, this material may be sent to trade papers and magazines. If the speaker is nationally known, and particularly if he occupies a position where his views make news, publicity can also be sent to national news magazines. The speaker himself may be associated with a business concern or other types of organization which has a publicity department that will send out news releases about him. Occasionally the organization conducting the program can arrange for the speaker to receive the press personally before or after the meeting. This may give a program the type of publicity which builds prestige for the organization conducting the meeting.

Organizing Panel Discussions

A panel discussion is ordinarily one in which two or more persons, generally with a chairman, discuss a subject which has previously been selected. For example, four persons with a chairman or moderator may discuss some phase of American foreign policy which is debatable. Two of the speakers may take the affirmative and two the negative. At the conclusion of the more formal discussion, the speakers may ask each other questions. The audience may also be permitted to ask questions. At other times each participant will simply present the part of a particular subject regarding which he is especially qualified. There may be no attempt to take affirmative and negative sides. To illustrate, a panel of business men may be asked to present, in a January meeting of an association of commerce, their views on business conditions for the coming year. A banker may express his views on the financial outlook, a department store president on retail prospects and problems, a manufacturer of steel on the outlook for his industry, and a construction authority on public and private construction. This type of panel and symposium, especially if questions are permitted, can be very effective. Each speaker will ordinarily be sufficiently different from the others, if the program is well planned, with sufficient variety so that it appeals to audiences with widely divergent interests.

When the Speaker Fails to Arrive

If a speaker advises the program chairman a week or more before the date he is to speak that he will not be able to fulfill his engagement, there may still be time to obtain someone in his place without too much trouble.

A more difficult situation arises if a speaker fails to appear at the last minute because of illness or another emergency. When it becomes necessary to obtain a substitute speaker upon short notice, it is always best to tell the person invited exactly the reasons for his being asked to speak at so late a date. He will wonder just what happened which resulted in an invitation that afforded so little time for preparation. If a prospective substitute is given all the facts, there is a possibility that he will accept in a spirit of good sportsmanship. In a predicament of this character it is often possible to find some highly qualified speaker who has a speech available which he has prepared for some other occasion and who will welcome an opportunity to deliver his talk before a different audience.

A farsighted program chairman should keep a list of several persons who may be called on to speak in emergencies. In small communities, for example, a local minister, or high-school superintendent, or an attorney may be willing to speak on short notice. The chairman may also prepare a list of subjects which would be suitable for discussion by the audience. The chairman can then announce that the speaker has suddenly found it necessary to cancel his speech, and that he himself, or some other person, will lead a discussion in which the audience is to participate. Possible subjects for discussion might be: (1) the question of how to promote a local improvement involving the addition of a park and baseball field for the young people, (2) the enlargement of the local public library, (3) what policies the community could pursue to induce new industries to locate in the city. Many other possibilities will occur to the chairman. In fact the scheduled speaker's absence may turn out to be a blessing. A meeting of this kind may be tremendously successful as each person present has a chance to participate in the discussion. Open discussions dealing with vital local issues should prove especially successful for clubs like Rotary, Kiwanis and the Lions, and for organizations of business men and civic-minded citizens.

CHAPTER 2

TECHNIQUES OF THE TOASTMASTER

SOMEONE in good humor once said of an eminent American statesman that he was certain the statesman was not a Baptist as he would never agree to submerge himself that long. The competent toastmaster submerges himself to give the speaker prominence. No person is a good toastmaster who is unwilling to make the speaker rather than himself the center of attention.

Length of the Introduction

It is clearly not the business of the toastmaster to be so incredibly dull that the speaker will seem to be a genius by contrast. But neither is it the toastmaster's business to speak at such length and with so elaborate an analysis of the speaker's subject that the speaker is left with the responsibility of saying briefly nothing.

There is an old story that when William Jennings Bryan was at the height of his power as a speaker he arrived in one city where he had an engagement to speak but had only a very limited time between trains. The chairman of the meeting felt called upon not only to introduce Mr. Bryan at length, but also to extend his remarks to include other subjects. When he had finished his introduction, only ten minutes remained for Mr. Bryan's speech. As Mr. Bryan was hurrying down the aisle out of the auditorium after his address, he heard one member of the audience say to another, "That man Bryan certainly is a great speaker." "Yes," said the other person, "he is an excellent speaker, and that fellow who followed him for ten minutes wasn't so bad either."

There is no excuse for the chairman to make so long an introduction that the audience rightly has some doubt as to who was to make the principal speech. The toastmaster is the starter for the engine, and not the engine. Consequently, the toastmaster must keep clearly in mind at all times his particular function in the meeting itself.

The average introduction need not take more than two or three minutes. If the biographical information about the speaker is lengthy, it is best to pick the most essential points and those of interest to the particular audience. The most distinguished persons may be presented effectively with short introductions. For example, in introducing the President of the United States, it is the custom merely to say, "Ladies and Gentlemen, The President of the United States."

Announcements, Entertainment and Other Parts of the Program

It is to be expected that there will be announcements of some kind in every type of program, but the announcements must be subordinated to the main part of the program. No effort is ever made to have the celery, olives and relishes at the beginning of a dinner substitute for the filet mignon, potatoes and peas. Likewise, the announcements should be announcements—not speeches. Bill Jones who has charge of the annual club golf tournament may feel that his announcement is the most important part of the program. He may use far more time than is allotted to him as he urges attendance and describes the tournament. Sam Smith is supposed to take five minutes to call attention to the ladies' night, but he appropriates fifteen minutes, and so announcements devour the time of a program. All of the announcements must be carefully planned for time and must be held to schedule.

Ventilation and Other Arrangements

It may seem unnecessary to comment on ventilation, but too many speakers have had to face audiences which were gradually being anesthetized by poor ventilation. Any one who prepares a speech carefully so that it merits the best thinking of an audience deserves physical conditions in the room which will help to make the audience receptive rather than drowsy. The author has found sometimes when he has spoken near the end of a long program that the members of an audience greatly appreciate being invited to stand and stretch for a moment while the windows are opened. It is better for a speaker to lose two or three minutes of his speaking time, if necessary, to assure himself of an alert audience. Check the ventilation and temperature in the room before the meeting starts and have someone at the back of the room watch the ventilation during the program.

Arrangements should always be made with the hotel or other meeting place to provide a lectern. Never wait for a speaker to request one. As presiding officer, the chairman will find a lectern helpful and convenient for notes and papers. Even if the speaker does not use a manuscript or notes, a lectern serves as a pulpit, and provides a place for the speaker's hands giving him greater ease as he speaks. *Always arrange for a lectern.*

The chairman should have enough helpers and committees to take all details of the meeting off his mind so that he can concentrate on his job of presiding. Committees should be appointed to handle reception, fellowship, table arrangements, and any other matters that may be complicated.

Brief Opening Comments

The objective toward which we are aiming is perfection in con ducting a program. Consequently, it is suggested that any announcements or brief comments which the toastmaster makes before presenting the principal speaker should be carefully prepared. There must be no stumbling in making the simplest announcements, no seeming unfamiliarity with the pronunciation of persons' names or geographical locations. The small parts of the program as well as the major parts must move smoothly.

Prepare Introductions in Advance

Place-cards should be used so the guests can readily find their places at the speaker's table. If there is a number of guests, the chairman should have before him a list of the guests as they are seated to his left and right. The guest list may also have information about each guest. This avoids embarrassment by keeping the chairman posted on important names or facts that may come up in the conversation.

In introducing guests remember always to give the guest's name last. To illustrate, "Starting at my extreme right, I am pleased to present the executive vice president of the Johnson Iron Corporation, a past president of the Augusta Association of Commerce, and now vice president of the Economic Club of Augusta—Mr. Richard D. Johnson." Always speak loudly and plainly so the audience hears each name clearly.

Sometimes a chairman may forget what he is going to say, like the Dutch gentleman acting as toastmaster in the old story who announced, "Chentlemen, dis is der distinguished chentleman who is going to address you dis evening. I have been selected to interduce him. I have done so, and he will do so." The story is also told of the Southerner who got so excited at the prospect of introducing Jefferson Davis, President of the Confederacy, that all he could say was, "Here he is!" It is best generally for the chairman to have a written memorandum of the comments to be made.

Getting the Good Will of the Audience

The chairman who has prepared in advance the various announcements, scheduled the meeting to run on time, advised the guests of their places at the speaker's table and arranged for the ventilation to be properly regulated, has already earned the good will of an audience. He may say as he introduces the speaker that "this audience is representative of the leading business and professional interests of our city—men and women who are vitally interested in the important problem our speaker is to discuss." Honest praise of the good qualities of an audience is permissible and is appreciated. As Cicero has said, "We are all excited by the love of praise, and it is the noblest spirits that feel it most."

Commending the Speaker

However, far more important than praising the audience is the whole subject of using praise or commendation in introducing the speaker. The chairman's praise of the speaker may be so faint that it appears the chairman is uninformed and is speaking with caution, or knows the speaker so well he dreads what the audience is about to experience (after all, the chairman may have to live with the audience for years after the speaker has left town). On the other hand, the praise of the speaker by the chairman may be so strong that no speaker can live up to the reputation the chairman has given him. Chauncey M. Depew, who was a great speaker, is reported once to have said that he preferred the taffy now rather than the epitaphy later.

Nevertheless, an introduction can be so extravagant in its commendation that even if the speaker is excellent, he never can reach the heights of the introduction. A great many American audiences believe Tom Collins of Kansas City, Missouri, is one of the best humorous lecturers of our time. He has told the author that he hoped this book would make it "clear that it is fatal to a speaker who intends to be humorous to promise his audience they soon will be rolling in the aisles with uncontrollable mirth. When a toastmaster begins to mumble about Will Rogers, you know you might just as well cut your wrists and go home, because you are ruined.

"Humor is not an exact science and it is dangerous to overpromise and build a hurdle no one can clear. I believe as cute an introduction as I have had in many a year came recently when a chairman said 'Our speaker is a veteran of two wars and has gone through hell for you. It is no more than right that you should now go through hell for him, and listen to what he has to say.' Certainly that is a lot better type of introduction than one in which the audience is promised one hour of uninterrupted laughter which, of course, they never get." No introduction should be so extravagant the speaker cannot live up to it.

After a member of one audience had listened to a long and highly commendatory introduction in which the chairman had given all the excellent business positions the speaker had held previously, the member said, "That speaker lost more good jobs than anyone I ever knew." It is advisable not to make it too difficult for the speaker by presenting what may sound like an obituary of him.

Good-Natured "Kidding" of the Speaker

On some occasions it is possible for the chairman to "kid" the speaker and to make remarks which seem to reflect unfavorably upon him. Ordinarily this type of introduction should be reserved by the chairman for those occasions where he knows the speaker very well or knows beyond doubt that no offense will be taken. In fact there are situations where the chairman and speaker may arrange between themselves for an introduction of this character with a suitable response.

Charles F. Pennock, past president of the Rotary Club of Philadelphia, has told the author that on an occasion when he introduced one of his best friends to an audience which knew both of them he did some good-natured insulting. He used the following simple pattern: (1) listed the speaker's real achievements; (2) stated that he could tell the audience a great many things about the speaker which they did not know, and implied they were things of which he would not be proud, but thought it was courteous not to air any dirty linen at that time; and (3) finally concluded by saying that he was very happy to introduce his good friend. If a toastmaster pokes fun at a speaker, it is often best to follow it with serious remarks commending the speaker just before the toastmaster turns over the rostrum to him.

Chapter 4 contains several introductions of this general type, such as Glen Miller's introduction on page 44, Edwin B. Moran's introduction on page 53, and Harold O. McClain's introduction on page 55.

Phil Hanna, financial columnist of the *Chicago Daily News,* once began an introduction of his associate, Bob Casey, ace war correspondent, as follows: "When the committee asked me to introduce our emaciated (Casey is a large person) speaker, I had no idea how interesting a job it would be." He then described, in good humor, Casey's automatic system for filing all his correspondence unopened in his coat pocket instead of answering it promptly. Ordinarily no chairman would make such a pointed reference to the speaker's waistline. But in this introduction it was all good fun. Mr. Hanna went on at length to tell the story of Mr. Casey's excellence as a reporter. Mr. Casey began his response as follows: "I don't know what I'm doing here—I'd much rather hear Phil Hanna talk (about Casey)."

Sometimes a chairman will make an unfortunate statement through a blunder in language or pronunciation, or in comments regarding the meeting or the speaker. To illustrate, De Witt M. Emery, president of the National Small Business Men's Association, tells of an experience he had as a speaker.

"I have in mind one experience which I shall never forget, and I hope that I may still have the opportunity of introducing the gentleman of whom I am to speak. He was chairman of a Town Hall Club in the far West. They had seven programs on their schedule for that year, and I was the seventh one. They had been having an attendance, they told me, of around 250 per meeting. For the seventh meeting, they had an attendance of, I should say, around forty.

"The chairman devoted fully ten minutes to telling all of the things he had done in trying to get out a crowd for that meeting, and then he turned the meeting over to me with this comment: 'Anyway, we have had six good meetings!' And I assure you, his statement was one hundred per cent correct."

Channing Pollock, author, playwright and dramatic critic, was once introduced to an audience with these words, "Now I am pleased to present Channing Pollock, author, playwright and distinguished dramatic critter." It was one of those unexplainable twists of the tongue for which both the chairman and speaker were unprepared. Only good luck or some quick wit by the chairman or speaker will help a situation of that kind. The chairman might have said, "I assure you that like the radio program, 'Information Please,' that comment was spontaneous and completely unrehearsed, but it was unintended."

A chairman should check himself on the pronunciation of all names, and the correctness of initials, titles and business or professional affiliations. Mr. Johnson is not Mr. Johnston. Mr. R. V. Smith is not Mr. R. D. Smith. The Old National Bank is not The Old National Trust Company.

Senator Owen Brewster of Maine states: "I had an introduction in Syracuse in which the chairman said he was now going to 'give the biology of the speaker.' I got a little worried about that. It worked out all right when he finally concluded by saying that they asked me because I came from Maine. They considered that it was a safe thing to have a person from Maine, because when he reached the Senate he reached the summit of all Maine men's ambitions, since they couldn't go any farther; so he thought a politician like that was likely to come nearer telling the truth. There is some advantage in having a fellow who arrives in the Senate and can 'put behind all hope ye who enter here.' " In this illustration the word "biology" was undoubtedly used deliberately and in good humor by the chairman.

Dr. Harold Moulton, president of the Brookings Institution of Washington, D.C., tells of a chairman without a sense of humor who introduced Dr. Moulton as follows: "Inasmuch as there are no reporters present, Dr. Moulton is going to take his hair down and give us the real inside." (Dr. Moulton is bald.)

Good-natured fun is permissible, in fact frequently desirable, but the audience and chairman must never forget that the speaker for any occasion is an invited guest. No rudeness should ever be shown to the speaker in introducing him. Poking fun at the speaker is permissible if the speaker is fully at home with his audience and the chairman, and understands it is wholly fun. Politeness and courtesy are essentials in conducting any program.

At the conclusion of the introduction the chairman gives the speaker's name in a loud and clear voice, turns toward the speaker, and waits until the speaker has risen to his feet before sitting down.

After the Speaker Is Introduced

The question of what to do after the speaker is introduced is simple. Unless it is absolutely imperative that the chairman leave the platform, he should remain in his chair until the program is completed and the audience has departed. Further, he should pay strict attention to the speaker, incidentally setting a good example for the audience.

After the Speaker Has Completed His Address

If the speaker makes a good speech, the chairman obviously should express his appreciation in the strongest terms. In Chapter 1 we have indicated other ways in which appreciation can be shown to a speaker.

If the speech was a poor one, the chairman can still thank the speaker but in less lavish terms. After all, the club is partly responsible, for the speaker was invited by the club.

Many audiences, particularly luncheon groups or those whose members must catch suburban trains home after an evening program, get up and leave the moment the speaker finishes and before the chairman

B

can say even a sentence of appreciation. If the club publishes a bulletin, sometimes a line is included urging the audience to remain for just a moment as a courtesy to the speaker while the chairman thanks him.

Introducing Several Speakers

It should be said again and again that it is better to err in having too few speakers and entertainment features on a program rather than too many. This is particularly true if one speaker, or one entertainment feature, is to be the principal event. A program which is too crowded is unfair to the participants and to the audience as well. It is simply disaster by plan. There is no good excuse for it.

As a rule, the principal feature is the last one—the grand finale. Exceptions may sometimes be made, for example, in political meetings where a governor or United States senator may be compelled to make appearances before several groups in the same evening; obviously all of the appearances cannot come last on each program.

In some cases a subject for discussion may be divided into two or three parts with one part assigned to each speaker. The speakers then will speak in the order which will permit the best development of the subject.

Whenever there is any danger that the program may be crowded, the speakers must be held rigidly to schedule and the introductions must be correspondingly brief. Any chairman who fails in that situation has not done his duty either to the speakers or to the audience

In conducting a program that is a bit crowded, the chairman can only hope that he does not have a speaker who begins by addressing his audience as follows: "How do I know what I'm going to say until I open my mouth and get going?" The chairman can say to himself, "You may not know what you are going to say until you open your mouth, but I know when you are going to close your mouth and permit other speakers to have their fair time."

W. B. Rogers, president and general manager of The Bond Hotels of Hartford, Connecticut, is an exceptionally able chairman. He is a strong believer in brevity as a general principle in presiding. He has told the author, "I once heard that if all toastmasters were laid end to end across the country, it would be a good thing. For that reason I have always believed that in presiding—brevity is next to Godliness."

In presiding at a meeting where there are several speakers, good sense is the best indication of what the length of the introductions should be. When in doubt, it is probably better to be brief rather than long. However, an introduction may be so brief that it fails utterly to do justice to the speaker or the audience. No introduction should fail to identify the speaker properly and give the audience sufficient information to establish him as one competent to speak on the subject. Thus, the chairman should describe the background of the speaker, state, if desirable, the reason for his appearance, and give the subject to be discussed.

A toastmaster's remarks may be as Lowell once said, "a platitude, a quotation and an anecdote," but his comments definitely must identify and establish the speaker in the minds of the audience.

Incidentally, in establishing the speaker's position in the field in which he is to speak, the competent chairman never tries to tell the audience what the speaker will say. If the chairman does make this error, he runs in danger, first, of making the speaker's speech and, second, of expressing opinions which the speaker later may be compelled to correct with considerable embarrassment to everyone.

It is an ironic fact that as a toastmaster becomes more competent he is more tempted to add to the length of his introductions and announcements. There is a danger that he will come to know that he is good, particularly after he has listened to the commendation of his friends. Under the spur of flattery he will lengthen his remarks until he not only begins to infringe on the speaker's time but also makes a speech of his own with each introduction. Eventually this type of toastmaster will lose the good will it may have taken him a long time to establish. He will then find that nothing recedes like success.

Handling the Heckler

As a rule it is best to ignore a person who interrupts the meeting, particularly if the interruption is of a minor character and is not repeated. If the person has asked an intelligent question, but is one of those individuals who is such an enthusiast that he cannot ask the question in its proper place at the end of the speaker's address, then the chairman or speaker should merely say that he will be pleased to consider the question at the conclusion of the address. If the speaker has not agreed to answer questions in an open discussion at the end of his address, he may be willing later to talk personally with those who would like to ask questions.

If a heckler is really rude, however, the audience ordinarily will resent his interruptions and will favor the speaker or chairman in any reasonable response made to the situation. The chairman may also state that the subject being discussed is highly controversial but everyone will agree that in a spirit of fairness the speaker should be entitled to express his viewpoint. The chairman may add that questions will be permitted after the speaker concludes, or that a speaker with a different viewpoint will address the club at a later date.

A heckler who continually disturbs a meeting must necessarily be requested to leave. However, it never pays to make a major issue out of an insignificant disturbance. Some member of the club sitting near the offender, or one of his friends, will ordinarily handle any unnecessary interruptions with little or no fuss.

Some time ago a candidate for the nomination for the Presidency of the United States was addressing an audience consisting in part of students. Some of the students in the front row came to the meeting with identical magazines, all of which had large pictures of one of the opposing candidates for the presidential nomination. Each student held his magazine so the picture was prominently displayed in a manner intended to disconcert the speaker. The candidate whose picture was displayed was a man of intelligence and of broad tolerance for the viewpoints of others. He would undoubtedly have disapproved of this display of discourtesy.

A demonstration of this kind is childish. Students who had reached any kind of maturity in their thinking would have no part in the pranks of children. Intelligent persons are always desirous of hearing both sides of issues that affect the national welfare discussed by those in positions of leadership in our national life.

By and large, no speaker or chairman ever has any serious problem with anyone wishing to heckle or interrupt a speaker. The good chairman, no matter what the situation, never loses his temper, has a sense of humor and uses good sense.

Last Minute Changes in the Program

If the program is carefully planned, the probability that changes will be needed is less likely. However, it may be necessary, as previously indicated, to shift speakers to accommodate a speaker who must catch a train or some other form of transportation. In the event a speaker becomes ill and is compelled to cancel his engagement, a local speaker may be obtained. It is best not to make too much of the absence of a speaker as it seems to imply that other speakers on the program are less important. Moreover, a substitute speaker, knowing the difficult situation he occupies, may make an extraordinary effort to do an outstanding job. The chairman should give him every consideration in introducing him. The audience knows the substitute is in a difficult spot, and if he does well they will give him a great deal of credit.

Use of Humor

A toastmaster tells a humorous story or uses an epigram of witticism to excite mirth or laughter. Washington Irving once said that, "Honest good humor is the oil and wine of a merry meeting, and there is no jovial companionship equal to that where the jokes are rather small and the laughter abundant." And it was Joseph Addison who said, "If we consider the frequent reliefs we receive from laughter, and how often it breaks the gloom which is apt to depress the mind, one would take care not to grow too wise for so great a pleasure of life." A toastmaster who is able to use humor well has an extremely effective speech instrument at his command.

Not to tell a humorous story well is a serious handicap in those situations where humor could serve to highlight an introduction. Chapter 4 contains many illustrations in which toastmasters have used humor to make interesting and entertaining introductions. Practice and careful study are required to make the best use of humor.

Perhaps it would be helpful to outline a few essential points regarding humor.

1. You may be able to think of clever comments and humorous stories "on the spot" as you act as chairman or participate in the program. If so, you are very fortunate. Most persons run the risk of complete failure if they rely wholly on extemporaneous humor. Humorous speakers and top-ranking radio comedians may sometimes speak humorously "off the cuff," but ninety-nine per cent of their humorous comments are carefully planned and are not extemporaneous. The average amateur toastmaster or speaker has no reason to assume he can do better than these professionals. Consequently, he should have his humorous stories and comments carefully prepared *before* he plans to use them.

2. No humorous story should be needlessly long. Excess words should be ruthlessly eliminated. A good storyteller can tell a long story, but he ordinarily intersperses short humorous quips as he proceeds to the conclusion of his major story. With experience a toastmaster can tell longer stories.

3. A good humorous story can often be changed to suit many types of occasions.

4. Do not say to the audience that you are now going to tell a joke, and "brother, this joke is really good." There is a great danger that the audience may dare you to be funny—a try-and-make-us-laugh challenge. A good storyteller can be in the middle of a story almost before the audience is aware of it. He ties it in subtly to his remarks.

5. Almost every humorous story has a punch line, which logically provides the climax right at the end of the story. To use the punch line two or three sentences from the end of a story destroys its effect. In other words, to keep on telling a story after you have passed the punch line will result in its losing much of its value. When you reach the climax of a story, the story is over. No story is so good that you repeat the climax simply because the audience liked it so well the first time.

6. If the chairman can tell a humorous story about himself, or can bring in local characters, he increases the possibilities for the success of the story. An audience likes names because they make the story more personal.

7. One should ordinarily not laugh at his own story.

8. The author does not believe in telling stories about serious physical handicaps from which some members of the audience or their relatives or friends may suffer. For example, this rule would include stories on such physical defects as stuttering or harelip. On the other hand, stories about nearsightedness or farsightedness are not objectionable, because millions of persons have these physical problems, perhaps the speaker himself, and the attention of the audience does not become centered on some one person.

9. Humorous stories should concern subjects which are known to the audience and with which they are familiar. To illustrate, a joke about golf may fall absolutely flat in an audience of farm people where only two or three may understand the game. A joke about some very general aspect of farming may meet with a favorable response from a large city audience, but a good humorous story that requires some fundamental understanding of farming may fail completely with a large city audience.

10. Always go over a story a sufficient number of times actually to make it a part of yourself. Then tell it casually in your own language.

11. If it is necessary for the toastmaster or speaker to explain just what is funny about a story, then it isn't funny.

12. Always keep the humor closely related to the subject discussed. Its relationship to the speaker or to the subject should be unmistakably clear. The humor should be timely and relevant. To tell a humorous story unrelated to the subject breaks the trend of the discussion, and may make the audience wonder why it was necessary. Did the chairman think perhaps that his remarks were too dry and uninteresting? A humorous story must emphasize the point he is making and then it may be most helpful.

13. Just as some humor is often worthwhile in an introduction, too much humor may not be good. After all, the audience wants some factual material in its introductions and not merely a string of anecdotes.

14. Finally, a toastmaster will find it an asset to have a few extra

anecdotes and epigrams ready for an emergency. Knowing the subjects to be discussed and the speakers, he can arrange to have pertinent extra material on a card available on a moment's notice.

The epigram, witticism and humorous definitions are terse comments that may be of great assistance in making a toastmaster's remarks colorful. Samuel Taylor Coleridge has given a good epigrammatic definition of an epigram as follows:

> "What is an Epigram? a dwarfish whole,
> Its body brevity, and wit its soul."

Chapter 7 contains hundreds of epigrams and witticisms suitable for use on many different occasions.

Chapter 6 has dozens of stories taken from actual speeches or introductions. Many of these stories are humorous. The source of each story is given so a toastmaster can say, "As Governor Brown of (name of state) once said," or "United States Senator Smith once told an interesting story on this point. Senator Smith said," and the toastmaster tells the story. Chapter 8 has hundreds of quotations suitable for use in introducing men in various professions and occupations, and for use on various occasions. Many of these quotations are humorous. Chapter 9 has scores of humorous stories and anecdotes. Thus the chairman will find a great many items, both serious and humorous, in this volume which he can incorporate in his introductions and speeches.

At the Close of the Meeting

At the close of the meeting, it should be emphasized again, do not forget to thank the speakers. The audience should not be allowed to start for the door until this is done. It does not call for a speech. It can be done in a minute. As the last speaker finishes and sits down, the chairman should rise immediately so there is no lapse in the program and no period during which there is no one at the lectern. Close the meeting rapidly, once it is over.

One Last Word

As we conclude these two chapters on the work of the toastmaster, we stress again the subject which has been re-emphasized repeatedly in these pages—careful preparation for every meeting. The author of this volume was given an interesting story on the importance of preparation by a man who had the unusual privilege of serving as president both of the Rotary Club of New York City and the Rotary Club of Chicago. This club president said, "The Rotary Club of Chicago met on Tuesday. Therefore I had a standing appointment at four-thirty Monday afternoon with the secretary of the club. We spent from thirty minutes to an hour and a half in planning and timing. Then with the biographical data on the speaker and any others who were to participate in the meeting, I spent such time as was necessary at home Monday evening preparing my introductions— actually writing them out in detail—then studying them. My notes were used only as a guide, and were not to be read. On Tuesday noon, fifteen minutes before the meeting, the secretary and I would double-check to determine any last-minute changes." Note how thoroughly this club president prepared for a meeting.

The chairman should be fully prepared for his part of the program. He should have a working familiarity also with the rules of parliamentary procedure so he will conduct every meeting fairly and with complete confidence in himself.

B*

CHAPTER 3

TEN FUNDAMENTALS FOR THE TOASTMASTER

1. Work out carefully every program for which you are toastmaster. You are responsible for seeing that the audience is fully rewarded for its time.
2. Conduct the meeting on schedule. Don't let it drag.
3. Give the speaker the opportunity to make the speech. That's what he is there for. The audience should never be in doubt as to whether the toastmaster or speaker made the speech.
4. Give the speaker every opportunity to succeed—a good audience, a quiet, well-ventilated room, and a carefully prepared introduction.
5. Give the speaker his full time. Don't cut him short or let him run way over the schedule.
6. Make the introductions brief if the list of speakers is long.
7. Express real appreciation to the speaker who has made a conscientious effort to do a good job.
8. Give the audience a chance to stand up and stretch during a long meeting. Then you know they are all awake.
9. Refuse to act as toastmaster for any meeting that is of no value, or is obviously too long. Why should you help to inflict mass boredom?
10. Make no apologies for your own unpreparedness. You have no right to be unprepared.

CHAPTER 4

ILLUSTRATIONS OF ACTUAL INTRODUCTIONS

THIS chapter contains dozens of actual introductions which have been used at meetings of many types, many of them to present nationally known and distinguished speakers. Anyone who is to act as the chairman or toastmaster of a meeting will find these illustrations of great practical assistance to him in preparing his introductions. The use of humorous stories and epigrams, and the exact techniques followed by some of the ablest chairmen are fully illustrated here, so the reader should find much material of value to him.

In some cases where the speaker made an unusual and interesting response to the introduction it is also given.

In addition, this chapter contains invocations, speeches made when gifts were presented to officers of clubs, remarks for beginning a discussion period, comments made in presenting a mayor to open a convention, a mayor's welcoming speech, brief remarks at the time of the death of a member of an organization, and other practical material for the chairman.

* * *

Paul A. Pratt, Vice President of The Borden Company of Milwaukee and a past president of the Rotary Club of Milwaukee, introduces Frederick C. Crawford, president of Thompson Products, Inc., of Cleveland, and then also chairman of the board of the National Association of Manufacturers, on the occasion of an annual meeting of the Milwaukee Association of Commerce.

And now, ladies and gentlemen, we come to the high point of our annual meeting program. Our speaker's national and international record as a leader of men, the close relationship of his business operations to those of Milwaukee industry, his many intimate friendships to be found among the business leaders of our own city, have combined to mark him as the logical man to bring a sound and valuable message to this meeting.

But, frankly, after reading the sketch of his business life recently published in *Milwaukee Commerce,* and then exploring other source material in search of information which might be of interest as an introduction to this audience, I found myself not only impressed—even awed—but, in a certain sense, discouraged. It seemed to me, from the written record, that we were doomed to have a "stuffed shirt austerity" of the Boston Back Bay variety on our hands tonight.

I carefully read his genealogy which indicated that he was born in Watertown, Massachusetts, of Coolidge stock—the "voluble" Coolidge—on the maternal side which came to the colonies from England in 1631, and, that on the paternal side the Crawfords were among those immigrants coming to us from Londonderry as recently as 1728. We Milwaukeeans, of firmly established lines extending well back into the nineteenth century, naturally resent the intrusion of such young upstart families coming upon our *own* American scene.

Then, I found that our speaker had graduated from Harvard University, Magna Cum Laude, and a Phi Beta Kappa—I suppose that makes you Brother Crawford—[when Mr. Pratt was introduced as toastmaster, it was mentioned that he was a Phi Beta Kappa] and then from the Harvard Graduate School of Applied Sciences. Well, that put the second strike on him. By the time I had perused a list of all the degrees which befell him thereafter, I was actually flabbergasted. My interest perked up a little when I found that in 1916—after all of this education—he actually went to work, entering the employ of the Steel Products Company of Cleveland as maintenance engineer. Since Milwaukee is rated the nation's largest steel customer, the subject of steel can even quicken the pulse of a local farmer and milkman. Our speaker began to look a little better to me when I found that only once in all these years has he taken leave from his company—now Thompson Products, Inc.—and then only long enough to serve in the U.S. Navy Aviation Corps during World War I. And then, when I found that by 1933 he had worked his way up to the presidency of his company he had begun to earn my respect.

What's happened to this gentleman in the past twelve years, however is almost terrifying. He is now not only president of Thompson Products, Inc., but also of all its subsidiaries. He has served his city as president of the Cleveland Chamber of Commerce. He has served as president of the National Association of Manufacturers and is now chairman of the board of that organization. He is an official of sixteen different trade associations, and is a director or trustee of ten philanthropic and educational institutions. Additionally, he serves his government as a member of the Management-Labor Policy Committee of the War Manpower Commission, the Management-Labor Council of the War Production Board, and the President's War Advisory Council of Business Men. While performing this multitude of public services, a fraction of which duties most of us would claim that we haven't time to perform, he has found time to distinguish himself as an engineer and as a pioneer in the manufacture of aeronautical products.

Reading the record I was impressed, but suspicious that a man so involved in business and civic affairs must be a stuffy sort of fellow to whom life is only real and earnest—in other words, a man who did nothing but work and worry. So I set forth to find out whether there was anything human about him, and I even put detectives on his trail. To my amazement, well authenticated reports came back that he persists in making life a song to himself and all those about him. It seems there's practically nothing that he doesn't like to do. He never takes a drink, but is the life of every party. He frequently vacations in Nassau and shocks the staid natives and visitors by always riding a bicycle backwards, and with fiendish skill. When he is on a boat, train or airplane he seems to spend all of his time exploring mechanical operations and fraternizing with workers in the engine room—and yet, he is a prime source of entertainment to the passengers. Off the record, it's my understanding that he loves to gamble on anything—and usually victimizes his friends. My operatives report that he is devoted to almost every kind of sport, is a topflight swimmer and badminton player. I further understand that as a host he is without a peer, except that at his parties hell is likely to break loose at any moment. In other words this man does not suffer at all from the "stuffed shirt" austerity that I originally feared, but is actually a human dynamo.

I give you these sidelights on our speaker so that all of you will know him and understand him. It is my high privilege to introduce one of the top gentlemen of the American business world—Mr. Frederick C. Crawford.

*   *   *

Harry L. Stone, manager of bank relations, International Harvester Company, Chicago, introduces James Conzelman, well known football coach.

Most Chicagoans identify the name of Jimmy Conzelman with football. His first experience as a college football coach was at Washington University in St. Louis, where he developed a team, which had been in the doldrums for years, into a three-time winner in the Missouri Valley conference. Ordinarily a coach's principal responsibility is to instruct his squad in football strategy and incidentally throw in a little character-building along with it, but with Jimmy Conzelman the multiplicity of duties was almost interminable. He discovered that one of his duties was to speak before high-school students, alumni groups, civic clubs, and university gatherings, and it was this which kindled Conzelman's determination to become a successful public speaker. His degree of success is best illustrated by an incident which occurred in Chicago. At a luncheon here, Jim preceded Pat O'Brien on a speaking program and when Pat took over he said, "Speaking after Conzelman is like following 'Gone With the Wind' with a magic lantern."

Jimmy Conzelman has had an amazing career and is a man of many accomplishments. He is an author, commencement orator, after-dinner speaker, radio commentator, actor, sculptor, band leader, piano player, song writer, champion boxer, football player, and coach.

Since the golf season is just beginning, it is interesting to note that mention of his golfing ability is conspicuous by its absence, but a man who has been so prominent in the field of sports couldn't help

but excel in this pastime. He most assuredly would not be classed as
a Civil War golfer—out in 61 and back in 65. Perhaps the following
recitation entitled "The Dissatisfied Golfer" would apply to his
prowess on the links. Here it is:

> Unto a golfer sick with shame
> Late one evening the devil came,
> And the Old Boy said with his oily leer,
> "Why are you sitting grieving here,
> What on earth do you want to do
> Would you sell your soul for a seventy-two?"
> The golfer cried to the grinning Nick,
> "For a seventy-two I'd sell it quick."
> "Done," said the devil, "put her thar!
> Tomorrow you'll shoot the course in par.
> Now get to your bed and rest content,
> I'll see you later"—and out he went.
> True to his bargain the devil kept,
> From tee to tee that golfer stepped
> Making the short holes and the far
> As had been promised to him, in par.
> Twice he had putts for a birdie three,
> But more than he asked for could not be.
> His friends rejoiced, as good friends do
> But he shook his head at that seventy-two.
> "Once I was stymied by a tree,
> There were two short putts I missed," said he,
> "And but for the rotten luck that's mine
> I'd have shot that course in sixty-nine."
> All that is left to be paragraphed
> Is that deep in Hades the devil laughed!

When the St. Louis Browns Baseball Team won the American
League pennant in 1944, there were comparatively few people who
realized that Jimmy Conzelman was in the background casting his
magic spell. He modestly disclaims all credit for the Browns' accom-

plishments, but those who know his capacity for laughing off his serious achievements were not deceived.

I have gone on at length and will now terminate with a story about a wife whose husband was ailing. The doctor in attendance advised the spouse that her husband was seriously ill and needed a good rest, and to accomplish this he left some sleeping powders. The wife inquired when she should give them to her husband, and the doctor replied, "Give them, nothing. You take them!"

It is now your pleasure to see me take a powder and present to you one of the most colorful figures in the sports world—Jimmy Conzelman.

*   *   *

Harold O. McLain, president of The Railways Ice Company, Chicago, introduces Francis B. Davis, Jr., chairman of the board of the United States Rubber Company. Following Mr. McLain's introduction the opening paragraphs of the address by Mr. Davis are given as an illustration of how a speaker may respond to an excellent introduction in a spirit of modesty and win the friendship of his audience.

I suppose Continental Europe in its entirety has natural resources at least equal to those of the United States.

Without doubt, the Soviet Union, covering one-sixth of the world's land area, has a wealth of latent physical resources enormously greater than our own.

The British Empire with all its far-flung lands, and Asia, and Africa, and South America, all possess natural resources, in large part undeveloped, which greatly surpass those of the United States.

Russia, Continental Europe, the British Empire, and Asia were old civilizations for centuries before the Pilgrims landed on our shores.

If these other world areas have had all these natural resources and the centuries to develop them, why does the world always have to come with its hat in hand to these comparatively small United States to aid and save it in time of trouble?

When disaster threatens, why is it always the United States that must and can and does supply the money, the raw material, the finished products, and the men in an avalanche of abundance and enormity that saves the world and enables these old and naturally rich continents and empires to survive?

What resources do we possess that enable us to supply our own needs and also to make up for the inadequacy of the rest of the world?

What asset do we own that other nations lack?

By what legerdemain and necromancy do we accomplish this mystical and sorcerous marvel?

What is the secret?

Well, there isn't any secret! The answer is obvious!

Our unique asset is constitutional liberty and the American businessman who exceeds in available freedom, capacity, effectiveness, initiative and vision and industry the businessmen of all the rest of the world.

Make no mistake about this unique and invaluable asset.

In spite of abuse and contumely, in spite of the long-haired boys and the short-haired boys, in spite of clumsy government tyros and world fixers, in spite of labor rackets, taxes, hell and high water, the American businessman, under and by virtue of our constitutional government, for one hundred and seventy-five years and down to this very second has done the most miraculous job and contributed more to the world's progress and well-being than any other one factor in the world.

Hear me!

In spite of his alleged faults, if you remove the American businessman from the history of the world in the last century, you must perforce rewrite the world's history in any scramble of desolation and despair your imagination may conjure.

You fellows of The Executives' Club are yourselves American businessmen and as such you should hold your heads high and be inordinately jealous and proud of your profession.

It is the greatest mass profession ever known to man, and those alien-minded individuals who would restrict and emasculate that profession are both stupid and vicious.

When some loose-lipped screwball rolls his eyes to Heaven in pseudo-sanctimonious and supercilious horror and chants the usual Red hymn, and says, "The American businessman and his profession of production for profit is outmoded and doomed"—when you hear that, you may reliably believe that you are listening either to a gullible fool or a malicious saboteur.

Now, these comments of mine here today, if they are pertinent at all, are pertinent only because our guest today is a typical American businessman.

He is the epitome and prototype of the American boy who, under the benevolence of our institutions, starts from a humble and obscure beginning and, by ability, courage and determination achieves leadership in a great industry.

Our guest is remarkable not because he is unique in America, but rather because he typifies and represents a group of men in this country of whom there are so very many.

To paraphrase Abraham Lincoln, God must have loved the United States. He put so many fine businessmen in it.

Our guest's record of achievement is magnificent, but nevertheless common to American business leaders and industrialists.

When I tell you about him I could be reciting the history of hundreds of outstanding leaders of American business.

Mr. F. B. Davis, Jr., our speaker today, is the president and chairman of the board of directors of the United States Rubber Company.

He was born in a little upstate town in New York, and after he had finished his preliminary education, he entered Yale University with a total capital of two hundred dollars to see him through.

. By selling calendars and clocks and waiting on the table, Mr. Davis successfully worked his way through the Sheffield Scientific School and graduated as an engineer.

His experience after graduation has been typically and increasingly significant with the assumption of heavier responsibilities.

He was a city engineer at New Haven, Connecticut; then an engineer with the Pennsylvania Railroad; then in the engineering department of the du Pont Company; then an assistant general manager of a division of General Motors Corporation; and then president of the Viscoloid Corporation.

He assumed the presidency of the United States Rubber Company at the zenith of its difficulties.

He led the company successfully during the depression, when it was confronted by heavy debt, reduced sales, and operating deficits.

Mr. Davis faced and fought and overcame those difficulties and, under his guidance, sales of the United States Rubber Company have risen from 78 million to nearly 500 million dollars a year.

Debt has been reduced to nominal significance.

Production of his company is at a peak point.

Mr. Davis has been through the bottom as well as the top of industrial experience.

He is a director of other important business corporations and banks and is interested in normal American avocations such as farming and outdoor sports.

Today Mr. Davis is to tell us about rubber, and certainly we are all interested in that subject, because our tires are getting pretty thin after two or three recaps, and some of us at least attribute our mounting golf scores to those horrible things we have been using as golf balls for the last few years.

It is a privilege for us today to hear the story of "Rubber, Your Obedient Servant" from Mr. F. B. Davis, Jr., a typical and successful American businessman whom we all admire and respect for his capacity and accomplishments—Mr. Davis.

The Introductory Remarks of Mr. Davis

It is gracious of your club to invite me here today. In fact, it is amazing—considering what my grandfather said about your city. About one hundred and twenty years ago, when my grandfather was a young man, he came here via horseback from New York. He took an option on considerable property that is now Chicago proper. After spending a month here he got on his horse and rode back to New York to stay. When asked why he returned my grandfather said: "That place out there will never amount to anything."

This confession is made now for two reasons. First, it shows just how wrong a Davis can be. Second, if any of my predictions today should miss the mark, you can charitably say: "He sure was off the beam, but at least he came by it honestly."

There has been much interest in rubber for some time now. Recently we received a letter from a lady asking if we could spare a few synthetic rubber plants—she said she wanted them for her garden.

This request led us to believe that perhaps our industry had not kept the public too well informed about our new baby—synthetic rubber.

* * *

M. Glen Miller of the M. Glen Miller advertising firm of Chicago, who is a past president of the Chicago Federated Advertising Club, introduces Arthur H. (Red) Motley, vice president and a director of the Crowell-Collier Publishing Company and publisher of The American Magazine. *Following Mr. Miller's interesting introduction, Mr. Motley responds with a humorous comment. (This was much enjoyed by the audience.)*

Distinguished guests and members: It is a considerable honor for me to have this little task today, because, for a long time, I have been a great admirer of Red Motley's. He is the kind of man to whom the people in the advertising business look up. In the advertising business we like to think of Red Motley as one of our sacred cows. I use that term in the more affectionate meaning, rather than that used by agronomists or in animal husbandry. I don't mean to imply, however, that he isn't sometimes referred to by the name of some other wild or domestic animal or its offspring. But he is the kind of man that we like to point out as an example of Horatio Alger success. He is the kind of man who has made his own way by hard work and perseverance and by knowing the right people.

Red Motley has done quite well for a boy. He has just turned forty, and, if any of you think life has just begun for him, you have something to hear a little later on.

He will undoubtedly tell you something about his religion and his political beliefs and his predilection for blondes. That probably is due to the fact that he came from Minnesota, where blondes are thick —I mean numerically thick.

He went to the University of Minnesota and later took law at Columbia, but this peculiar episode was brought to a quick finish when he got his first client. It seems he took a case for a merchant who had had an altercation with one of his customers, and the case came up in court just at a time this merchant had to go out of town. So he left word with his fiery young attorney to let him know just as soon as the case had been decided. After it was over, Motley sent a telegram to his client, which read: "Right has triumphed." Shortly thereafter, he got a return telegram from his client, and it said "Appeal the case."

Red Motley doesn't mince words. He cuts right through to the core of things, and I think his forthrightness and honesty are probably responsible in a great degree for his success. When he was made publisher of *The American Magazine,* I wrote him a little note of congratulations. It was a pleasure for me to have had such a thing happen to someone I knew, and I wrote a very nice affectionate piece of copy. It was a masterpiece of copywriting, to tell you the truth. After an appropriate interval, an envelope came back with the Crowell-Collier mark on it, and I opened it and inside was a little slip of scratchpad paper and across it was scrawled, with a red pencil, "Thanks. Red."

You will hear a talk today that I guarantee will grip you from beginning to end. Red is in very fine fettle today. I know from talking with him briefly before the meeting. I might tell you about one meeting that he addressed. During the course of the long and arduous talk, Red had become a little hoarse, and after it was over and the people began to come up and talk to him, there was a man with a little boy and Red said to him, "Well, how did you like it?" The boy looked up at him and said, "You need a new needle."

I think it's no more than right for Red to stand on his own feet from now on, and it is a good deal of pleasure for me to introduce to you Mr. Arthur H. Motley, vice president and director of the Crowell-Collier Publishing Company and publisher of *The American Magazine.*

Mr. Motley began as follows:

Well, I made it. There was a minute there that I thought I was not going to get a chance to make the speech. I thought Miller was going to make it.

*   *   *

*Percy Wilson, president of Percy Wilson Mortgage &
Finance Company, introduces Emil Schram, president of
the New York Stock Exchange.*

Distinguished guests and fellow members: Ever since my early youthful invention of how to get rich quick was blown to smithereens by the New York Stock Exchange, I have always wanted to hear from the president. One of the things that I wanted to ask was why, out of 130 million people in the United States, the Exchange always decided it was the stocks that I bought that were too high. Another thing that has always been rather curious to me is, why is it necessary to have both bulls and bears? I would be much in favor of shooting the bears, which reminds me of the man who, having overspeculated in Wall Street, lost his money; and a friend of his said, "Well, George, were you a bear or a bull?" The victim shook his head sadly and said, "Neither—just a plain, simple ass!"

Now, from the hunting ground of the bears and the deep-walled canyons of the bulls, comes the shepherd out to the pastureland, to talk to the little Lambs.

You know, the present incumbent of the high-backed chair of that mysterious and unpredictable barometer of corporation earnings, deficits and tips was born down here in Peru, Indiana. For my part, I am awfully glad that the New York Stock Exchange finally selected a farmer, who understood us out here, and who himself is operating one of the largest farms in Illinois. It is one of the additional credits to the great State that a farmer from Illinois can do the kind of job of running a farm that makes him the man to be selected for running the New York Stock Exchange.

It was in 1933, because of the successful operations of one of these farms of Mr. Schram's, together with the many interrelated business enterprises connected with it, that he was selected as a chief of the Drainage, Levee and Irrigation Division of the Reconstruction Finance Corporation, and, three years later, the President appointed him a member of the board of directors of the Reconstruction Finance Corporation, of which he was elected chairman of the board in 1938.

It is very significant that, during the last three or four years, the New York Stock Exchange has undoubtedly enjoyed greater mass confidence and suffered less public criticism than at any time in its history. . . . I would like to call your attention to the fact that perhaps this record dates back to the Ark and Noah, who was the only other man able to keep so many companies afloat while the whole world was in liquidation.

It is with a great deal of pleasure that I have the honor to present to you a fellow citizen from Illinois, who will speak to us on the subject of "Venture Capital"—Emil Schram. Mr. Schram.

* * *

An interesting illustration of how the president of a club emphasized in his introduction the qualities which were the exact opposite of those possessed by the speaker is given in the following example. Charles W. Wooldridge, then president of the Rotary Club of Dallas, Texas, introduces Carl Bolte, who was then a director and vice president of Rotary International and a militant crusader for anything he believed to be right. Some of Mr. Bolte's friends said of him approvingly and in good humor that he was sometimes bombastic.

It is now my pleasure to present our guest of honor and principal speaker.

All of you have known, I am sure, some fellow who at all times and under all circumstances makes a supreme effort to agree and be agreeable; the type of fellow who keeps his counsel for fear of asserting some principle with which all of his hearers do not agree; the type of fellow who nods affirmatively to compliment and flatter his adversary; the type of fellow who never takes a definite stand on any issue for fear of creating some ill will among those who take the opposite stand.

It is now my pleasure to present to the Dallas Rotary Club a man who is the extreme opposite of the one I have just described, the Honorable Carl Bolte.

*   *   *

Ralph Budd, president of the Chicago, Burlington & Quincy Railroad Company, introduces Charles F. Kettering, famous inventor and then a vice president and director of General Motors Corporation.

It is an unusual thing, even at an Executives' Club luncheon, to have a man of such truly great distinction as the guest speaker of today. He ranks as the foremost leader in the realm of science and invention. He is, moreover, an extremely practical man, as his position of vice president in one of the greatest corporations of the world attests. Besides that, he possesses, in a rare degree, the gift of expression which enables him to tell about abstruse and technical subjects in a language that all can understand, and in a way that is most entertaining.

All of you know him or know of him, and I shall not take your time and his to relate in detail his many inventions, the humanitarian and scientific activities in which he participates or the formal honors which have come to him in recognition of his accomplishments.

The subject which is assigned to "Boss Ket," as he is affectionately known, is "Some Secrets of the Postwar Period." I can't help being a little amused at that, because I remember hearing him say, on several occasions, that, when he was asked "What will the cars be like next year?" his answer was "We don't know. If we did, we would build them this year."

Now, here we are twelve hundred strong, eager to share this secret, and if it is a secret, twelve hundred of us, including the press, will do our very best to keep it for you.

Literally, seriously, we are delighted with the opportunity to hear you, Dr. Charles F. Kettering.

*   *   *

W. W. Touchstone, past president of the Rotary Club of Los Angeles, introduces Dr. Francisco Villagran, Consul

General of Mexico in Los Angeles, at an international
meeting of Rotary Clubs in Mexicali, Mexico.

This gathering tonight is more than a meeting of Rotary Clubs of different cities. It is a meeting of fellow Rotarians of different nationalities and different languages. We here exemplify the true ideals of Rotary International.

Our speaker tonight fits perfectly into this meeting. He is a Mexican, a fellow citizen of you who are members of the Mexicali Club and who are our gracious hosts tonight.

He acquired a good part of his formal education in the United States at Jefferson College in Louisiana. Moreover, in the good American tradition he worked in the United States to earn his way through that college. He returned to Mexico to complete his education at the University of Mexico, and in the years that have gone by has become one of the outstanding educators of Mexico. He was chosen by his government to become the Consul General of Mexico at Los Angeles, the most important consular post in the Mexican diplomatic service. Possessed of a keen insight into human nature, he has acquired an amazing understanding of the characteristics of the people of the United States. In addition, he is a fellow Rotarian, a member of the Rotary Club of Mexico City.

No other man is better qualified to be the principal speaker at this meeting—a meeting of Mexicans and North Americans—a meeting of Rotarians, men brought together through the fellowship and ideals of Rotary.

We in the United States have learned to admire and respect him as much as you admire and respect him. It is with a great deal of pleasure that I present to you, Doctor Francisco Villagran, Consul General of Mexico.

*   *   *

James B. Blaine, past president of the Executives' Club
of Chicago, and executive vice president of John F. Cuneo
Company, Chicago, introduces United States Senator Claude
Pepper of Florida.

It would be impossible to have a Southern gentleman with us to-day who is more Southern than Senator Claude Pepper. He has spent one-third of his life in Texas—and one-third in Florida. It's true that he lived only nine months in Texas when he was five years old, but any good Texan will tell you that this is equal to fifteen or twenty years anywhere else.

Senator Pepper has had an active political life since his early days in law school. While a student at Harvard Law School he campaigned for the democratic nominee who was opposing Henry Cabot Lodge on the issue of the League of Nations. He has been an advocate of international understanding since that time.

In 1928, four years after his graduation from law school, he was elected to the Florida legislature. Six years later he made his first campaign for the United States Senate. He did not win that election in 1934, but he was elected for a two-year unexpired term in the Senate in 1936, and was reelected in 1938 in a walk-away. Actually, in Florida, one is not elected to office—one simply fights to get the Democratic nomination. Then one sits back to see whether it is a unanimous vote or whether a republican has dared to go South.

During the bitter days immediately before Pearl Harbor when every one seemed to be either isolationist or internationalist, the Senator had a unique distinction. He was hanged in effigy before the Capitol building. His friends were both angry and pleased. Angry at the insult—pleased that only the effigy had been hanged.

I suspect that there were others who would have been just as pleased if the situation were reversed. Senator Pepper is a man loyal to his party, as he has shown by his negative response to Henry Wallace's third party. And he has proved that he has a loyalty that stretches beyond party, beyond sectionalism, to the place he feels America must play in the world of nations.

It is with sincere pleasure that I introduce to you the United States Senator from Florida, the Honorable Claude Pepper.

*   *   *

Even the introduction to club members, perhaps at an annual meeting, of persons who may be employed in the

*club office can be done in an interesting manner. Thomas
R. Mulroy, Chicago attorney, made the following brief but
clever introduction:*

First, may I present Miss Moore, that lovely and gracious lady
who, at this very moment, is transcribing my poor words on the right
here. Miss Moore is a skillful secretary, court reporter, stenotypist,
and ticket seller. Verily, she is the quintessence of an amanuensis.
And since you may not have the time to look up those words as I did,
I would tell you that they simply mean, in the current slang of our
children, that Miss Moore is on the beam, she's in the groove, and
she's cooking with gas!

* * *

*The same Mr. Mulroy, past president of the Executives'
Club of Chicago, introduces Ilka Chase, radio, stage and
screen star.*

It is a tradition of this club, Miss Chase, that the president in introducing an *artiste* such as you must attempt to be satiric and sar-
donic—but not today! You, my dear lady, are a dangerous woman,
and I would not think of letting you have the last laugh.

You know there is an old adage that God made women without a
sense of humor so that they could love men instead of laughing at
them. Our guest is a devastating exception to that rule.

Anyway, it is too hard to introduce women. You have to select
your words with such infinite care. For example, you may call a
woman a kitten, but you must not call her a cat.

You may call a woman a mouse, but definitely not a rat!

You may call a woman, as a term of endearment, "duck," but you
simply must avoid "goose!"

You may, and I recommend it to you gentlemen, greet your wife in
the morning with a cheery: "My dear, you certainly are a vision,"
but, please, oh, please, never say, "My dear, you certainly are a
sight!"

But men are queer, too. They say the main difference between man
and beast is man's brains, but there the difference ends, because man

is lion-hearted, chicken-livered, pigeon-toed, busy as a bee, sly as a fox, blind as a bat, gentle as a lamb, drunk as a hoot owl, stubborn as a mule, strong as an ox, vain as a peacock, happy as a lark, or crazy as a loon—depending upon your particular point of view.

Miss Chase gained stage fame on Broadway by her portrayal of the part of the brazen cat, and I don't mean kitten, in the play entitled *The Women*. She is now a scintillating movie star.

Miss Chase is the author of two successive best sellers, *Past Imperfect* and *In Bed We Cry*. I read *Past Imperfect* and liked it very much. I read *In Bed We Cry* . . . period!!

Abraham Lincoln once wrote a review of a book—not Miss Chase's, of course—from which I wonder if I might adopt his comments as my own view of *In Bed We Cry*. Mr. Lincoln wrote:

"For those who like this kind of book, this is the kind of a book they will like."

Miss Chase has always been years ahead of her time, a genuine prodigy.

At the tender age of fourteen, she was valedictorian of her graduating class in a secluded convent school, and on the occasion of her address she delivered this sweet, idealistic and unsophisticated philosophy of true love (with my own apologies to Dorothy Parker):

"Dear fathers, mothers, and classmates, I would like to recite a poem about true love:

> "When you finally swear you're his,
> Shivering and sighing.
> And he vows his passion is
> Infinite, undying,—
> Classmates, make a note of this:
> One of you is lying!"

Here is indeed the truly soft-spoken woman's woman, incorrigible romanticist, shy rosebud, as we next find her at the age of twenty-five. One evening an old friend of the family rushed in to her and said, sobbing: "Ilka, some man has taken my car and run away with my wife!"

"No! No!" exclaimed Ilka, "not your *new* car!"

Now that all my bad jokes are concluded let me say in all earnestness that this huge gathering today is a dramatic tribute to Ilka Chase, one of America's brilliant women.

I do now present to you with a genuine feeling of privilege the one and only Ilka Chase.

* * *

Edwin B. Moran, manager of the Central Division of the National Association of Credit Men and author of The Credit Side of Selling, *introduces E. N. Ronnau, assistant vice president and general credit manager of the Cook Paint and Varnish Company of Kansas City, Missouri.*

When our next speaker was asked for biographical data, and told not to be modest, he wrote:

"When modesty was made a virtue, it was a great day for fools, for it brings the genius and the fool down to the same denomination."

It was really difficult to trace this speaker's "Who's Who" but the Credit Interchange Department of the Credit Men's Association never fails—we got all the dirt.

He was born in the state of Kansas, but you can't hold that against the state.

After the usual growing pains of youth, St. Mary's College gave him a B.A. degree, but shortly after he left there, the school closed.

He has a charming and smart wife, from whom his three sons and one daughter inherited their good looks and intellect.

He has five grandchildren, and from his bragging, we know they are chips off the old block, with all modern improvements.

While not advertising it, he admits he has all known vices, but tries to keep them under control.

His hobby is hunting. He has just returned from a pheasant-hunting trip in South Dakota, and if you believe him there is no need for any of you to plan a trip there because he got all there were.

He has been active in the Credit Men's Association at Kansas City for more years than he admits his age to be; he has served as chairman of too many committees to enumerate, as director, vice president and then president, during which term he brought the membership to its all-time high.

He is now a director of the National Association of Credit Men and in his spare time serves as assistant vice president and general credit manager of the Cook Paint and Varnish Company.

A fellow who does a grand job of being a true friend.

He will represent the credit man's point of view in this forum discussion on "Sales and Credit Methods in Promoting Distribution and Profits."

My very good friend—Ed N. Ronnau

*   *   *

Harry L. Stone, manager of bank relations, International Harvester Company, introduces Gen. Carlos P. Romulo, Resident Commissioner of the Philippines.

General Romulo, The Executives' Club of Chicago is delighted to have the privilege of hearing you speak on the subject, "America's Stake in the Pacific."

On the occasion you spoke to us before, I do not recall that any description was given you of The Executives' Club, but, in the very apt words of our ex-president, Tom Mulroy, "Our Club is composed of fourteen hundred Chicago executives, many of whom were born in the country, where they worked like the devil so they could live in the city, where they worked like the devil so they could move back to the country." That is a brief and reasonably accurate statement describing this club.

Being an army man, General Romulo would undoubtedly be interested in an episode concerning army personnel, but I seriously doubt if he witnessed the following: An army sergeant was drilling his underlings, and, with that cold fishy stare that only could emanate from the glaring eye of a top-kick, he bellowed, "Attention!" One lowly private in an oversized uniform was singled out for special criticism, and his ears were greeted by, "Didn't you hear me give the order, 'Attention!'" To which the private replied, "I am standing at attention, sir. It's my uniform that's at ease."

General Romulo is a business executive of the Philippines. Indeed, he is one of the most distinguished and most articulate sons of his native land.

He holds honorary doctor of laws degrees from Columbia and Notre Dame universities. After achieving his master of arts degree at Columbia University in 1921, General Romulo returned to the Philippines, where he soon became editor and publisher of two prominent newspapers and managing director of two radio stations.

Our speaker has been during his career a publisher, editor, author, university professor, playwright, Pulitzer prize winner, and at present Resident Commissioner of the Philippines. As a colonel and now a general in the United States Army, he served on the staff of his good friend General Douglas MacArthur during all of the tragic but gallant fight to save Bataan and Corregidor. Later, he continued to serve General MacArthur as aide-de-camp at his headquarters in Australia.

General Romulo is perhaps to us the best known Filipino. This brilliant, courageous, forthright hero is admired and revered not alone for his inimitable platform eloquence, but also for his championing the cause of the Philippines in this country.

Gentlemen, I give you General Romulo.

* * *

Harold O. McLain, past president of the Executives' Club of Chicago, introduces Thomas R. Mulroy, attorney.

It is a great pleasure to be here today, but I at once admit that I realize it is exceedingly hazardous for me to attempt to be either fatuous or facetious with Mr. Tom Mulroy. To attempt verbal jousting or repartee with him is, of course, to court the whirlwind, and, on the other hand, to phrase his serious qualities too patently is to emphasize the obvious to you fellows who have known him so long and are already his admirers and friends.

In spite of these difficulties of approach, however, I suppose I should accord some compliance with the traditions of this rostrum, and so, as the fellow said in the Turkish bath, "Won't you please bear with me," while I follow the plan of the Texas steer, with a point here and a point there, and a lot of bull in between.

Now you know that Tom, even as a youth, and as a child, indicated remarkable precocity and sagacity and erudition. That was evidenced when he was just a little fellow in a primary class—and under the tutelage of a very stout schoolmistress. The teacher was emphasizing to the children that animals have capacities that sometimes physically exceed those of men, and she told them of the little yellow canary she had at home, how it could sing, and she propounded this question to the children: "Can you tell me what my little canary, at home in his cage, can do that I can't do?" Tom, who was of a practical turn of mind, volunteered, raised his hand, and said, "Teacher, I know what he can do that you can't do—he can take a bath in a saucer."

A little later, one day, one of the school trustees visited the room. He mounted the teacher's platform, and, to test the children on their powers of observation, he moved from one side of the platform to the other, meanwhile taking a pencil out of one vest pocket and putting it into another. Then he turned to the children and said, "Can anybody tell me what I have just done?" Again Tom volunteered. "I know what you did, sir," said Tom, "you walked in front of our teacher without saying 'Excuse me.' " He was very bright.

Advancing in his school work, he was one day asked in an economics class to explain some of the uses of cowhide. Tom had ready answers. "The main use of the cowhide," he said, "is that it helps to hold the cow together."

In a class on anatomy, he was once asked to define the word "anatomy." Tom said, "It consists of three parts—the head, the chest and the stomach. The head contains the brains, if any," which showed that he was perspicacious, even in those days. "Then," he said, "the chest contains the liver and the lungs. The stomach contains the bowels, of which there are five—a, e, i, o, u."

As he progressed a little higher in his school work, one day they were discussing inflation. Tom volunteered the information that inflation was a bad thing, in that it caused two to live more steeply than one, but in one way, inflation had its virtues, because, said Tom, "under inflation, when you forget your change, you don't lose so much."

Then, as he got a little older, he finally very zealously began the pursuit of real knowledge. Sometimes it was diurnal, sometimes matutinal, and very often nocturnal.

Tom is a great host. He entertains people hospitably and bounte-ously. Recently I was at a stag poker party in his home. We sat down at the table at eight o'clock in the evening. We were just starting to play when we heard the patter of little feet and the chatter of little voices up above.

Tom said, "Just a minute, fellows. Those are my little children, and at this time they always come to bring me a goodnight message. It makes me feel very humble and reverent to have those little fellows come and talk to me at night. Let's listen."

We listened, and a small voice piped up and said, "Daddy." Tom said, "Yes, Mary, dear, what is it?" Mary replied, "Daddy, I wanted to tell you that little Willie found another bedbug in his bed."

Of course Tom's drive and energy and vitality often make him a little hectic. I commented on it and sympathized with his wife, Dorothy, one time, on that problem. She said, "I'll tell you, Harold. Tom means well, and I try, always, to be patient and philosophical with him, and I always try to remember, too, that it is better to have loved and lost than never to have loved at all."

Away from his home, Tom is primarily an athlete, and a man among men. I love to play golf with him. His innate ability as a golfer, and his capacity for sharp and dishonest trading for strokes on the first tee is outstanding.

Recently I had a game of golf with him at Exmoor. As he came in and sat down in the locker room and disrobed to put on golf clothes, I noticed some big numbers tattooed on a certain portion of his anat-omy. I said, "Tom, why do you have those numbers tattooed on you?" He said "Those numbers aren't tattooed on me; that's where Dorothy hit me with the license plate when I held the door open for her to drive the car in the garage."

Now, isn't that just like a woman? A woman can go through an eighteen-inch aisle in a Walgreen store and never knock a thing off the counter, and then go home and drive the car into a twenty-foot door and knock both fenders off both sides of the car.

Well, as I said, we started to play golf. We got around to about the third hole when a dog ran out from under a fence and attacked Tom. The dog snapped at his heels and then at Tom's legs. In self-

c

protection Tom pulled his niblick out of his golf bag and made a pass at the dog with the steel head of the club. The club hit the dog back of the ear and knocked him out.

The dog's owner came over the fence just then, picked up the dog, and said to Tom, "That was a dirty trick, knocking out my dog."

Tom said, "Well, what did you expect me to do? The dog was trying to bite me; I had to defend myself."

The dog's owner said, "Why didn't you use the handle end of the club? Why did you have to hit him with the head?"

Tom said, "I would have used the other end of the club, if it had been the other end of the dog that was attacking me."

Going on with our game, we got around to the eleventh hole, when Tom sliced a long ball over into the rough. He went over there, found the ball, and stooped down and picked up a few leaves. Then he took a club out of his bag, put it back of the ball, and picked up some more stuff. Finally my partner, Harry Stone, said "What are you trying to do, Tom? I thought you might possibly have a spoon lie here, but if you keep on with that, you'll soon be able to hit with your driver."

Well, we had a fine game, and Tom enjoyed himself, and, as usual, he insisted on keeping the score. He won $3.75. After the game he drank five old-fashioneds, ate a double order of rare roast beef with two pieces of pie à la mode, and then climbed into his car, completely happy, and drove away smiling, all set for another week of hard work in his law office.

I know I'm taking a lot of time here, but I'm doing that purposely. I propose to take so much time that when it comes Tom's turn, he will either have to give up his speech or else abandon those insidious and castigating sarcasms he is prepared to heap on me. He won't even have time to take a bow.

But let's take up where I left off with Tom, back in his office. You know, gentlemen, when you get Tom in his law office, it is time to abandon these stupid inanities and be serious about him.

Tom Mulroy is a conscientious, indefatigably industrious and serious student of the law. He is one of the youngest lawyers with high rank in his profession, or, if you prefer, he is one of the highest ranking lawyers who is young in his profession, in this Chicago area.

He is to tell us today about a subject which is significant to all of us; he is to describe and talk about a legislative enactment which is perhaps one of the major enactments since the beginning of the war.

The Taft-Hartley Act is the most discussed, cussed and praised act in many moons. Tom is going to tell us about it, and I guarantee to you that no lawyer in the United States could bring to you a more thoroughgoing and yet commonsense and understanding analysis of that act than it will be your privilege to hear today in this place.

I think Thomas Mulroy is exactly the right man, at exactly the right time, with exactly the right subject, and I think you will all agree with me that Tom Mulroy also is in exactly the right place when he is here today at the Executives' Club, among his admirers and friends and wellwishers.

I hope you will all indicate to Tom how grateful we are to have him here to speak to us on the subject of the Taft-Hartley Act. Thank you very much.

*　　*　　*

James B. Blaine, executive vice president, John F. Cuneo Company, introduces James E. Gheen, humorous lecturer.

Members of the Executives' Club of Chicago and guests: Despite the fact that this is National Laughter Week and all of us should be prepared to laugh at anything or anybody, I shall not introduce James E. Gheen as a humorist. Instead, I shall say that today we have with us one of the wisest of all men. Because fortunately wisdom and solemnity are not always the same, I do not claim that he is a solemn man.

Mr. Gheen's wisdom is found in three unique abilities which he has developed:

1. He can laugh at the idiosyncrasies of a world chasing its own tail.
2. He can get others to laugh with him.
3. He can laugh at himself. And as the famous Greek oracle said, "He who can laugh at himself can laugh with the gods on Olympus."

I do not know what makes a humorist. There is some wisdom and some mercy and a great deal of whimsy in the humorists I have known. I suggested intelligence as a necessary ingredient, but Mr. Gheen said I was wrong.

Mr. Gheen, after spending a most enjoyable hour with you, I have come to a real respect for your deep understanding of human nature and I want to present you to this meeting today not as a humorist but as a humanist.

And now, Mr. Gheen, I give you this bunch of sour-pussed curmudgeons, otherwise known as the Executives' Club of Chicago, to do with as you please.

*   *   *

Thomas R. Mulroy, attorney, introduces Bainbridge Colby, former Secretary of State.

In 1860 Wendell Phillips said, "You can always get the truth from an American statesman after he has turned seventy or given up all hope of the Presidency."

Now, I think that is a cynical exaggeration. The fact remains, however, that Mr. Colby has turned seventy and is not a candidate for the Presidency. Our guest has always been noted for his courage, for his forthright candor on public issues. Bainbridge Colby is a statesman, richly skilled in affairs of state, abundantly endowed by education, background, and sagacity to perform with gracious efficiency the complex responsibilities of high diplomacy.

A lawyer of international fame, Mr. Colby served with great distinction as Secretary of State in the Cabinet of Woodrow Wilson. Along with Henry Stimson, he is the only living ex-Secretary of State. The toga of an elder statesman has long since rested on the shoulders of Bainbridge Colby and, thus richly and justly enrobed, he has sat at the ringside of history, watching with true perspective, uninhibited by personal ambition or political office.

It is through the keen eyes of such an impartial observer that we are today to see certain vital world and domestic problems and panaceas

Mr. Colby comes to us in the constructive spirit of another great American, the spirit expressed in the midst of the Civil War in these ageless words:

"With malice towards none,

With charity for all,

With firmness in the right as God gives us to see the right,

Let us strive on to finish the work we are in;

To bind up the nation's wounds;

To do all which may achieve and cherish a just and lasting

peace among ourselves and with all nations."

Gentlemen, the former Secretary of State of the United States, Hon. Bainbridge Colby.

* * *

M. Glen Miller of the M. Glen Miller Advertising firm of Chicago presents Edward J. Jeffries, Jr., mayor of Detroit.

Mr. Chairman, gentlemen, and you in the cheaper seats: It has always been my assumption that an introduction was intended to identify a speaker, to qualify him on his authority or to apologize for the poor cuss.

As one of the country's outstanding politicians and municipal planners, Mayor Jeffries needs no identification. As mayor of America's fourth largest city, he needs no apology as an authority on municipal government. And that leaves me with but one alternative.

Now, I cannot apologize for a man who was elected to the Detroit city council at the ripe old age of 31, who was elected to the office of Mayor at the age of 39, and who, after three terms, is still only 44 years old.

I cannot apologize for a man whose favorite vegetable is spinach, who, although a promising young son-of-a-judge of Detroit, went to work as a boy, cutting lawns, cleaning sidewalks and running errands for neighbors, and who, when he was old enough, worked in theaters, the post-office, and in Henry Ford's atelier of automobile production.

Matriculating at the University of Michigan when only 16, Mayor Jeffries took his A.B. and LL.B. degrees and then went bounding off to jolly old prewar London, where he spent four delightful terms of study on the exhilarating and fascinating subject of Roman and British constitutional law.

A great high-school football player, Mayor Jeffries now would rather play golf, in which he is good enough to have won the championship of his own club.

An excellent bowler, he slings a mean bridge hand, is a formidable opponent at any kind of card game, and if his purpose was not so serious today, could regale you with a variety of ingenious card tricks from this platform.

His Honor smokes a pipe, and his wife objects to it no more than most wives do. He drinks only enough to escape solicitation for membership by the W.C.T.U.

Married to a musician, he loathes concerts, but obediently accompanies his spouse, sits quietly and awake during the program, and reaches home without making any nasty remarks.

Now, I ask you, how can I apologize for a guy like that?

I don't want to tell you about his municipal administration. I hope he will do that. But I do want to remind you that shortly after taking office he was able to reduce his city's financial indebtedness to a point where he saved some forty-two million dollars in interest charges.

I don't think it is seemly for me to apologize more for Mayor Jeffries. I feel that he should be presented to you in person and apologize for himself.

Gentlemen, Mayor Edward J. Jeffries, of Detroit, Michigan.

*   *   *

Peter Grimm, chairman of the board of Wm. A. White & Sons of New York City and past president of the Chamber of Commerce of the State of New York introduces V. K. Wellington Koo, distinguished Chinese statesman.

The name of V. K. Wellington Koo, as a most accomplished and effective representative of his country, is perhaps more widely known in the capitals of the world than any other diplomat. I find myself enjoying an unusual sense of gratification in presenting him to you as our guest today, for we were undergraduates at Columbia University at the same time. That would seem to make us contemporaries, which our looks may perhaps belie. If, indeed, he does look to be a good deal younger man than myself, perhaps we see in him another product of the serene life which his Oriental ancestry makes possible.

I recall many things about Mr. Koo as an undergraduate, of which perhaps he is altogether unaware; but one only I will recount. We both lived in Hartley Hall, facing South Field at 116th Street and Amsterdam Avenue. I recall no single time that I passed Mr. Koo's apartment coming home in the evening, at whatever hour, that I didn't see the blind drawn, the apartment all alight and hear the typewriter aclatter. That devotion to his work; that very evident consecration to duty that he knew the future life of his country demanded, made an impression upon me that can never be removed. That earned for him here, though he will count it a minor distinction, the line in *Who's Who* which describes him as "the most brilliant student in the history of Columbia University."

His life from that day has been one long record of continuous service to China and we of the chamber take real and deep satisfaction in paying tribute to one who has made so conspicuous a mark in the world.

He was born in Shanghai in 1888. At Columbia he edited both the *Spectator* and the *Columbian*. He got his A.B. in 1908; his A.M. in 1909; his Ph.D. in 1912 and an Honorary LL.D. in 1917. To read his record of service to China from that point on would be to present a very long list indeed, and most of it you all are familiar with. He was an ardent and hard working representative of his country at the League of Nations. At home in China he has served as Finance Minister, Minister of Foreign Affairs and Prime Minister. He was also at one time a member of the International Board of Arbitration at The Hague, and before he became the ambassador here, he was ambassador to a number of other countries, notably France and Great Britain. He did yeoman work in the organization of the United Nations at San Francisco in 1945; and now we are glad to have him here as his country's representative.

I understand that Mr. Koo's talk will have most to do with trade relationships between our countries. China and the United States are most natural traders—China needs many of the things we have and make, and we, on the other hand, need and want many of the things that only China can produce. In this respect the two countries are natural complements one to the other. When all is well in the economic relations between the two countries, the barometer will stand at fair, and if it does not stand there today, I hope the ambassador will tell us why it does not; that he will explain what the situation is and how the two countries may be brought together and enjoy, fully, the trading advantages which they present one to the other.

It is with the greatest of pleasure and feelings of the honor paid us that I present to you Dr. V. K. Wellington Koo.

* * *

Chancey I. Weaver, past president of the Rotary Club of Columbus, Ohio, introduces Dr. Rees Edgar Tuloss, president of Wittenberg College, to the Columbus Rotary Club.

Because I live in Springfield, Ohio, I was tendered the honor of introducing my distinguished fellow townsman, the president of Wittenberg College, to this club, composed about one half of the garden variety of business men and the other half of president and members of the faculty of Ohio State University. To prepare this introduction, I read a number of books, including one by Emily Post. In her book, she says, "An introduction should do several things: first, quiet the audience; second, qualify the speaker as having sufficient information adequately to cover his subject; third, to warm the speaker to the audience and create a friendly atmosphere for his message." I also noticed a footnote, which said, "It is considered good form to leave a little time for the speaker."

This man is distinguished for his work in the Lutheran Church, for his long and capable service in education, and for his business accomplishments, including a bank presidency, the operation of his own private business and his able speaking and writing in this country and abroad.

To those members of this club, who, like myself, mingle in the lowly marts of trade, Dr. Rees Edgar Tuloss is a man of parts, to those of you who tread softly in the halls of higher learning, this man is an intrepid and untrammelled exegete.

* * *

Peter Grimm, past president of the Chamber of Commerce of the State of New York and chairman of the board of Wm. A. White and Sons of New York City, introduces Dr George Gallup.

A wise observer of human affairs once said that there are at least two reasons for one's actions—a good reason and a real one. I could not help but think of this when I asked my friend, Dr. Gallup, if he would not come today to speak to my fellow members of the chamber. The good reason I had was, of course, to furnish a treat to you all and, at the same time, to honor Dr. Gallup on the remarkable contribution he has made to the modern scene by what is commonly known as the Gallup Poll.

And now I must confess to what the real reason was. I want him to solve what has been a mystery to me, and must be a mystery to most of you, and that is this. Who participates in all these Gallup Polls? Where are the polls taken up? And how are they taken up in such great numbers, without our knowing they are being done? Has anyone ever stopped you on the street, or come to your office, or called you on the telephone, to ask your opinion on the myriad of questions on which the Gallup Poll utters its dicta? Well, we have Dr. Gallup here now and we will ask him these questions. But we will not forget to serve the good reason we had in inviting him here and that is to compliment him on the great and original accomplishment his poll is. Yet, I hope he will address himself, at least in part, to the mystery that surrounds the poll.

Dr. Gallup's boyhood was spent in Jefferson, Iowa, where he was born in 1901. It was while he was a student at the state university of Iowa that he got this idea of measuring public opinion, public tastes, public anything. In a very few years he developed the idea into a successful organization, which is known as the American Institute of Public Opinion, which now has affiliates in nine countries in Europe, South America and in Australia. That organization was founded as recently

C*

as 1935 and immediately attracted wide public attention when, in its first year, it made an amazingly accurate prediction of the Presidential election in 1936. Since that time, Dr. Gallup has increased his prestige by successfully predicting the outcome of numerous national and state elections, as well as reporting successfully the public opinion on vital public issues and ascertaining public tastes.

In 1940, Dr. Gallup founded Audience Research, Inc., which carries on continuous audience surveys for a number of the motion picture companies. He is the author of many articles and books on public opinion and reader research. Two of his best known books are *The Pulse of Democracy*, published in 1940, and *A Guide Book to Public Opinion Polls*, published in 1944. I hope Dr. Gallup won't take occasion to tell us that, if we had read his books, we would not be asking the questions we did. We would much rather have him tell us the answers.

Dr. Gallup has had honorary degrees conferred upon him by Northwestern University, Tufts College and Drake University. And I should like him to feel that the old institution of the Chamber of Commerce of the State of New York, more deeply steeped in tradition than any of these, wishes to confer an equivalent honor upon him and express our gratitude for his coming to us today.

*   *   *

Mr. Grimm introduces Thomas E. Dewey, Governor of the State of New York.

I know that I am expressing the feelings of all of you when I say to Governor Dewey that we are exceedingly pleased to have him with us, and that he does us honor by coming to us on this occasion. As chief executive officer of the Empire State of the Union, he has added luster to its prestige and considerable to his own reputation. I think it can be said that Thomas E. Dewey needs no introduction to any American audience. It would, of course, be presumptuous to introduce him to this New York audience.

I like to think that Tom Dewey first captured the imagination of the people, not only of our city, but also of this country, by his work in the early thirties as special prosecutor. Other communities throughout our land with similar problems watched his work with anxiety, and then with deep satisfaction, as Thomas E. Dewey, then Assistant District Attorney, fought the enemies of society and brought them to book for their crimes. But his rise and his accomplishments did not stop there, for he went steadily from one success to another.

The administration of Mr. Dewey as our governor will be remembered for many reasons. But there are three reasons which, while they are cause for the gratitude of the entire community, have a special significance to the businessmen of this state. One of these is the manner in which he met the problems of the veteran. It is a sad commentary, but true, that in the past each party tried to outdo the other in the appearance of liberality. That was not Governor Dewey's way. We shall be forever grateful for the wisdom he exercised in appointing a bipartisan committee to weigh the problem of the veteran and thus pull it out of politics.

A second reason lies in the fact that Governor Dewey was the first in a long line of governors who made state home rule a reality. He did more than pay lip service to the idea of home rule; he actually gave local communities home rule, at the same time using all the facilities of the state to help these communities with their problems.

The third and perhaps the most important reason why businessmen of the state are grateful to our governor is his accumulation of a surplus of 500 million dollars. All of this sum, except 57 million dollars, was accumulated in his own administration. As a result, the entire state rehabilitation program is being financed out of this fund. In the same period the debt of the state was reduced by more than 20 per cent. And in this year of heavy peacetime taxes he has reduced the state tax burden on the people by 25 per cent.

The chamber is happy in this opportunity to make grateful public acknowledgement and appreciation of these accomplishments. Too often public office in this country is an invitation to public criticism. A man who rears his head in politics above his fellows finds he is a ready target for many a blow. I count it a great privilege on this, my first meeting as president of the chamber, to recognize on your behalf this good work of our governor, and to tell him we are proud of him.

*   *   *

Ferre C. Watkins, Chicago attorney, introduces Robert A. Taft, United States Senator from Ohio.

When Athens fell before the onslaught of the Spartans, some of its greatest thinkers walked amidst her ruins and dreamed and talked of a perfect government. In the peaceful grove of Academus, Plato told of the qualifications of those who should rule an ideal state. He said that among the youth of the nation those with the greatest sense of justice, of loyalty to their country, and the greatest promise of intellect and character should be chosen to serve the highest function of human-kind, that of governing one's fellows.

Twenty-three centuries later, a boy was born in a distinguished fam-ily in Cincinnati, Ohio. His grandfather had been a prominent judge; a famous Secretary of War; an Attorney-General. His father was Governor-General of the Philippines, President of the United States, Chief Justice of the United States—the only man ever to hold those two positions.

Senator Taft lived with his father in the Philippines and in the White House. He was steeped in the atmosphere of training and learning that Plato discussed twenty-three centuries before.

The Taft tradition is one of amazing service to our country. Senator Taft's mother was the daughter of a United States district attorney; his wife, nationally known for her charm and brilliance, is the daughter of a former solicitor-general of the United States; his sister is dean at Bryn Mawr College; his brother, Charles, is an authority on both mu-nicipal and diplomatic affairs; the Tafts' four sons all were in the late war, Robert, Jr., having participated in the landings at Guadalcanal, Sicily, Salerno, and Normandy.

Such a background as Senator Taft has, living in the shadows of great ancestors, would have obscured a smaller man, but he, in his own right, has carved out a career that is proper to stand beside that of any of his ancestors.

At Harvard, in the law school, he was first in his graduating class. At Yale, he stood number one. In the Ohio bar examinations, among members of his profession, he ranked first in that test. No man ever came to Washington better prepared by training, background, and character than Senator Taft.

He served six years in the Ohio House of Representatives. He was Floor Leader and Speaker, and was elected to the Ohio Senate. A leading lawyer of the nation, he is now serving his second term as United States Senator.

But there is something very interesting about this man. Despite his eminence and his unquestioned leadership in the Senate, he still serves as chairman of his county republican committee; as committeeman of his own home precinct; and as republican chairman of his township.

Amidst the storms of recent years, his clear, calm voice has sounded from the bridge, pointing out the shoals ahead and charting the path to escape them. In an age of confusion, ill-considered utterances, and hasty decisions, Senator Taft has met great issues with Olympian calm, unawed by opposition, uninfluenced by political expediency.

We have the honor to hear today from one of the nation's leading statesmen, a man of reasoned judgment, fearless action, and unwavering devotion to his country's cause—the senior senator from Ohio, the Honorable Robert Taft.

* * *

Elmer T. Stevens, president, Charles A. Stevens & Company of Chicago, introduces Paul G. Hoffman, president of The Studebaker Corporation, before the Rotary Club of Chicago.

My introduction may be of the thumbnail sort. I met Paul Hoffman first in 1926. Through a lack of sales resistance, I found myself chairman of the State Traffic Committee of the Association of Commerce. I was completely equipped for that job. I knew nothing whatsoever about state traffic—didn't know there was such a thing as state traffic —and it had not occurred to me that state traffic might be a subject for a scientific study.

When I went to my first meeting, I faced a group of uniformed policemen who looked at me with pathetic hope—that here was a Moses to lead them out of their troubled spots—and I knew I had "the bear by the tail."

Somewhere I had heard that there was a young man who had lately come from Los Angeles to South Bend to be in charge of the sales of the Studebaker Corporation, who had that ability to look ahead which my job required. We got him on the phone. He came to Chicago. He talked to our committee, and the scientific study of state traffic engineering became a fact.

The Chicago study has been and still is one of the greatest studies on state traffic that has ever been had.

Paul Hoffman in Los Angeles had been foreseeing enough to know that it would be necessary to solve those problems if the automobile was not thoroughly to lick the municipality.

I got to know him; learned that he had been in Chicago; educated at the University of Chicago; had gone to war; after the war he had been a salesman of Studebaker automobiles in Los Angeles, and such a good salesman that he ultimately and shortly owned the agency—the largest in the corporation's organization; and then had been brought, as vice president in charge of sales, to South Bend.

That organization has demonstrated that it is forward looking, too, by the car that they have on the streets today. Forward looking depends upon having a right kind of view after also—and that car certainly has a view after.

My first introduction to the Studebaker automobile came in 1926 after I had met Paul Hoffman. I went to Los Angeles to look over his work there, and I drove back in a friend's car—a Studebaker—and that was some car! It was heavy, it was powerful, it had guts, and it had a brake, whose sole purpose in life was to stop that car. I drove it occasionally, and every time I applied the brake we stopped to pull my passengers out of the windshield.

I hope that I look reasonably fresh right now because at eleven-thirty last night I finished a twenty-five hundred mile drive in one of these "go as you please, either direction" cars. It was a twenty-five hundred mile afloat and glide ride, and my passengers did not at any time go into the windshield. It has a forward-looking performance there.

In fact, I would say that this man, Hoffman, has three characteristics—a capacity for terrifically hard work, ability to look ahead, and ability to associate with himself men of high enthusiasm and ability.

He is not a one-man show in any sense of the word, and the things in which he works are not one-man shows.

During this time of which I speak, he developed a family of five sons and two daughters. The five sons went to war and all five came back. The mother carried an almost parallel activity in war activities, and Paul, himself, was busy in war production; but all the time during war production he was groping with the fact, indisputable, but not often considered, that a postwar time was coming, and with that postwar time would come problems—some new and many old—and not previously solved, the solution of which would be necessary if the American way of life—that way of life which is pledged to the sovereignty of the individual—was to endure. Then the Committee for Economic Development was born.

In a little bulletin gotten out by the Kiplinger Letter the other day, they said it was the best type of thing that businessmen had contributed.

CED is a remarkable effort on the part of intelligent leaders and broad-gauged scientists to solve the economic problems in a way which is fair to everyone and on the basic premise that that which is best for the whole country is best for everyone in it.

It is an interesting development and a fundamentally sound and important thing in the economic history of our country. I think you will find it of extreme interest and importance.

Paul Hoffman has been the chairman of CED since its formation, but it is not the shadow of Paul Hoffman alone, but of the type of men with whom he has been associated.

Please don't misunderstand me. They have done a tremendous amount of work, and they deserve credit for it, but it has not been a hardship. They have been happy in the doing.

I would like to have you meet Paul Hoffman today as a man who has been the leader in this and who has been happy in the fact that he believes, and I believe, and everyone else who was in contact with the organization believes, that we are making a most worthwhile contribution to our history.

Gentlemen, Mr. Paul Hoffman.

* * *

John C. Lewe, Judge of the Appellate Court of Illinois, introduces Dr. Norman Vincent Peale, Minister of the

Marble Collegiate Church of New York City and author of
A Guide to Confident Living.

Our speaker is the Minister of the Marble Collegiate Church of New York City. This is the oldest Protestant church in America, now in the 312th year of its history. Every Sunday morning and evening, I am informed, it is filled to capacity, which suggests a story that my father once told me about an elderly Christian lady who was dissatisfied with her pastor. In recounting his many failings, she said, "Six days a week he is invisible and on the seventh day he is incomprehensible."

For almost a decade, Dr. Peale has been speaking on a nationwide radio hookup over the National Broadcasting System, on the radio program known as "The Art of Living." To his parishioners, and millions of listeners throughout the land, this crusader of modern Christianity is both visible and comprehensible.

Dr. Peale is active in many civic and church organizations. He has written two excellent and well-known books, *The Art of Living,* and *You Can Win.* Our speaker was graduated in 1920 from Ohio Wesleyan University. He has honorary degrees conferred upon him by Syracuse University, Ohio Wesleyan University and Duke University. It is indeed a high privilege to present to you Dr. Norman Vincent Peale, whose subject is "The Art of Living in America Today" —Dr. Peale.

*   *   *

Earl M. Wanacek, Milwaukee attorney, introduces Charles A. Eaton, Member of the House of Representatives from New Jersey, and Chairman of the House Foreign Affairs Committee at an annual meeting and dinner of the Milwaukee Association of Commerce.

We are privileged this evening to have as our speaker a man whose background and experience is as varied and as extensive as would be the case with two or three average individuals.

Our speaker was born in Nova Scotia and was graduated from Acadia University and from the Newton Theological Institute in Massachusetts. He was ordained a Baptist minister and among his pastorates was the largest Baptist church in New York City.

A man of wide and varied interests, he turned his talents to the field of journalism and served as Sociological Editor of the *Toronto Globe,* Canadian correspondent for the *New York Tribune* and the *Boston Transcript,* special correspondent for the *London Times,* and editor of *Leslie's Weekly.*

With the entry of the United States into World War I, Dr. Eaton's authoritative grasp of industrial relations was recognized by his appointment to head the National Service Section of the United States Shipping Board Emergency Fleet Corporation. In this capacity he toured American shipyards and industrial plants and addressed over a million workers to sustain high productivity of war shipping.

Dr. Eaton later devoted himself to the field of industrial relations, becoming head of the industrial relations department of the National Lamp Works of the General Electric Company, and serving other companies as industrial relations consultant.

He was urged to run for Congress in 1924 and was elected on the Republican ticket in the State of New Jersey. In every succeeding campaign he has been reelected and has served most prominently on the House Foreign Affairs Committee.

Dr. Eaton is a firm advocate of United States participation in matters of world peace and cooperation, and has a consistent record of support of legislation which follows these lines.

His concept of internal conditions and of the world viewpoint is not equaled by many men in the world today. He is recognized as one of the most able speakers in Congress and his words are received with the authority his experience and knowledge command.

It is a privilege and a pleasure for me to present to this meeting Representative Charles A. Eaton, of the Congress of the United States, and Chairman of the House Foreign Affairs Committee. His subject will be "Business and the New Congress."

* * *

John C. Lewe, Judge of the Appelate Court of Illinois, introduces Tom C. Clark, Attorney General of the United States

Only a few decades ago some facetious writer said that Texas was "The place where there are the most cows and the least milk, the most rivers and the least water in them, and where you can look the farthest and see the least." What he did not see was the enterprising and indomitable spirit of the Texans. Today, Texas is one of the great states of our union, ranking sixth in population and, to hear the Texans tell about it, it is first in every other respect.

Our speaker was born in Dallas forty-six years ago. He attended Virginia Military Institute and served with the 153rd Infantry in the first world war. Afterwards he studied at the University of Texas and was admitted to the Bar there in 1922. In a few short years, while associated with his father in the practice of law, he won an enviable place in the community. His fine talents and attainments had provided him with a lucrative law practice, but this he gave up in 1937 for an appointment as Special Attorney in the Department of Justice, Bureau of War Risk Litigation. He did not labor very long in obscurity. His sound common sense, his legal acumen and diligence in the discharge of his duties, were soon recognized in Washington. In 1940 he was made chief of the West Coast offices of the Anti-Trust Division. In 1942, he was appointed chief of the War Frauds Unit, and in 1943 Assistant Attorney General in charge of the Anti-Trust Division. He rose from the bottom level of the Department of Justice lawyers to attorney general of the nation in the short space of eight years. Though young in years and young in the point of service, in this exalted position he is boss of the biggest law office in the world.

Tom Clark is an earthy and homespun Texas lawyer with the smack and tang of elemental things—the rectitude and patience of the cliff. His subject is "The Attorney General and the Business Man."

I count it a high privilege to present to you the Attorney General of the United States.

*　　*　　*

Nathaniel Leverone, chairman of the board of the Automatic Canteen Company introduces Billy B. Van, "Ambassador of Good Will from New England," at a ladies' day luncheon of the Executives' Club of Chicago.

I share Billy Van's opinion of this audience because he mentioned to me as we talked and gazed at you lovely ladies how magnificent you appeared, as beautiful and stately as lilies, and that he couldn't help but comment as you sat there among the male bipeds whose names you bear, how you seemed to look up above them the way a lot of beautiful birds of paradise would among a lot of old buzzards.

Then he said he was very happy to be here because he thought he might learn something about homely philosophy and our beautiful women. I'm glad I didn't get my adjectives transposed.

I have known Billy Van for many years. I have known him back when he was a star of that famous musical comedy, *Sunny Days* with the supporting cast made up of such stars as Jeanette MacDonald, Fred Stone, Sheehan and many others. Billy, the great outstanding star, gave it up because he wanted to go back and live in New Hampshire in God's country, as he called it, and live like a decent human being.

To me, Billy has always been a great man. He has known almost everybody in the United States, and they are all glad to see him as an old friend. So it delighted me when Sheriff Mulcahy said to me, "Is that the real Billy Van? Why I remember when my old man"— I wouldn't express myself like that, but Sheriff Mulcahy said "my old man" and I want to pick up the vernacular of political life as much as possible—"I remember when my old man used to take my hand and lead me to the theater to hear Billy Van." Then he said, "Is that old bird still alive?"

But Billy has been a great man; he has been too busy to grow old doing fine things for his fellow human beings. Among those who know him, he is noted for his wisdom, for his wit, for his political astuteness, and for the ability to express himself.

The stage would be better today if they had more men of Billy's type. Billy's humor is a splendid type—clean and delightful. It is real humor; it is spontaneous; it is almost unconscious, like many of our bureaucrats. As for his ability to express himself, when he started using these amazing adjectives, these astonishing adverbs, and mystifying metaphors with his fascinating phrases and figures of speech, he would make almost any college professor become bewildered. Sometimes his words are as soft and low as the sweet memory of a meadow brook in the springtime. At other times, they are as fascinating as the gentle fall of sweet-tinted petals in the apple orchard in May. Sometimes his words sparkle as do the dewdrops in the hayfield in the early dawn. When he finishes speaking, you feel as sad and depressed as when the bright lights disappear in the deep dark night and the gay music fades into silence.

He seems to possess the wisdom of Socrates, the wit of Mark Twain, and the political astuteness of Ed Kelly, former Mayor of Chicago.

Billy has lived a full life: Billy has lived through an abundant life. Billy remembers back before the days when a man had to support the United States government, and various other governments, plus his own family, on a single salary. I knew Billy in the early days of New Hampshire when he thought a bureau was a piece of furniture in a bedroom, but he has learned differently from visiting Washington.

Somehow or other, I think that Billy is best described by this old Quaker proverb—some of you may know it. It is the one that my mother gave me, and I used to have it on my desk at Dartmouth College. This old Quaker who loves human beings the way Billy does used to say, "I expect to pass this way but once. If there is any kindness I may show, any good thing I may do for my fellow men, let me not defer or neglect it, for I shall not pass this way again." Or perhaps Daniel Webster might have given me the thing that reminds me of Billy. Daniel Webster was being twitted by some senators after a speech he had delivered. He was being particularly twitted by a senator from the Middle West who said, "What have you got up in New Hampshire except a lot of scenery, granite hills, mountains covered with pine trees, and valleys filled with lakes and streams? What do you raise there?" Daniel Webster, referring once more to those granite hills, said, "among those mountains, God Almighty has stuck out a great sign"—referring, of course, to the old man of the mountain—"saying that up there he raises men" and as proof of that I want to introduce to you Billy B. Van, known in New Hampshire as the Ambassador of Good Will from New England. Billy B. Van!

* * *

Frank Spencer, department manager of Socony-Vacuum Oil Company, introduces James A. Farley, chairman of the board of the Coca-Cola Export Corporation, and American statesman.

First of all, I want to say that after our guest speaker has made his address, there will be a short period during which you may ask some questions, and Mr. Farley has agreed to answer them.

Less than sixty years ago, down in a place in New York called "Glassy Point" or Stony Point—I can't get it quite clear—the Irish parents of our speaker today, who christened their son James A. Farley, decided right off the bat that their son was going to be a democrat. How did they decide that? Well, the facts are these.

There was a republican politician in that neighborhood who was looking about, casting about to get some Farley votes, so he went around and in order to develop a little favor with the Farley family, he tried to kiss little Jim, but little Jim bit him on the nose. In a recent nationwide broadcast, Mr. Farley admitted that was his first real public service to the democratic party.

When I assumed this job of introducing Mr. Farley, the first thing I did was to get a book: *Jim Farley's Story of the Roosevelt Years.*

This book has interested me very, very much indeed because it disclosed a lot of things that I and a lot of other republicans have suspected for many years and never knew.

I have been advised by some of my friends what I should do and what I shouldn't do in connection with making this speech or should say in this introduction.

James Farley has been one of the wheelhorses of the democratic party over a period of thirty-five years. It was he who contributed more than anyone else to the political campaign which elected the first democratic president since Woodrow Wilson. His party loyalty has been unparalleled. He loyally and consistently supported his chief year after year, frequently under difficult circumstances, until the time came when he felt that "the boss," as he always referred to President Roosevelt, had departed from those party principles in which James A. Farley believed.

Mr. Farley's thirty-five years of political service to the democratic party have given him the intimate close contact with people of all walks of life which has contributed tremendously to his present-day success in the status of a businessman. As chairman of the board of the Coca-Cola Export Corporation, he has helped spread the gospel, even into foreign fields, of indulging frequently in "the pause that refreshes."

It has been sixteen years since Mr. Farley was elected chairman of the national committee of the democratic party and that election took place right here in Chicago. Since that time, Mr. Farley has been in and out of Chicago hundreds of times, but this is our very first chance to welcome him here as a business executive. As such, he is naturally interested in his subject of today, "World Conditions," from an economic view. But as a man who will always live with at least a corner of his heart belonging to the democratic party, he is vitally interested in world conditions as they will affect national policy. It is therefore with great pleasure that I present our guest speaker of today, the Honorable James A. Farley.

*   *   *

Portion of the humor in an introduction used by Thomas R. Mulroy, Chicago attorney, when he introduced Miss Sylvia Porter, financial editor of the New York Evening Post *and Leon Henderson, chairman of the Research Institute of America and economist, who were to debate before the Executives' Club of Chicago.*

I have talked privately with each of our two debaters, as to what each thought of the other, and I got quite an earful because they have been fighting over economics for years. For example, when I asked Miss Porter what she really thought of Leon Henderson she said, "In any list of the ten best economists in America, Leon Henderson would rank eleventh."

I asked Mr. Henderson if he reads the brilliant daily column that Miss Porter writes in the *New York Evening Post,* of which she is financial editor. He said yes he does. I said, "How do you like her as an economic writer?" He said, "Well, in my judgment Miss Porter either ought to put some fire into her writing or vice versa."

* * *

T. Louis Chess, past president of the Lions' Club of San Francisco, presents the following introduction which he used at a meeting of the American Legion, as an illustration of a concise introduction. Ordinarily it is necessary to give a more detailed introduction in order clearly to establish the speaker's authority to discuss the subject and to give the audience the proper background.

My comrades: Our speaker today has a message of great importance and of interest to every good American. It is my pleasure to present Admiral —————, Chief of Operations of the United States Navy, whose subject will be "American Defense on the High Seas."

* * *

Harry L. Stone, manager of bank relations of the International Harvester Company, introduces the four members of the Executives' Club of Chicago who engaged in a contest with the Quiz Kids of the well-known Quiz Kids' radio program.

The last time the representatives of the Executives' Club engaged in mental combat with the Quiz Kids, the aftermath was very appropriately described by past president Tom Mulroy as the acquisition of many new inferiority complexes or retreads of same. However, this will not happen today. Observe the contestants on our team, men laden with a vast amount of brain power, certainly more than sufficient to hold their own with the Quiz Kids—we hope!

On your left you see the Quiz Kids, who will be introduced later by their genial quizmaster, Joe Kelly. On your right are our own Whiz Kids whom I would like now to introduce to you. As I read your names, gentlemen, will you kindly rise so that you may be properly identified to the audience.

First is Nat Leverone, chairman of the Automatic Canteen Company. Nat is an old hand at this game, having given a scintillating performance against the Quiz Kids at our previous meeting. He is a very loyal alumnus of Dartmouth College, and there is a song close to the hearts of all Dartmouth men, entitled "Men of Dartmouth," which contains these strange words, "With the granite of New Hampshire in their muscles and their brains." Our fervent hope is that there will be no granite in Nat Leverone's brain today.

Now we shall pass on to our next contestant who is Sidney Moody, one of Chicago's prominent attorneys. I understand that Sidney Moody really excels as a cross-examining lawyer. One time when he was asking a witness when a certain crime occurred, the witness began by saying, "I think—" He was immediately cut off by Sidney who said, "We don't care what you think. We want to know what you know." With that remark the witness said, "Well, I may as well get off the stand. I can't talk without thinking because I'm not a lawyer!" Today the tables are turned, and Sidney is the witness being cross-examined.

Our next able contestant is Phil Hanna, financial editor of the *Chicago Daily News*. He is also a veteran, having vied with the Quiz Kids before. Phil enjoys traveling and I understand during one of his meanderings around the universe, he was taken captive in the Cannibal Islands where the chief of the cannibals asked, "What was your business before you were captured by my men?" "I was a newspaper man," answered Phil. To which the chief retorted, "An editor?" "No, merely a financial editor," said Phil. "Cheer up, my man," spoke up the cannibal chief. "Promotion awaits you. After dinner you'll be editor in chief."

When Phil appeared on this program before, someone was mean enough to contrive the idea of quoting from Mr. Hanna's editorial of several days before and asking "Who wrote this?" No one, not even Phil, could identify his priceless pearls of wisdom, which prompted him to say, "I guess I'd better start reading my own stuff."

Next is Glen Miller, president of the advertising agency which bears his name. He was a little reluctant in accepting this assignment, but his determined monologue finally convinced him that he was our man. Our experience in clinching Glen brings to mind a story about a man walking into his friend's office where he noticed hanging on the wall a handsome mounted fish, below which was an inscription. Unable to restrain his curiosity, he went closer to read it, expecting to see the size, weight, and date of this prize catch, but here is what he read, "If I hadn't opened my big mouth, I wouldn't be here." I guess maybe that applies to Glen today.

That completes my biographical sketch of our four able representatives, who, believe me, have our wholehearted appreciation for tackling this assignment.

Our scorekeeper is Mr. Elliot W. Frank, vice president of the La Salle National Bank. Being adept at figures, this job should be duck soup to him.

And now it is my privilege to present to you the man who has filled an unusual niche in the entertainment world. All of you who have heard the Quiz Kids over the air know it is not necessary to emphasize how well he has performed. A number of people tried out for this position. Among them were college professors, prominent radio announcers, a famous lecturer, and others, but none seemed to measure up to the performance of Joe Kelly. His remaining off the program for even one week creates a clamor of protest which may be summed up this way, "Give us back our Joe Kelly, who is like a father to the Quiz Kids."

Mr. Kelly, the platform is yours.

*   *   *

Thomas Robert Mulroy, Chicago attorney, and past president of the Executives' Club of Chicago, introduces Harold O. McLain, president of the Railways Ice Company and past president of the Executives' Club of Chicago.

Harold McLain is such a beloved and brilliant personality that I thought you would like me to tell you today something of his background so that you might better understand his climb up the ladder of life.

May I say at the outset that—if I may coin a phrase—Harold was born. He did not exactly come from a good family—he was sent.

In the Chicago public schools he pursued his studies, never quite overtaking them.

Harold was graduated from the University of Michigan, and then went on to Columbia University Law School in New York, where, as a result of Broadway's bright lights, he was as broke as the Ten Commandments.

After leaving law school Harold did a short term in the army with Teddy Roosevelt at San Juan Hill.

Out of the army, Harold took a short fling as a pioneer radio announcer, and I am delighted to find from extensive research that his idea of a proper and effective commercial was considerably different from what is considered effective today. His first commercial went like this:

"Mothers, go now to your nearest store and buy Quaker Oats.

"Are Quaker Oats shot out of a gun? Do Quaker Oats greet you with vibrant freshness? No! They just sit and sneer at you!"

He left radio and then spent fourteen years as a practicing lawyer in Chicago, and I say to you that Harold McLain wrested from reluctant juries triumphant verdicts of acquittal in every case in which his clients were clearly and unmistakably innocent.

Yes, Harold McLain was a fighting lawyer who gave no quarter—as any bellboy will tell you.

Since 1926, Harold has been president of the Railways Ice Company and a leader in the ice industry in this country and Canada.

About a year ago, alas! Harold entered politics—politics, ah! sweet politics—where they pat you on the back so they'll know where to stick the knife.

Harold was elected president of the Highland Park Republican Club and campaigned very vigorously for Tom Dewey in 1944. Yes, in October, 1944, Harold entered politics; the day after election day Harold gave up politics!

As a matter of fact, he really did a good job for Tom Dewey. Dewey ran very well in Highland Park; he placed.

Chairman Brownell of the Republican National Committee, in speaking of the effective work Harold did for Dewey in 1944 in Highland Park, said, "Quote (pause) unquote!"

That concludes my thumbnose sketch of Harold McLain.

Now that my poor jokes are finished, may I express, with deep sincerity, the profound affection and respect which every one of the fourteen hundred members of this club shares for Harold McLain. As our president for two years Harold, in his weekly introductions, was invariably a great attraction and certainly a better orator than the speaker of the day.

In any discussion of Harold McLain I hold these truths to be self-evident: that he is an outstanding business executive; that he is a public-spirited citizen; that he is a gentleman rich in character and charm; but this above all, that he is constructively articulate.

In these times that try men's souls here is no summer soldier or sunshine patriot who shirks from the service of his country; here is a man with the courage to stand up and be counted on the contentious issues of the day; a man who has a genius—and this I stress—for espousing with powerful force and clarity the aims, the ideals, and the record of American industry.

I know no more persuasive advocate at the bar of public thought than our great and good friend; I know no more dynamic exponent of the American system of free enterprise; I know of no more winsome fireside philosopher.

Gentlemen, I give you the "favorite son" of this great club, Harold McLain.

*　　*　　*

A portion of Mr. McLain's response to the above introduction by Mr. Mulroy.

I tried so hard to get a chance to see what Tom's jokes were and to see his script. He told me that he would have nothing to say about me except serious, well-intentioned stuff; that he wouldn't think of making any jokes about me. So I am really in a spot that deserves your complete sympathy.

I am highly appreciative, of course, of this honor and privilege of coming before you because all of us who are in the Executives' Club understand and appreciate deeply what an honor it is to occupy this forum. I am very grateful for the things Tom Mulroy said.

For perhaps the past ten years since we became acquainted in this organization, and even before, Tom and I have been very close friends, and we have had a good many business transactions to-gether. In those transactions I have always tried to be friendly with Tom, and certainly he has been exceedingly close with me.

Seriously, I am glad to have this chance to declare there just isn't anything I wouldn't do for Tom Mulroy, and I am encouraged to believe, too that there just isn't anything he wouldn't do for me. That is the way it has been with us in the past ten years: There just isn't anything we have done for each other.

Of course, we have a good deal in common because we have both occupied this rostrum here. We both have used this same springboard, but he has been making swan dives, and I have been making belly-flops. That is because he is a top, first-class presiding officer. He is the best.

There isn't anything second-class about Tom. He is in reality first-class. He is the top at this kind of thing. You know, ordinarily a chairman or a toastmaster is supposed to be sort of the punk that starts off the fire, but on the contrary, Tom is the luminous incan-descence that contributes a scintillating sparkle and brilliance to these otherwise drab programs.

He is articulate, erudite, and oracular. He is prophetic, provoca-tive and vocal. He is ubiquitous, vehement, and loquacious. He is in-deed an orator, and he is a raconteur. He is the embodiment and the epitome of *cacoethes loquendi.*

He is just a top guy at this kind of thing, and I am not going to waste any more time trying to live up to the stuff he handed me.

I have a rather heavy subject here today that is certainly by every test a contrast to this persiflage in which we have been indulging here, and as Alderman Kenna used to say when he would get up in the city council to discuss an important subject, "Leave us face it."

*   *   *

Dr. Franklyn B. Snyder, president of Northwestern Uni-versity, introduces Dr. Alfred P. Haake, economist and economic consultant, and Professor Harold Laski, British economist, who debated the subject, "Socialism vs. Free Enterprise."

We are here today to listen while representatives of two branches of the English speaking family of nations discuss a question of great and timely interest. Whatever you may think of the merits of the two philosophies which will be expounded, we all agree on this: It is good to meet in this way and to talk together and think together on controversial and important matters. We are grateful to the Executives' Club of Chicago for having given us this occasion.

The privilege of free assembly and of free discussion is very precious to the Englishman and to the American, and we agree that there must be no curtailment of this privilege—no censorship, no thought police. I add, to preserve this privilege, we must use it as we are proposing to do today.

The two contestants who are going to take part are experienced battlers in the ring. I might call them intellectual "Golden Glovers" and of the heavyweight class.

In this corner, the representative of the United States and in this corner that of Great Britain.

The story of Dr. Alfred P. Haake's life is a typical American story of hard work, of ambition, of the ability to find in this new world satisfying opportunities of many sorts. He was a boy who worked his way through college, too, and claims the University of Wisconsin as his alma mater.

He tells me he has been a truck driver, a grocery clerk, a journalist, a business man; he must be something of a politician to have gotten himself elected mayor of Park Ridge, and we know he has an interesting and honorable relationship to General Motors. He is widely known for his ability to make men listen and make them think about important questions.

Professor Harold J. Laski, as you know, is a subject of his Britannic Majesty and an eloquent advocate of those policies which we Americans associate with the present government of England.

A graduate of New College, Oxford—it was new in the year it was established, the year 1379—where he took a "first" in modern history, a man who, even as an undergraduate, was recognized as a man of unusual intellectual power even in the Oxford environment. He soon became an influence in the thinking of his own country and of the United States by virtue of his eloquent and cogent writings and addresses.

He has had many contacts with American universities. He, too, makes people think and in academic parlance some people who listen to him give him an "A," some people give him an "F," but nobody gives him a "C—."

You might have expected the boy who worked his way through a midwestern institution to represent the point of view of labor—of socialism. You might have expected the graduate of an Oxford college, traditionally associated with the old way of doing things, to represent capitalism and free industry. But both of them, gentlemen, have reversed their fields and Dr. Haake speaks, as you know, for free enterprise and Professor Laski for socialism.

The rules of the contest which have been handed to me are very simple and both contestants profess to know them. Dr. Haake will speak first, Professor Laski second; then each will be given two brief periods in which to say, in simple and understandable English, what he really thinks of his opponent's arguments.

One last word before we call these men into the ring. This contest is conducted strictly under Marquis of Queensberry rules—no hitting below the belt, no rabbit punches, break clean if I tell you to, don't hit after the bell and go to the neutral corner if the other man hits the canvas. And may the best man win!

*   *   *

H. G. Evans, vice president of the Hamilton Manufacturing Company of Two Rivers, Wisconsin, introduces and pays tribute to Miss Eva Wirth on her retirement from Washington High School, Two Rivers, Wisconsin. (Students, faculty and townspeople were present.)

This is to direct your attention in this brief moment to a life that has affected the lives of everyone here. It has been felt particularly by the 2,834 students who with this class have graduated during the past twenty-five years from the halls of this high school. This life is truly representative of a profession. In paying tribute to Miss Wirth we do so because she has given faithful service of unusual length. She vitalized her subject matter in an unusual fashion.

She knew her subject ... and to a point where it became a part of her very thinking, a live issue of her heart. When anyone is so in love with one's work that it becomes a part of one's very being, one can well be likened to "a tree planted by the rivers of water that bringeth forth his fruit in his season, his leaf also shalt not wither, and whatsoever he doeth shall prosper."

In any line of work a thorough knowledge of the subject brings to the individual four very important moral qualities. They are mentioned because therein lies a lesson for all of us. They are courage— and it takes courage to initiate anything; confidence, for self-assurance is demanded whenever we carry out a responsibility effectively; poise, for we must command respect of others if we are to gain their cooperation; and above all, enthusiasm, because to hold the attention of others we must fire and inspire them with the same interest for the subject matter.

An outstanding teacher always displays an unusual ability to teach the subject matter to students. Miss Wirth won not only state but national recognition in her work as a student and teacher of geography. This subject, a required part of our sophomore course, is not so presented in any other school in the state and probably in the United States, and this institution is pointed out as having the best equipped geography rooms in Wisconsin.

All of this is evidence of the work of a teacher who knew how to vitalize the subject matter. Her Pan-American Conference and Mock Coal Conventions have been copied by other schools. The annual exhibits of her classes, of course, have been outstanding.

But more important than all these is this fact, the one that marks any teacher's efforts as a work of lasting value: she did not teach a class—she taught the individual student. Lives have been changed, thinking corrected and directed toward the building of a better citizenship for the future.

Should you visit Edinburgh, Scotland, and famous Princess Street in that city, you will find on one side the heights that border the street. On top of the heights is the Scottish war memorial. This memorial stands out as an unusual one. Every man's name, every Scotsman who made the great sacrifice in the first world war is engraved there in stone. Above these names is a simple inscription very carefully chosen because it best applied to every single man whose name is commemorated. Yet the inscription is far more appropriate for those who are giving all in their living than for those who gave all in their death. They are the words of a man who wrote two thousand years ago, and in their simplicity this is what we read: "The whole earth is the tomb of heroic men and women. Their story is not graven only on stone over their clay, but abides everywhere without visible symbol, woven in the stuff of other men's lives."

We pay tribute to Miss Wirth, to a faithful service of twenty-five years, to a teaching profession and responsibility which she reflected so faithfully in her services to the people of Two Rivers. We are sorry she retires at this time, but we are nevertheless thankful for the example and inspiration that she leaves to the other members of her profession and to the rest of us who carry on in our own work.

*   *   *

Dr. Alfred P. Haake, economic consultant, introduces Samuel B. Pettengill, vice president of the Transportation Association of America and former congressman, to the Rotary Club of Chicago.

I am grateful for the opportunity to present our speaker of the day. In the past few years I have had the privilege of presenting some of the most notable and highly regarded persons in America, but the honor accorded me today is unique—unique not in that this man is famous and is lauded in *Who's Who* with his listing as congressman and author of several best-sellers and organizer of numerous undertakings for the saving of the country; or even as a member of a political party which some years ago was swallowed up in a new political order and now threatens to free itself from the chains of its humiliation; nor even for the fact that he is an honorary member of a sister Rotary Club, the chairman of our own Rotary Commission, a man with an unblemished record and congenial fellowship.

Not for all of those things is he unique, but because he is one of those all-too-few individuals who stand four-square for what they believe. If there is one thing that stands out above all others in Sam Pettengill's record, it is that he has refused to let personal interest or the desire for popular favor emasculate his uncompromising devotion to truth. I give you a crusader whom history will record as one of the men who saved his nation—a man in his own right—Sam B. Pettengill.

* * *

Dr. Paul J. Misner, educator, introduces Dr. Arthur B. Moehlman, professor of education at the University of Michigan.

The opportunity to introduce your speaker today is indeed a pleasure and a real privilege. I have known him intimately for a period of more than fifteen years. I have known him as one of the few really great teachers with whom I have worked. I have known him as a friend whose interest in his students continues after the college days are ended. But I want you fellows to know him today as one of the few leaders of American education who is fearlessly and courageously fighting for the preservation of sound social and educational principles.

As an author and editor he has pioneered in his interpretations of the role of public education in a democracy. He has consistently maintained that the public schools belong to the people. He has steadily resisted the efforts of those individuals and groups who would transfer control of our public schools either to professional educators or government bureaucrats.

Your speaker belongs neither to the right nor to the left. He is, on the contrary, one of those rare individuals who in these hectic times have been able to stay on the straight and narrow path that alone leads to the fuller realization of the democratic way of life.

I am proud to present my teacher, Dr. Arthur B. Moehlman, who

D

will speak to you on the subject of "Looking Forward in Education: A Civic Challenge."

*   *   *

The chairman frequently is called upon to introduce guests at the speaker's table. Edwin B. Moran, manager of the National Association of Credit Men, once told the following interesting story prior to introductions he was called upon to make.

The president of this club at each and every meeting, as he comes to the presentation of the speaker's table, has a very delightful privilege.

He can say anything he wants to about these distinguished gentlemen arranged on his right and left, and they can do nothing about it. Thus, he may give expression to suppressed desires long lurking in his system.

You know, the other evening one of the grand ladies of the city, renowned for her elaborate dinners, discovered just before the guests were expected that her butler was ill, and therefore unable to perform his usual duty.

So in the emergency she summoned from her staff of servants Mrs. O'Brien, a trusted employee in the family for many years, and she said to her:

"Now, Nora, you stand at the drawing-room door and call the guests' names as they arrive."

Nora's face lit up at the very prospect of such a privilege, and she said: "Thank you, ma'am, I have been wanting to do just that to some of your friends for the last twenty years."

*   *   *

J. L. Hemery, assistant to the general manager of the Clearing Manufacturing District of Chicago introduces Lynn Saylor, advertising manager of the Ingersoll Steel Division of the Borg-Warner Corporation.

Our speaker, in addition to being a past president of the Magic Carpet Luncheon Club of Chicago, is one of our founders. He hails from the beautiful state of Iowa. Lynn has a prolific imagination. He injects his energetic personality into strange things. He dreams up and brings out of them practical realities. His outstanding ability has attracted the attention of such concerns as Certain-Teed Products, Warwick Manufacturing Company and the Ingersoll Steel Division of the Borg-Warner Corporation. Of course, as the demand for Lynn's services grew, Lynn's demand for remuneration increased so that now he is the high-salaried advertising manager of the Ingersoll Steel Division.

The other day I called at Lynn's office and while waiting for this busy executive I overheard two of his young lady employees discussing his eligibility. Miss Green said, "I know he is rich, but isn't he too old to be considered eligible?" Miss Brown replied, "My dear, he is too eligible to be considered old." Lynn grows younger every day. He has been a power behind our club since its inception. His subject is "Advertising for Prosperity." I present Lynn Saylor.

* * *

James B. Blaine, executive vice president, John F. Cuneo Company, introduces Clare Boothe Luce, author, playwright, and former congresswoman from Connecticut.

There are some of us who are naturally bystanders in the world, seeing and weighing and making private judgments of which few others know. There are others of us who are caught up in the midst of activity, whirled almost by a power beyond us, by a love of being in the activity of the world. And then there are the rare few who, while acting as catalytic agents and creating activity, are able to stand aside and observe. Our speaker today is one of these rare persons.

She has been a doer in life. As a young suffragist she was a crusader who made herself heard. As a journalist she has had her ear to world events for many years. And as a writer she has evaluated what she has done and what she has seen, and fortunately, she has made these public in a truly creative manner—in her books and in her excellent plays.

Her clear-sighted weighing of the serious and of the frivolous of life has made her a menace to all stuffed shirts. Her satire, which is outrageously clever, can be biting and damning to those of us who have great pretenses of our own worth.

As I mentioned, Clare Boothe Luce has not been one to stand aside and watch only. She has accepted fully her responsibilities as a citizen, not by condemning, but by entering into the ways of America fully to understand them and to do her share in making them better ways. As a freshman congresswoman, she early stirred Congress with her forthright addresses. Driven by her feelings of responsibility, she worked long and hard for laws she felt necessary to promote peace in this country and in the world.

Her name has been one of the most publicized in the country despite her drawback of being the wife of a publisher who mentions her in his publications only with reluctance. And with her fame she has suffered having every private decision of hers made a matter of public debate. She has borne this invasion with courage and with unusual tact, and we sincerely compliment her on this quality.

While Mrs. Luce has withdrawn from a political office, she is keenly aware of the political issues of the day and knows the political story facing us from both the inside and the outside.

Mrs. Luce has kindly consented to answer questions from the floor at the conclusion of her address.

It is with pleasure that I present a onetime representative of Congress and an all-time representative of the American woman, Mrs. Clare Boothe Luce.

*   *   *

Harold O. McLain, president of the Railways Ice Company of Chicago, speaks on the occasion of the retirement of a club president from office.

The retiring president evidences the poise of Pericles, the power of Daniel Webster, the humor of a Bill Nye, the delicate imagery of a Thomas Moore and the magnetism and lure of a Lauren Bacall! He is as adamant as John L. Lewis, and his voice is as mellifluous as the limpid notes of the sweet wind, and as persuasive as the dulcet strains of the Oriental flageolet. As he approaches a myopic and melon-shaped forty, he bursts like a lovely, incandescent rocket on the scene, which, under his guidance, has run the gamut of variety from a Babylonian weenie roast to a Guy Fawkes Day in Cheapside.

*   *   *

Edgar L. Schnadig, president of The New Boston Store of Chicago, introduces Dr. Gerald Wendt, editorial director of Science Illustrated.

Science today is serious business. It reminds me of the story of the psychopathic patient who suffered from the hallucination that he had a cat in his insides. Unable to disprove this, the psychiatrist simulated an operation. When the man came out of the ether, he was shown a black cat, and was told his troubles were over. He replied, "I'm sorry, doctor, but the cat that is bothering me is gray."

So it is with science today. You reach for a cat called U-235, and you come up with a flock of kittens called neptunium, plutonium, uranium 233 or something else. Like a Chicago winter, the elements are overpowered. The alchemist of old, the first nuclear scientist, on his deathbed begged for one more day to discover the secrets of the universe. Now scientists produce secrets of which the universe never dreamed.

Our speaker today is Dr. Gerald Wendt who knows about science as it is, and as it may be. Dr. Wendt has been a professor of chemistry at the University of Chicago, dean of the Pennsylvania State College, director of the Battelle Institute of Industrial Research at Columbus, Ohio. He has been a scientist in the government service, and editor and author. Dr. Wendt was born in Davenport, Iowa, and received his professional degree at Harvard. He completed his training in war plants, and has traveled extensively in Europe.

Dr. Wendt is author and editor of numerous textbooks in several sciences. His best known book is *Science for the World of Tomorrow* published when he was director of science at the world's fair in New York. As consulting editor to *Time, Life, Fortune* and *March of Time*, his interpretation of scientific news reached a wide audience. *The Atomic Age* by Dr. Wendt appeared in 1946, ten days after the bomb hit Hiroshima. His pet phrase is "The best is yet to come," and so it is. I am proud to present, and you will be happy to hear, Dr. Gerald Wendt, editorial director of *Science Illustrated*.

*   *   *

J. C. Wakefield, formerly chairman of the program committee of the Kiwanis Club of Boston, introduces Robert A. Walsh, member of the staff of the Massachusetts College of Pharmacy, with a concise statement of the speaker's background.

It is a rare occasion when one has the opportunity to introduce a guest speaker from his own chosen field of endeavor. That is my privilege today.

This is National Pharmacy Week. The observance is being conducted by the American Pharmaceutical Association, and carries an additional theme of Cancer Control in cooperation with the American Cancer Society.

Our guest speaker is a member of the staff of the Massachusetts College of Pharmacy, presently teaching bacteriology, physiology, and professional relations. He is also chairman of the medical board of the E. L. Patch Company, and national vice president of the Phi Delta Chi Fraternity.

On this most timely occasion, it gives me a great deal of pleasure to introduce to those assembled here a man those of us in pharmacy consider to be one of our most outstanding representatives of the profession in the commonwealth, Mr. Robert A. Walsh.

*   *   *

Harry G. Hoffman, president of Hoffman & York, Inc., Milwaukee, introduces Morris Sayre, president of the Corn Products Refining Company and president of the National Association of Manufacturers, at the 87th annual meeting and dinner of the Milwaukee Association of Commerce.

We come now to that portion of the evening program which all of you have been eagerly awaiting. When I first learned that Mr. Sayre had accepted the association's invitation to be our guest speaker this evening, I was elated. I had heard much of his reputation from stories in the press and from many friends who had met him on previous occasions.

I realize that a man with the background of our speaker needs comparatively little introduction, and I feel that perhaps I can be like the Scotchman who went into a florist's shop on the eve of his wife's birthday. By way of introduction, the florist said, "Why not say it with flowers? How about a dozen roses?" "Well," replied the Scotchman, "I am a man of few words. Give me two."

It seems to me, however, that it would not be doing justice either to the man or to the organization he represents, and it would not provide the necessary springboard for his talk, to limit the introduction merely to his name and his connections. As briefly and as quickly as I can, therefore, I should like to summarize my introductory remarks as follows:

To my mind, our guest speaker clearly represents and typifies the American way of life. His experience is an outstanding example of the fact that ours is a land of opportunity, and a classic illustration of an American tradition backed by thousands of real-life success stories.

Mr. Sayre began his business career in 1908, shortly after his graduation from Lehigh University as an engineer—washing boilers—at the Granite City, Illinois, plant of the Corn Products Refining Company. He has been associated with that company ever since. From this unromantic job, he became successively assistant master mechanic, assistant superintendent, and superintendent of the Granite City plant. Transferred to the company's Argo, Illinois, plant, he served there as manager from 1916 to 1928.

In 1928 he went to New York as general manager of the company and in the following year was elected to the board of directors. He became vice president in 1933, executive vice president in 1942, and president in 1945.

In spite of the demands of his business life, he has always managed to find time for civic organizations, club affiliations—and even public office. While living in Illinois, he was elected mayor of La Grange. While serving as senior warden of the Episcopal Church in that city, he was a member of the committee charged with the supervision of rebuilding his church after it was destroyed by fire. This experience aroused in him a deep interest in church architecture and, as a result of his studies in that field, he is considered a lay authority on that subject.

His successes are entirely his own—he earned his education at Richmond College through a scholarship and later financed his education at Lehigh by tutoring, running a summer boarding house during vacation times, and selling to housewives the stereoscopic views which once were a mainstay of home entertainment. When he went to work for the Corn Products Company at seventy-five dollars a month, he stretched his pay far enough to help put a brother and sister through school.

Tonight he is with us as the head of the National Association of Manufacturers. He has been a director of N.A.M., has served on many important committees and recently was elected to the presidency.

Ladies and gentlemen, it is a real honor to introduce to you a man whose background and achievements are so much in keeping with the principles of democracy which his organization represents, and I deem it a great privilege indeed to present to you the president of the National Association of Manufacturers, Morris Sayre.

*   *   *

Edwin B. Moran, manager of the National Association of Credit Men, introduces Louis Ruthenburg, president of Servel, Inc.

Our speaker admits his hobbies are horseback riding, fishing, agriculture and armchair farming, which one might understand if he looks at *Who's Who* and sees that he is a member of the Engineers' Club in New York City, the Wall Street Club in New York City, the Metropolitan Club in Washington, D.C., and the Evansville, Indiana, Country Club.

He was born in Louisville, Kentucky. He studied mechanical engineering at Purdue University, which gave him a degree in 1907.

He has had an interesting and broad industrial background, which included a year of engineering work in Europe.

He has been associated with such organizations as:

The E. C. Walker Manufacturing Company

The Kentucky Wagon Works

The Dayton Engineering Laboratories Company

General Motors Research Laboratories

General Motors Truck Corporation

Yellow Sleeve Valve Engine Works

In 1929 he became president of the Copeland Products, Inc., and at the same time, chairman of the refrigeration division of the National Electrical Manufacturers' Association.

He was given an honorary M.E. degree from the University of Detroit.

The speaker is:

President of the Indiana State Chamber of Commerce

Member of the executive board of the American Gas Association

Member of the board of trustees of Purdue University

Director of the National Association of Manufacturers

Director of the Mississippi Valley Association and

The Indiana chairman of the Committee for Economic Development.

All this would cause you to believe he is very busy, but he has another main sideline at the present time which provides him with spending money. He is president and general manager of Servel, Inc., of Evansville, Indiana.

Our guest and speaker, Louis Ruthenburg.

* * *

William Given, vice president of Young & Vann Supply Company, Birmingham, Alabama, introduces Hugh Comer, a past president of the American Cotton Manufacturers Association, and executive vice president of Avondale Mills, Birmingham, Alabama, at a meeting of the Kiwanis Club of Birmingham.

D°

Sometime during the year 1897, over a half-century ago, a new enterprise was launched in Birmingham. It was known as the Avondale Mills. This enterprise was of particular interest and importance to Birmingham and to the South for the very good reason that its operation was that of converting the South's principal agricultural product into finished goods, thereby bringing to the South economic advantages heretofore enjoyed by distant points.

The successful launching and developing of this new enterprise— over good times and bad—into one of Alabama's great institutions was due largely to the vision, genius, and dogged perseverance of one man, and one man only, a distinguished Alabamian and one of Alabama's greatest of all-time governors. I have reference to the late Governor B. B. Comer, the father of our speaker.

It was against this background that our guest, his brothers and associates, continued the affairs of this fine company to further accomplishments and greater usefulness.

We of Alabama can well be grateful not only for this company's fine accomplishments, but also for the influence their successful pioneering no doubt had in bringing about the shift of the important textile industry to the South.

It is under this environment that our speaker has grown to his present stature as a leader in the religious, civic and industrial life of our state. There are many things which could, and might well be said, about our speaker and his fine company, but I shall resist the temptation to encroach further on his time, except to say I know of no one better qualified to speak on the subject of "Cotton and Cotton Manufacture." I am happy to present a man who has dedicated his life and talents to the development of the cotton textile industry in Alabama and the South; a man who has won local and national recognition; a past president of the American Cotton Manufacturers Association and presently a member of its board of directors; a past president of the Alabama Cotton Manufacturing Association; a member of the National Cottor Council, and of the National Cotton Textile Institute; a man bred, born and educated in Alabama and one of whom, as Alabamians, we are all proud, our friend, a distinguished Alabamian.

Ladies and gentlemen, our speaker, Hugh Comer, executive vice president of Avondale Mills, Mr. Comer.

* * *

Opening remarks of an introduction for a ladies' day meeting of the Executives' Club of Chicago by Harry L. Stone, manager of bank relations of International Harvester Company.

This is the first occasion I have had of addressing this club at a time when the audience is graced with the presence of the fair sex. We must admit it takes the women to add the sparkle, the warmth, and the proper balance to these affairs. And so ladies, we extend you a very cordial welcome.

I believe it was man that first described woman as nothing but "a rag, a bone and a hank of hair." And I am certain it was woman who termed man as nothing but "a brag, a groan, and a tank of air."

* * *

Edwin B. Moran, manager of the National Association of Credit Men, introduces Henry L. Porter, sales promotion manager of the Standard Oil Company of Indiana.

At a recent meeting I introduced our chairman of this evening in great detail.

Duplication hardly seems necessary this evening, for is there a man so dumb or inactive in this club, that he knows not Henry Porter?

Therefore, only to some few newcomers, I remind you that this man, chairman of our program committee for the year. is:

A farmer by birth

A teacher by profession

A sales manager by choice

Vice president of the American Marketing Association by election

A member of the National Society of Sales Training by desire

A member of the Chicago Sales Executives Club by wisdom

The sales promotion manager of the Standard Oil Company of

Indiana, and a charter member of that company's sales research department by the wisdom of its officials.

We owe a great deal to this man for the conscientious effort he and his committee are putting forth to develop practical, timely and interesting programs for us.

Your program committee chairman, Henry L. Porter.

*   *   *

Sometimes a chairman is called upon to open a discussion after an address. Paul A. Mertz, director of company training of Sears, Roebuck & Company and past president of the Industrial Relations Association of Chicago, opens a discussion meeting with the following pertinent story.

We hope this is only the beginning—that this is really going to be an industrial conference.

I attempted the difficult task myself when addressing the National Association of Cost Accountants at their Southern Division convention in Nashville, Tennessee, of trying to prove to them that they were paying for a personnel program in their industry whether they had one or not. I was reminded of that story which no doubt most of you know of the traveling salesman who turned in his account after a trip, and on the good old swindle sheet he had charged a suit of clothes. When he handed the sheet in, his manager said to him: "Sam, you haven't done anything wrong, but there's one thing you've got to understand about your expense account. You can't include any of your personal expenses in it. For instance, if you buy a suit of clothes, that must come out of your own personal budget and must not be charged to your expense account with the company."

Well, after his next trip Sam came back with a pretty satisfactory expense account, and his manager, after looking it over, said to him this time: "Now you've got the idea, Sam. Everything is accounted for properly, and there are no items here which are of a personal nature." It was just too much for Sam, and he smiled all over as he said, "Well, there's a suit of clothes in there anyhow."

However, I think that in an audience like this our speaker really has an easier job than the one I had. I would like to see you get back at him. Try to make him prove that his program does work and that it does accomplish what he says it accomplishes. Who has the first question? Maybe you are just starting a program of this kind? Maybe you are planning one? Maybe you don't have any at all? Or perhaps you have had one in existence in your company for nineteen years? Let's have your questions.

* * *

Edwin B. Moran, manager of the Central Division of the National Association of Credit Men and author of The Credit Side of Selling, *introduces J. C. Aspley, president of The Dartnell Corporation, who is to serve as chairman for a luncheon program for the Rotary Club of Chicago. Mr. Moran and Mr. Aspley are close friends and Mr. Moran good-naturedly "kids" the chairman.*

And now! I present the chairman of the day.

Usually, this is a pleasure. Today it is only a duty.

I have personally known him for ten or twelve years, which is too long. For ten or twelve years before I met him, I read his publications and editorials, which proves that credit men are gluttons for punishment.

He claims Hamilton, Ontario, Canada, as his birthplace, although I have never heard that Hamilton has done any bragging about it.

I have heard that he is a naturalized citizen of the United States, although I have never seen his papers.

He was educated at the University High School and Armour Institute of Technology, but is not known to have won any distinction or special honor at either.

He really got a good start in the advertising department of Swift & Company, where he told them how to utilize the squeal in the pig, but he wandered away, to the editorial staff of *Printer's Ink,* and now is editor and publisher of *American Business* magazine, which is devoted to sales, advertising and public relations, and occasionally has a good article on credits. (Incidentally, the subscription is $3 annually, or two years for $5.)

He is president of The Dartnell Corporation, sales research counselors, whose monthly services can be obtained for a most moderate cost.

He is author of a number of books devoted to sales, sales management, advertising and competitive trade practices.

When he isn't busy telling folks how to spread the oil of successful selling, he may be telling you about his former forty-five-foot power cruiser, which holds the distinction of being the winner of the only Chicago to Mackinac endurance cruise.

He organized and was the first president of the Chicago Sales Executives Club, and later was president of the National Federation of Sales Executives.

He has served Chicago Rotary on the metropolitan area committee as chairman of our club publications committee, and as vice president in charge of the club service division.

I now present in this corner at 198 pounds, your chairman of the day, John Cameron Aspley.

*　　*　　*

Many times a chairman is called upon at the opening meeting of a convention to present the mayor of the convention city, who gives an address of welcome. Often this introduction is liable to be stereotyped. At a meeting of the National Foreign Trade Council, Philip D. Reed, chairman of the board of the General Electric Company and former chairman of the United States Associates, International Chamber of Commerce, Inc., introduced the mayor of St. Louis in the following interesting manner:

This great convention is not and cannot be legitimately and appropriately launched without our having a word from the mayor of this city. It would be inconceivable that we should carry on these deliberations without knowing whether or not he is glad to see us, whether or not he is pleased to have us here, eating our gray matter away with consideration of these tremendous problems. So I give you, and I hope he will say a word to us—the Mayor of St. Louis.

*　　*　　*

Harold O. McLain, president of the Railways Ice Company, Chicago, speaks upon the occasion of his retirement as president of the Executives' Club of Chicago, at which time he is presented with a gift.

This is, indeed, a very beautiful token of your continued generosity and charitable tendencies in your treatment of me. I assure you that I should like to respond to Mr. Nelson's levity in like manner, but I really do not feel just like it. I give you my deep expression of gratitude for your continued support, and also for this very fine token which will be a permanent reminder of that support and generosity.

I hope you will please bear with me this one last day if I indulge in continued use of the first person. This moment of my retirement from the presidency of the Executives' Club is one to which I have looked forward with anticipated delight and with contemplated dread.

The realization that each Friday after today I may sit quietly and mute in the body of this audience and visit and enjoy the program without responsibility is, of course, an appealing and delightful prospect. However, the knowledge that no longer shall I experience the particular personal elation with which I have been suffused when some of our events seemed to be especially appropriate and successful is in contrast a rather dreadful and gloomy aspect of my retirement. In the main, however, I shall be entirely happy and content to join the large group of our honorable and potent ex-presidents, to which unfortunately I shall bring perhaps more than my proper share of senility.

I am glad that our orthodox, traditional procedure permits me to make acknowledgment of the heavy debt I feel to the members and officers and directors of this club. To me that debt is very real, and I mean its acknowledgment to be entirely sincere.

In spite of my administrative mistakes and amateurish blunders, for two long years our officers and directors and committees, without one single exception, have been charitable and courteous and enthusiastic and patient, and above all continually and infallibly loyal to me. May I refrain from naming any one individual because I am so greatly indebted to them all, and I am anxious thus publicly to acknowledge my debt and to tender my most sincere gratitude and thanks to them all?

And to you members, I am likewise head over heels in debt. In our effort to hear both sides of many problems, on occasions we have had speakers here who have violated your own proper convictions and views. On those occasions, or when our programs were below standard, you smiled charitably and inscrutably, but voiced none of the bitter criticism to which you were fairly entitled. However, when the program was good and the speaker struck a responsive chord, you turned loose unreservedly with expressions to me of sincere approval and congratulation which warmed my heart for days.

With such backing and support from members, officers and directors my experience here for two years has been unparalleled in its importance and significance to me. Best of all I have made many new friends. Necessarily I have gained a confidence in speech which although unwarranted is indeed comforting on many occasions. As your president I have been permitted to greet and meet many delightful and important persons. I have been exposed to cultural and educational influences which surpass any similar influences to which I submitted in either college or law school. And then, too, at home I have gained an appropriate status and a proper dignity and honor which has long been due me from my wife and children, but which went unrecognized and unsung until I became the president of the illustrious Executives' Club. For all these delights and privileges I am truly grateful.

Today you have selected gentlemen as your new officers and directors who assure a standard of excellence for the coming year which will surpass in every way our puny efforts of the past. Your new president is as capable and as reliable in his Americanism as he is brilliant and charming in his personality. I know you will give him and your new officers and directors your full and unstinted devotion and help.

And now, in conclusion, may I avoid the emotion and sentiment which lies in wait and very near the surface this moment to grip me, and for all your kindness, for all your loyalty, for all your patience, and for all your support which I shall never forget and which shall always be one of my treasured memories, I express finally my deep and my abiding gratitude. I thank you very much.

Now I have the opportunity and the privilege and pleasure of turning over this meeting to, and asking him to carry on from this point, your new president, with whom we are all so much in sympathy and whose election delights us so much.

*   *   *

Harold O. McLain, president of the Railways Ice Company, Chicago, introduces David Seabury, eminent consulting psychologist, author and lecturer.

It is, of course, an obvious truism that the most important components of our world are those elements whose mysteries are the most difficult to pierce and chart. The first is God whom every thoughtful man recognizes but no wise man can translate to a purely mundane equation. The element of mystery second in importance to our life is the human soul and its fellow the human mind, the mechanics of which have baffled the world from the beginning.

Physical, social and political science have run the gamut of varied progress for two thousand years, but psychology, the knowledge and natural history of the mind, has probably made more progress in the last fifty years than in all preceding centuries. Now faintly we begin to catch inspirational glimpses of the wonder and beauty and divinity of the human mind.

There are wise men who contribute to the scientific knowledge of the mind and who, even more, apply their intimacy with psychology to helpful and strengthening procedures with their fellow men. Such an eminent consulting and applied psychologist is Mr. David Seabury, our speaker today.

Of course, you remember that Mr. Seabury has appeared before this Executives' Club now for the fifth time. Each time has been a delightful, stimulating, educational experience for us. You know that he is an author of books whose scientific depths are so delightfully leavened with simplicity that we unenlightened laymen can enjoy as well as learn in their reading. You await impatiently, I know, the development of his subject, "Understanding Our Times," which Mr. David Seabury brings to us today, so I shall delay him and you no longer.

*   *   *

P. D. Houston, chairman of the board of the American National Bank of Nashville, Tennessee, the then newly-elected president of the American Bankers Association, presents a gift of silver and a scroll of honor to the retiring president of the American Bankers Association, Robert M. Hanes, president of the Wachovia Bank & Trust Company of Winston-Salem, North Carolina.

The final session of our annual convention always brings a pang of regret as we witness the retirement from the presidency of the association of the man who has carried the burden of the office for the year preceding. All the men on this platform who have borne the responsibilities of this office will admit that their load was made easier by the loyalty, patience, and understanding of that splendid group of women who, each in turn, have met the responsibilities placed upon the president's wife. As a token of its appreciation to them, the association through the years has offered the retiring president an enduring gift in the form of silver for use in his home. And so, Mr. Hanes, while we offer this gift to you, we really mean it for Mrs. Hanes, your helpmate through the years.

Mrs. Hanes, I know the delegates would like to greet you tonight. May we ask you to stand a moment?

I could speak at some length of the fine contributions Bob Hanes has made to the work of the association through the years. You heard me say a few minutes ago what I thought of his work as president. No man could have done more. Further praise from me at this time, which he richly deserves, would only be a source of embarrassment to him. Modesty is one of Bob's distinguishing characteristics.

However, on your behalf, the executive officers of the Association have inscribed on parchment and bound in leather a single sentence which is designed to give expression to our high regard and which we hope will remind him throughout the years of our debt to him for his leadership.

The wording of the parchment is as follows:

"Brilliant leadership as president of the American Bankers Association during the year ———— has earned for Robert M.

Hanes this testimonial from the membership as an expression of its admiration for his vision, his dynamic energy, and his profound wisdom in the direction of association affairs."

On behalf of the association I am asked to offer you this parchment and to transfer to your permanent possession this gavel as the symbol of authority as president of the American Bankers Association for the year ———

* * *

Some clubs make special announcements at weekly luncheon meetings relative to birthdays of members and also make announcements at the time of the deaths of members. Edwin B. Moran, some of whose introductions are included in this chapter, has used the following statements on such special occasions.

Birthdays

Birthdays are like stepping-stones
Along the path of years;
Here's hoping you will always find,
As each new one appears,
That it's a stepping-stone as well
To joys and pleasures new,
To still more happy hopes fulfilled,
And still more dreams come true.

* *

A happy birthday to each and every one of you

* *

Count your garden by the flowers,
Never by the leaves that fall.
Count your days by golden hours,
Don't remember clouds at all.
Count your nights by stars—not shadows,

Count your life with smiles—not tears.
And with joy through all your lifetime,
Count your age by friends—not years.

* *

A happy birthday and many more of them to each and every one
of you.

* *

Death

No one hears the door that opens
When they pass beyond our call;
Soft as loosened leaves of roses,
One by one, our loved ones fall.

Regretfully, and sorrowfully, I ask you to dwell for a moment
upon the passing of two friends and fellow Rotarians, —————
and —————.

The shadows flit across the face of the earth, and are gone.

So it appears sometimes with our lives.

But like the sunshine, and the shadows, and the rain, which have
their eternal effect upon nature, so also is the influence of our lives
eternal.

We take pride as Rotarians that the influence of Ernest and Henry
was of the very finest, and will be remembered throughout our days.

Let us bow our heads in silent prayer in memory of these two, never
to be forgotten, fellow Rotarians, ————— and —————.

* *

"His life was gentle, and the elements so mixed in him that Nature
might stand up and say to all the world, 'This was a man!' "

So wrote Shakespeare, and so can we think and say of —————,
for in every sense of the word, he was a man, a gentle, kindly man,
whom we shall miss in fellowship, and in friendship.

"Brownie," as he was affectionately known to all Rotarians, had a
devotion to his duties, as well as the principles and ethics of Rotary,
which endeared him to all members.

O, for the touch of his vanished hands,
And the sound of his voice, that is still.

"Brownie" left us a week ago today. For him the play is done; the curtain drops.

We say "Farewell."

Let us bow our heads in silent remembrance and prayer for our friend and fellow Rotarian, —————.

* * *

An invocation by Rev. George M. Gibson before a national convention of the Office Management Association.

Oh, Almighty God, Eternal Lawgiver, Maker of all things, Judge of all men, Giver of every good and perfect gift! We invoke Thy presence upon this assembly today; and be with these Thy people in their deliberations, and grant that their vision will be widened and their hearts strengthened for new tasks. Be Thou with them all personally that they may serve an even wider field relative to the work of their hands and of their minds to the growing righteousness of the world. Grant to each one of them a new birth of freedom and righteousness and of justice.

Bless our land and all the lands of the earth today that men dwelling in them may find a new commonwealth of life; and eliminate conflicts everywhere, so that those who labor with hand and those who labor with mind may find that comradeship of spirit with spirit which is like unto that above. We pray Thy blessing upon this assembly and upon each one here. Be Thou with us in our undertakings, and grant that there may go from life to life and heart to heart throughout the whole world a new faith and devotion and confidence on which our institutions may rest. We ask this in Thy name. Amen.

* * *

An invocation by the Rt. Rev. Daniel J. Gercke, D.D., Bishop of the Tucson Diocese, before a convention of the Arizona Bankers Association.

Oh, God, our Father, all wise and loving, to know Whom is to be truly wise; to serve Whom is to reign in this and in the world to come —look down upon us, gathered here on this memorable occasion, and bestow upon us Thy loving benediction. Oh, God, from Whom are holy desires, right counsels and just words, give to Thy servants that peace which the world cannot give. Direct, we beseech Thee, Oh, Lord, our actions by Thy holy inspirations, and carry them on by Thy gracious assistance, that every prayer and word of ours may begin always from Thee and through Thee be happily ended. Amen.

*   *   *

An invocation by Dr. Charles Ray Goff, pastor of Chicago Temple, First Methodist Church, before the convention of the National Fraternal Congress of America.

O Eternal God, our Father, we give Thee thanks for Thy goodness and Thy mercy to us. We thank Thee for this wonderful land. We thank Thee for all the fine relationships of life. We thank Thee for our friends and associates. Now, as this convention gathers here, we pray Thy blessing upon every member, and upon all that is done. We ask Thee, O God, that we might each seek in some way to build in this world something of the spirit that moved in the heart of Christ. We pray for the world, for our part in it, to ask that soon the day may come when wars may cease to the ends of the earth.

O God, we pray Thee that something new may be born in the world, that we may find a new spirit moving in the hearts of men. During the hours, we pray Thee, of this Congress, may that spirit be born in the hearts of those that are here. God bless us all and forgive us for our failures in the past. Give us, we pray Thee, Thy spirit. We ask it in Christ's name. Amen.

*   *   *

H. Lee Huston, an Iowa banker, presents an ivory gavel to Vivian W. Johnson, president of the First National Bank of Cedar Falls, Iowa, upon completion of his term of office as president of the Iowa Bankers Association.

Members of the Iowa Bankers Association, and friends: It is indeed a privilege and an honor for me to take part in this ceremony—this ceremony so emblematic of the passing of another milestone; this ceremony so expressive of the thanks of a group of people to their leader at his departure—the presentation of a token of esteem and affection, which will be cherished by its owner through the years to come.

Will the retiring president please stand? Each year this same ceremony is performed and each year another past president of the Iowa Bankers Association is born. But think how few there are of you, "the leaders," and think how many there are of us, your followers and admirers. There are very few of you who are born to be leaders; there are many, many of us who are born to be followers. It must be a great satisfaction to you now to join that distinguished and exclusive fraternity of the past presidents of this association.

To be chosen by this association to be its president is an honor of the highest degree. It is not just an office sought by the climber to be used for his own selfish whims and advancement. It is more the acknowledgment of a career of prominence in our field, banking, that is worthy of reward. The man chosen to be president of this association should represent the ultimate in integrity, ability, personality, sincerity, honesty, and all those qualities most admired and most necessary to the highly successful banker.

That you possess all of these qualities is evidenced by the successful year just closing and by the legion of friends you have throughout the state.

> No person was ever honored for what he received;
> Honor was the reward for what he gave.
> Great has been your effort;
> Greatness is your reward.

And now on behalf of the Iowa Bankers Association and with the compliments of its members, I hand you this ivory gavel. With it go our complete thanks for services rendered well; with it go our sincerest wishes for continued prosperity and happiness.

We trust that it will always bring fond memories of the many, many friends you have made throughout the state as president of the Iowa Bankers Association.

* * *

A mayor of Tucson, Arizona, welcomes the Arizona Bankers Association to Tucson.

I feel highly honored this morning to be asked, as mayor of this city, to greet you and extend to you the courtesies of Tucson. I feel that we are also very highly honored in having you select our city for your convention. There must be some attraction, or you would not come.

We hope that all your deliberations here will be entertaining and profitable to you and also to us, and we hope that it will not be long before our attractive city may attract you again, in the near future.

During your stay here, I again as mayor, and for the city, extend to you hearty greetings and all the privileges that the city can give you.

* * *

Thomas R. Mulroy, Chicago attorney, introduces Sir Norman Birkett, judge of King's Bench, England.

Sir Norman Birkett is an illustrious name throughout all England. Reaching the heights as a barrister, he was in 1924 appointed King's Counselor, and for almost three decades has participated in many of the most famous trials in the English courts. His talent long since attracted the envy and affection and the interest of American lawyers. Last fall he was honored at the convention of the American Bar Association where he delivered a masterful address.

Sir Norman was twice elevated to Parliament, and in June of 1941 King George knighted him. In November of the same year Sir Norman was elevated to the highest court in all England.

In a desire to obtain colorful data about our brilliant guest I asked *Time* magazine to send to me such stories as it may have published about him. I received two lengthy articles relating to two trials in which he had appeared as defense counsel.

Time said our guest was Britain's outstanding criminal lawyer and described him thusly:

"Norman Birkett, who got Wallis Warfield Simpson her divorce, and who is England's top criminal lawyer."

Unfortunately, however, the jurors in those two trials apparently had not read *Time* magazine, because in both of the cases they rendered verdicts licking Sir Norman. What is worse, his opponent in the libel suit was a woman, who wasn't even a lawyer. Her name was Elsie Florence Eva Borders and, according to *Time* magazine, at the conclusion of the trial she made this courteous, modest, cultured comment about Norman Birkett: "I wiped the floor with him."

At that point in his career I wonder if Norman Birkett, the most illustrious lawyer in all England, might have had the thought expressed by a young office boy in a large Chicago law firm, who quit after working there only two or three months.

"What's the matter, Jimmy," asked the managing partner jocularly, "didn't you like the law?"

"No," said Jimmy, "and I'm sorry I ever learned it."

In any event, what Elsie Florence Eva Borders did to Norman Birkett is proof of what I have always said about controversies with women: "The only way to fight a woman is with your hat: grab it and run."

Our system and principles of jurisprudence all originated in England. We owe England a great debt for this. What of our stewardship? Much of it has been splendid, such as the fine work done by the American Law Institute in restating in simple language the law of the land, and the procedural reforms accomplished through the cooperation of the judges and the bar association.

Even the "to-wits," and "aforesaids," and the "know-all-men-by-these-presents," and the "parties-of-the-first-parts," although still in good standing in too many law offices, are considered by most alert lawyers to be eighty-seven-cent words which they cannot afford to use in careful draftsmanship.

An exception may prove this rule, I hope, because I regret to report that only recently a legislature in one of our great states enacted in all seriousness the following requirement:

"It is hereby enacted that no bond shall be valid in this state unless signed by the secretary of the corporation in the SOUTHWEST CORNER thereof."

Nevertheless, we have come far, particularly in trial technique. For example, take the discouraged judge way back in 1871 in Chicago who, at the conclusion of a jury trial, felt it necessary to give the following instructions to the jury before they retired:

"Gentlemen of the jury: The attorneys on both sides in this case have been so unintelligible, the witnesses for both sides have been so thoroughly incredible, and both the plaintiff and defendant are such notorious characters, that to me it is of no consequence how you decide the case."

There has been some improvement. Nowadays lawyers are at least articulate, if not always intelligible. The story goes that one day a young lawyer, in making his closing address to a jury, decided to reply to, and in his opinion effectively answer, the reference made earlier by his opponent to a famous passage from the Old Testament. Listen:

"It may be true, as my opponent has said, that the battle is not always to the strong, nor the race to the swift, but, believe me, that's the way to bet."

I cannot present Sir Norman to you without first expressing to him our profound affection and respect for the English people in their historic fight for freedom.

I give you a man rich in character and distinction—a magnificent orator—a gentleman, Sir Norman Birkett.

*   *   *

Harold O. McLain, president of Railways Ice Company, Chicago, introduces Alvin N. "Bo" McMillin, football coach at Indiana University. Mr. McMillin's response follows immediately after the introduction.

Our program today consists of three addresses of fifteen minutes each by Mr. McMillin, Mr. Stuhldreher and Mr. Elward, each of whom is a well known and capable football coach.

It is always proper in any program to begin with a humorous and buoyant and witty note, and it is accordingly appropriate that we start our program today with "Bo" McMillin, who deservedly bears the reputation of being one of the most effective and proficient humorists and wits in the coaching profession. How a fellow can be a humorist and wit and a football coach at the same time is a mystery to me. If a human being can stand all the trials and tribulations and the infamous slings and arrows of fate which daily assail a football mentor, and if at the same time he can retain his humor and wit and be noted as a jolly and sparkling speaker, he is the kind of a fellow that could sing "We won't get home until morning" while riding to the guillotine or sitting on the electric chair. Ordinarily a coaching job has so many problems and uncertainties that it would knock all the fun and humor out of anybody.

I have a feeling of real respect and indebtedness to our first speaker, "Bo" McMillin, because I remember my grandfather saying at one time that in the early days in Scotland the McLains got their start by stealing sheep from the McMillins, and so to that extent I no doubt owe something to "Bo." He has a delightful charm and ability to enchant those upon whom he turns his oratory.

As you all know, Mr. McMillin is a Texan who made a nation-wide and sensational reputation as a football player with the Praying Colonels at Centre College. Since his graduation he has devoted his time to coaching, and after assignments at three or four colleges he finally became the coach at the University of Indiana, where he has had great success. He appears before us today as the conquering hero and victor, having defeated Purdue, which may in part account for his jollity and good humor in his recent speaking engagements. We welcome most heartily "Bo" McMillin, the football coach at Indiana, who will talk to us about any subject he chooses, just so it has some reference to football some place in its content. I am delighted to present Mr. McMillin.

*　　*　　*

Here is Mr. McMillin's response.

Members of The Executives' Club, and friends: I am afraid the reputation the chairman has built up for me is going to be lost by the time I get through. I am going to take what he said with a grain of salt, just like I plead with my football players not to think too much about what these wonderful sports writers have to say about them.

What Mr. McLain has said reminds me of a story about a little old country boy down in Texas that I used to know pretty well. This boy used to come into the little town about three or four miles from his home and stand in front of the drugstore, and watch the boys and girls who had a nickel, or a dime, go in and partake of those beautiful ice cream sodas, the strawberry variety, and he kept telling his ma about it. He said, "You know, Ma, I sho' would like to have one of those sometime."

She said, "Well, son, why don't you save up your money and get you one?"

So he started saving, and after some little time he got a dime together, and he went down, and walked into the drugstore, just like he saw those other boys and girls do, and he walked up to the soda fountain. The fellow said, "Well, what are you going to have?" He said, "I don't know what they call it, but," he said, "give me one of those things, will you?", and the soda boy brought out a strawberry ice cream soda, and the other boy took his straw and he sucked his straw, and he ate it, and he went home. His mother asked, "Well, son, how did you like it?" He said, "Do you know, Ma, that is just sweet wind."

And what your chairman has been saying about me, I am going to take it just like it is, "sweet wind."

CHAPTER 5

ILLUSTRATIONS OF HOW SPEAKERS RESPOND TO TOASTMASTERS

I N THIS chapter there are presented many actual illustrations of the opening remarks of speakers as they have responded to the introductions of toastmasters. These examples should be helpful both to speakers in preparing their responses, and to toastmasters, who may find stories and interesting comments which they can adapt and use.

* * *

The introductory remarks of football coach Wally Weber of the University of Michigan as he responds to an introduction by Kenneth L. Wilson, athletic commissioner of the Intercollegiate Conference.

Executives, vice presidents, office boys and assorted taxpayers: I'm not much of an after-dinner speaker, but I'm always after the dinner, as you can see by my rotund girth, so round, so firm, so fully packed, so free and easy on the draw.

Not knowing the quantity of the fine victuals I might expect with your hospitality, I took it upon myself to participate in some sustenance in one of your more unhygienic beaneries over on Wabash Avenue, to sustain my anemic figure until I got to the banquet hall.

Incidentally, I haven't seen Tug Wilson in a good many years. You know, he has reached the metallic age—gold in his teeth, silver in his hair and lead in his feet. But he has a very nice personality, a man of charming personality and great force in the Western Conference.

He said something about Weber playing on the last Yost team. It was really the highlight in my rather abbreviated career. It seems that in those days Mr. Yost was featuring a tremendous aerial game. It was featured by the throwing arm of the son of an impoverished tailor named Friedman, now a purveyor of jeeps in the city of Detroit, who threw passes into the receptive digits of a young man named Oosterbaan. My only function was to inflate the ball, which I did with consummate skill.

* * *

Tom Collins, from Kansas City, Missouri, who is widely known as one of the best humorous philosophers and speakers in the country, began an address as follows:

Thank you very much, sir. Ladies and gentlemen, good afternoon. I appreciate that gracious and very brief introduction, which leaves me little to live up to except to be a humorist and a philosopher. If I can get over those two hurdles, I probably will get by this without falling flat on my puss.

I obviously feel very much at home here. After that election which I just witnessed, anybody from Kansas City would have a very homelike feeling. [The club before which he was speaking had just held its annual election with only one slate of candidates.] I do feel it my duty to tell you that about a third of my town went to the penitentiary for holding elections in just such brisk manner as that. If you can get over that one, I'd think you could get by with pretty nearly anything.

Now, obviously, nobody would have asked a fellow with as silly a name and obvious lack of background as I have to come down here today, had you wanted to be set right on anything. If you wanted a cultured message, you well know you wouldn't have gotten me, and I know it. And so I have but two promises to make to you—this will not be dignified; it will not take long. I have a watch and I know how to tell time. And I believe that speakers should be guided by an old Biblical adage: "He who thinketh by the inch and speaketh by the yard ought to be kicketh by the foot."

I am here, frankly, ladies and gentlemen, to listen to my own favorite speaker on your time.

* * *

The opening paragraph of an address given by United States Representative Dewey Short of Missouri offers an interesting suggestion for beginning an address when a speaker has been honored by being asked to speak several times before the same audience.

When first I was invited to address this organization I felt highly honored. The second time you had me here to speak to you I really felt flattered, but now that I have been invited for the third time to appear before the same group I am really beginning to wonder whether I am great or you are just dumb. Anyway, I am overwhelmed by your capacity for punishment.

* * *

Roscoe Drummond, Chief of the Washington News Bureau of the Christian Science Monitor, *responds to an introduction.*

The generous introduction which I received reminds me of the press seminar, which was held in Washington. It is customary, as you may know, at the time of the President's annual budget for the budget director to attempt to explain the budget to newspapermen. I recall that we were having an interesting session with the budget director and his colleagues when there appeared to be a noticeable discrepancy of about sixteen billion dollars in comparing two tables. It developed, in the conversation, that there was a reasonable explanation. It was a matter of using different comparisons, and one of the speakers was able to explain the discrepancy of at least fourteen billion dollars. However, a persevering newspaperman said, "What about the other two billion dollars?" "Well," the representative of the budget said, "What do you want me to do, explain it down to the last penny?"

Well, I am willing to say and grateful to say that the introduction was approximately accurate.

* * *

Joe R. Hanley, Lieutenant Governor of the State of New York, responds to an introduction.

Mr. Chairman, ladies and gentlemen: I do not know how many of you have ever undertaken to make a public speech. I assure you, if you ever have attempted it, you appreciate the difficulty I find myself in, because of this beautiful and splendid introduction. I didn't realize who he was talking about, most of the time. And I did wish that my children could have been here to recognize what a wonderful father they had.

This introduction in spots made me think of the soap my mother used when I was a boy—soft soap and it had a lot of lye in it.

* * *

Ellis Arnall, former Governor of Georgia, responds to an introduction.

I appreciate the introduction accorded me by the chairman, and only hope that I may some day have the happy privilege of presenting him to some of my friends. While I know I could never present him with the ease and grace which he manifested in presenting me to you, I promise you and I promise him that I shall present him with the same utter disregard of the truth.

Now I never make an address or speech or lecture; I just talk, and I talk about things that I like to talk about, and talk about things that I think need to be talked about all over America today.

* * *

Dr. Deane W. Malott, Chancellor, University of Kansas, responds to an introduction.

It is an honor to have this opportunity to be with you, and a pleasure to renew an old friendship with the chairman. I have not seen him for ten years. He has not quite as much hair as he once had, and I assume, from the introduction, that it is because so many ideas have gone over his head.

With such an introduction, one really ought to collapse, because it would have made such a wonderful obituary.

* * *

Adm. Richard E. Byrd, famous explorer, responds to an introduction.

I certainly appreciate all those fine things the chairman just said about me. I don't begin to deserve it, but I must admit I'm human enough to like it just the same.

A schoolgirl got on the train which brought me here, and she wanted an interview. She recognized me, and wanted an interview for the school paper, as she was one of the editors. We talked a while, and presently she said, "Admiral, where did you get that Southern accent—the South Pole?"

Sometimes, as I go around, I am introduced by ladies. The other day I was introduced by a lady as follows: "Ladies and gentlemen— Rear Richard Admirable Byrd."

This morning, on the train, a man asked me the difference between the top and the bottom of the world. He asked, "What do you miss down there from civilization? What do you miss the most?"

Well, of course we missed a lot of things. Some of them we didn't mind missing, and others we did; some we were very glad to get away from.

I was discussing that very thing in the middle of the six months' night with one of the Irishmen in the camp, Jack O'Brien. It was right in the middle of the long Polar night. We were missing things, and we were also glad to get away from some things. I said, "Jack, what are you missing most from civilization?" He answered without any hesitation, "Temptation."

* * *

Rilea W. Doe, vice president, Safeway Stores, Inc., Oakland, California, responds to an introduction.

Mr. Chairman, and gentlemen: I, of course, would not be honest if I didn't say I appreciated that very generous introduction. As a matter of fact, it is almost the way I wrote it. He left out only a point or two. The next time, Mr. Chairman, don't forget that during World War II, I was an air-raid warden.

E

* * *

Senator James W. Fulbright responds to an introduction.

It is very unusual for me to have an introduction like that. I think it's the first time I've been called a statesman since I have been outside my own state.

It reminds me a little of a story that they tell in Arkansas about the farmer who was taking a little white-faced calf down a country road, on the end of a rope, and he was having some difficulty in making headway. He came to a little bridge over a shallow creek, with a dry creek bed, and the calf wouldn't move forward. He was tugging on the rope when a man drove up behind him in a car. The car couldn't pass because of the calf in the road, so the driver thought he would urge him on, and he let out a loud blast on the horn. The calf responded by jumping sidewise, over the edge of the bridge, and fell down in the creek.

The man walked up to where the farmer stood looking at the calf. He saw that the calf had fallen and broken its neck, and was dead, and he didn't know what to say.

Finally the farmer looked up and said, "Well, stranger, I appreciate your intentions, but don't you think that was an awfully loud toot for such a little calf?"

*   *   *

Harold E. Stassen, former Governor of Minnesota and statesman, responds to an introduction.

I count it an honor to respond to your invitation to meet with you on this delightful luncheon occasion here, in the hub of America. I might say that your gracious invitation, relayed to me, was very persuasive, because it expressed the thought that most of the members of the Executives' Club of Chicago knew me only as a character in a color cartoon on the front page of a newspaper. The view was expressed that it might be of mutual interest to us to meet together in a direct and frank session at one of your outstanding luncheon occasions here in Chicago.

Seriously, in responding to your invitation, I wish very directly and frankly to discuss with you some of the current questions before our country, not from a standpoint of saying to you, "Here are the answers to them"; not to say, "I want you to agree with me in detail"; but rather in the hope that as we think together in the real American spirit, we might find our way through—in America—to better answers than if we are coy and evasive and do not confront the issues of the day.

＊　＊　＊

Dr. Norman Vincent Peale, Minister of the Marble Collegiate Church of New York City, responds to an introduction.

I assure you that it was worth a trip from New York to Chicago to hear such a fine introduction. It has served to build up my ego. My ego was recently deflated in what was to me a most embarrassing manner. I was the speaker at an annual banquet of a bankers' association in a certain Eastern state, and arrived at the city where the banquet was to be held about an hour late. I went to my room, put on my tuxedo, and descended in the elevator to find that all of the bankers had gone into the banquet, save one stray banker whom I encountered in the elevator.

This banker, I am sad to relate, unlike most members of his profession, had obviously been communing with spirits which were certainly not religious spirits. He was weaving rather unsteadily on his feet. He looked me over speculatively; apparently he had no thought I was a minister; then he fixed a thin watery eye on me and said, "Hello there, Buddy." Well, it wasn't the form of address to which I was accustomed, but I answered in kind and we had a conversation for a moment or two which might be described as jocular. Finally, growing more confidential and apparently talking to me, he said, "Where are you going tonight, Buddy?" "Oh," I said, "I'm going to the banquet of a bankers' association. Where are you going?" "Oh," he replied, "I suppose I'll have to go in there, too, but I don't want to, because it won't be any good." I said, "Why won't it be any good?" "Oh, they've got some preacher from New York to speak in there today." I said, "You don't mean it!" He said, "It's a positive fact!" "Well," I asked, "why on earth have they got a preacher to speak to a bankers' association?" He replied with, "You've

got me, Buddy, unless it must be they are running out of money."
"Well," I said, "I guess I'll go on in anyway." He said, "I guess I
will, too, but it won't be any good." I said, "I know it won't be any
good." Having agreed that it wouldn't be any good, I went in, took
my seat at the speaker's table, and forgot about him. He went out of
my mind until I stood up to speak. As fate would have it, the first
man whose eye I caught at the end of the room was this man, and he
threw up his hands in a gesture of dismay and almost collapsed.

He listened to me, however—I saw that he did, for I fixed an eye
on him that wasn't thin or watery. I made my speech, and, when it
was all over, I was standing there at the table, shaking hands with
such people as came forward, when I saw him coming up from the
left. He had a shy and embarrassed smile on his face. I could see that
he hated like sin to come up and speak to me, but he thought he
ought to. And I liked him, because, when he got up to me, he proved
that he was a dead game sport, for arriving in front of me, he put
out his hand and he said, "Put her there, Buddy. We were both
right, weren't we?"

*   *   *

*S. Kendrick Guernsey, executive vice president of the
Gulf Life Insurance Company of Florida and a past president of Rotary International, responds to an introduction.*

President Lester, ladies and fellow Rotarians: I think I shall never
hear an introduction of that kind without recalling an experience
I had in Atlanta, Georgia, several years ago when I was going to talk
on the program of the district conference. I came into the conference
room a few minutes before time for my talk, took a seat in the last
row of chairs just in time to hear two men seated in the row in front
of me mention my name. You know how, in spite of noise, you hear
your own name called. So I naturally listened and this is the conversation I overheard.

One man said, "Who is this fellow Ken Guernsey who is going to
speak next?" His friend replied, "Oh, he is a fellow who has been
active in Rotary ever since I can remember. He was past district governor, past vice president of Rotary, served on many committees,

and the general line you have just heard." His friend said to him, "Well, I'll tell you, Jim, whenever you hear of a man who is giving that much time to one of these civic clubs, one of two things is the case. He is either a politician or he is a darn fool." Just at that moment the chairman spied me in the rear of the room and he said, "I see Ken Guernsey back there. Ken, come to the platform." These fellows turned around and caught me looking into their faces and realized I had heard what had been said. So after my talk one of these men came up and said, "Ken, I am not going to deny what I said. I know you heard me. But after hearing you speak I don't believe you are a politician."

*   *   *

Samuel B. Pettengill, vice president of the Transportation Association of America and former congressman, began an address with the following interesting illustration.

During the height of the Supreme Court fight, my old friend John Garner was called to the White House for a conference. He said, "Chief, do you want it with the bark on or the bark off?" I am going to try to give it to you today with the bark on. I think you can take it.

*   *   *

Harold E. Stassen, former governor of Minnesota and distinguished statesman, responds to an introduction.

After hearing the introduction by your distinguished chairman, my pleasure at being invited to speak to you has changed to regret that I was not appearing before a court, because if I were at this moment before a court, I would say, "Your honor, I rest my case." Surely nothing that I can say from this point forward can do anything else than decrease your estimate of me.

*   *   *

Dr. Preston Bradley, pastor of the Peoples Church of Chicago, responds to an introduction by Paul Westberg.

I listened to the very magnanimous and gracious words spoken about me, and it reminded me of the time when I was invited to come up to St. Peters, Minnesota, to speak up there at a civic dinner at which all the luncheon clubs united. I was in Duluth, and we drove over to St. Peters. On the outskirts of the city, just as we were entering, is a very big billboard. That billboard says, "You are now entering St. Peters, Minnesota, home of five governors." And it is true that that little city has produced five governors for the state of Minnesota. But down below it, in small print was this sentence, "We have natural gas too."

* * *

Tom Collins, publicity director of the City National Bank and Trust Company of Kansas City, Missouri, responds to an introduction which included only his name and his title.

Good afternoon, ladies and gentlemen. That was a very gracious and painless introduction. It reminds me of Mark Twain who said the best introduction he ever got was from the fellow that said, "I know two things about Clemens—he has never been in jail, and I don't know why." That seems to be the way I was pitched out here, with nothing to live up to, and I enjoyed it very much.

Obviously, I do not have the effrontery to come here to set you right on anything concerning the banking business. I am newly come to it, just a little over a year ago, and am very grateful for a chance to mingle with my betters. I would be stupid if I came here to tell you anything about the technical side of banking. You know I don't know and I know I don't know, and if I tried it I would run out of answers.

I would be like a gentleman who came to his local school and said, "Isn't it fine to come down here and get educated. To learn that two times two is four, and seven times eight is fifty-six—nine times twelve—(pause)—and then there is geography." I would be that way, too, I would run out of answers.

* * *

When R. R. Brubacher, president of the Toy National Bank of Sioux City, Iowa, was elected president of the Iowa Bankers Association, he responded with the comments which follow.

Mr. President, ladies and gentlemen of the Iowa Bankers Association. I want you to know that I have spent a very enjoyable two days here, which have reached their conclusion and consummation in rather flattering nomination speeches. I only wish I had half the qualifications mentioned. Perhaps some of you remember a play called *The Lion and the Mouse.* That play was a great success, but the same author wrote another play called *The Ne'er Do Well,* which wasn't. It seems when the curtain fell on the last act of the play, *The Ne'er Do Well,* in New York a young lady sitting behind this author touched him on the shoulder and said, "When the curtain rose on your play, I took the liberty of cutting off a lock of your hair. Now I would like to give it back." Now, I hope I can conduct the affairs of the association so that none of you, figuratively speaking, will want to return that lock of hair.

Seriously, I am deeply appreciative of the honor which you have just bestowed upon me. I will do well if I can fill the office as capably as have my predecessors. I can only say that with your cooperation I shall do the very best I can. Thank you very much.

*　　*　　*

Dr. William H. Kiekhofer, for many years professor of economics at the University of Wisconsin, responds to an introduction.

After this altogether too generous introduction by Dr. Haake, who was one of our most brilliant students at the University of Wisconsin, and who later became one of my own delightful colleagues for some years, and always remained a devoted friend, my feelings are not unlike those of a certain bachelor-girl whose somewhat belated engagement was reported. When confronted with the story she blushed, but her eyes twinkled as she said, "Modesty and honesty compel me to deny the report, but thank heaven for the rumor."

I am quite willing to have Dr. Haake, at my time in life, go on and say nice things about me even if he has to stretch matters very considerably.

* * *

Alben W. Barkley, United States Senator from Kentucky, responds to an introduction.

I am deeply grateful to the chairman for the very generous words with which he has presented me to this fine audience of men. I would not be entirely frank if I did not tell you that I do not deserve what he has said about me, and I would not be entirely frank or truthful if I didn't say that I am glad he said it.

I want to say at the outset that my remarks are entirely extemporaneous. I haven't had time to reduce these remarks to a manuscript, and I do not like to read a speech anyway. I read one once, and when I was the guest of the host who had invited me, I asked him what he thought of my speech. "Well," he said, "I have three criticisms to make. First," he said, "you read it; secondly, you read it poorly; and, thirdly, it was not worth reading."

* * *

Dr. Franklyn Bliss Snyder, who served for many years on the faculty and as president of Northwestern University, responds to an introduction by Harold O. McLain, president of the Railways Ice Company, Chicago.

I was just going to say most of that myself.

I appreciate the gracious technique of the toastmaster, Mr. Mc-Lain. It is not that which one usually experiences on such occasions. Not very long ago, looking into the faces of an audience a little larger than this gathered in my home town of Evanston, the chairman, looking at her watch, said: "Now we have come to the serious part of the evening: An address by Mr. Snyder. Some of us have heard him before and some have not. Those who have not are looking forward with great pleasure to hearing him now."

The bald literalism of that statement contrasts pleasantly with your very gracious exaggerations, and if I had to choose between the two, I would much prefer Mr. McLain's technique.

* * *

Dr. Carroll Sibley, biographer, author and lecturer, responds to an introduction.

Thank you, Mr. McLain for that unusually gracious introduction. I think there is nothing so rare on this earth as a superlatively good presiding chairman, but a presiding chairman like Mr. McLain presents one great difficulty. It keeps an audience wondering when the program is over why in the world they imported a speaker from two thousand miles away when they have an acre of diamonds in their own front yard. When I make that statement, gentlemen, I am polishing no apples, or, as we say in California, simonizing no citrus.

Mr. McLain referred to my published works, and while it is true I have written a number of books, I sometimes suspect that my literary following is so small that it might almost be said that my writings are confidential.

I understand that you have had the pleasure of several addresses from Lloyd Douglas, and it happens that Dr. Douglas lives very near our family in Southern California. Not long ago Mrs. Sibley and I had the privilege and pleasure of breaking bread with Dr. and Mrs. Douglas. As you recall, he is a man with a great sense of humor, and with a twinkle in his eye. After we had our fine meal, he said he suspected it was true in the case of each of us that the intellectual income of both of us was so much less than our oratorical output that we were both constantly in danger of mental bankruptcy.

Now I promise you several things about whatever I may say. In the first place, I shall give you no political oratory, which a friend of mine defines as: "The art of making deep sounds from the chest sound like messages from the brain."

And then I promise you another thing: I am going to be brief, because I have always felt that a speech in order to be immortal need not necessarily be eternal. I shall never forget the time that a certain well-known speaker came to Yale to address a class, and he took as his text the letters which are used in the word "Yale." And so he

E

spoke for about thirty minutes on "Y"; how important "you" are to life, and how important life is to "you." Then he came to "A" which stands for "ambition," and how important that is, and without which no one ever got very far. And "L" stands for "loyalty," and he devoted about thirty minutes to loyalty to your friends, loyalty to your family, loyalty to your employer. Finally he came to "E", which he said stands for "energy" without which nobody can get very far in life. He talked about two hours, and one of the students upon leaving the lecture hall at the conclusion of his remarks was heard to say to a friend: "Thank heavens, we are not students at the Massachusetts Institute of Technology."

* * *

Dr. Neil Carothers, for many years on the faculty of Lehigh University, responds to an introduction.

The kindly introduction of your chairman reminds me of two other occasions on which a chairman introduced me.

On one of them the chairman was most inexperienced, and he said that never having undertaken such a task before he had gone to a veteran toastmaster and asked him what the rule of introductions was, and this veteran told him that it was a very simple rule: "If the man is a big-shot and really amounts to something, simply state: 'We have with us today,' and say no more. But if he is small potatoes and does not amount to much in his home town, say just as much as you can about him." This young fellow then started with my birth and moved on down for the next fifteen minutes.

And on another occasion that I am reminded of, because of the perfectly beautiful way in which your chairman in only five minutes has presented to you the economic problems that now face us, I was introduced by an ex-Governor of the State of New Jersey who was, without doubt, the greatest orator that state had developed, but who had no terminal facilities whatever.

They warned me in advance that they had confined his introduction to ten minutes, which was far too long, but that I might expect the worst. The old gentleman did all right until he came to the subject of government policies at Washington, about which he appeared to feel very deeply. Instead of completing his introduction at that point, he talked about government policies at Washington for the next forty minutes.

When I got up to deliver my simple thirty-minute address, I told him that he reminded me of the Irishman who was trying to learn to ride a horse and who was mishandling the horse until the horse ended up by putting his back foot in the stirrup. The Irishman looked around at the horse and said: "Be gorrah, if you are going to get up, I am going to get down."

*   *   *

Harold O. McLain, president of The Railways Ice Company, Chicago, responds to an introduction.

That is a very pleasant introduction and commentary your chairman has accorded me. You know someone has said that the three hardest things in the world to do are to climb a fence leaning toward you, to kiss a pretty girl leaning away from you, and to acknowledge with proper humility a flattering introduction. In spite of many failures, I've had some success with the first two, but the last one has me licked.

I am glad what your chairman said really applied to me. Not this time, of course, but sometimes a chairman or toastmaster indulges in a little flattery about the speaker which doesn't carry conviction. That happened to the mayor of Des Moines a few years ago.

That official, who was plagued, as are most of us, with embarrassingly forgetful moments, was to introduce at a large civic banquet the guest of the city, Mr. Wiley Post, who had just completed his remarkable solo flight around the world. In his introduction the mayor said something like this. "Fellow citizens, this is the proudest and most triumphant moment in my life. I am to present to you perhaps the greatest explorer, the most magnificent navigator, the most brilliant aviator in all history. He has just completed his astounding feat of circumnavigating the globe in solo flight. The feats of earlier explorers and navigators like Columbus and Balboa and Ponce De Leon and Coronado pale into insignificance beside the accomplishment of our guest, the great pilot at whose feet the world bows in homage and whose name is on everyone's lips. It is the high privilege of my career to present to you our guest, the world renowned . . ." and then a horrible blank look came over the mayor's face as he experienced a lapse of memory. He stooped down and said in an audible whisper to Wiley, "What did you say your name is?", and receiving the reply he straightened up and declared dramatically, "the great Wiley Post." Wiley arose in acknowledgment of the introduction and said:

"Friends, as your honorable mayor has intimated, I have been a great traveler. I have felt the charm of Oriental Tokio and Shanghai, the mystery of St. Petersburg, the courtly brilliance of Vienna, the fascinating lure of Berlin, Paris and Rome, and the sturdy enormity of London. I have had the privilege of being entertained by the crowned heads and ruling potentates of most of the countries of the world, but I want to say to you that never have I visited such a delightful and charming city with such magnificent parks and boulevards, such splendid public buildings, and peopled by such beautiful women and hospitable and capable men as this your own world renowned city of . . ." and then Wiley allowed a blank look to come over his face as he leaned over and said in a loud and hoarse whisper to the mayor, "What did you say is the name of this burg?"

* * *

Jans J. Vander Graff, formerly Protestant chaplain at the Vaughn General Hospital, Hines, Illinois, responds to an introduction.

The introduction sounded somewhat like an obituary, and I hope I can live up to all the things the chairman has just told you. I feel just a little bit like the man who had recently been married and didn't know just how he was going to stack up with his wife when he came home late one night, so when he put the key in the door, he said, "I wonder what I am letting myself in for." I don't know whether you know what you are letting yourself in for today.

* * *

Tom K. Smith, president of the Boatmen's National Bank of St. Louis, Missouri, began his acceptance of the presidency of the American Bankers Association with the following paragraph.

In accepting the presidency of the American Bankers Association I am fully aware of the responsibilities which go with this high office, and I am deeply impressed with the honor you have seen fit to confer upon me. I earnestly hope for the strength of mind and body which will justify your confidence in my ability to meet the obligations imposed upon me as leader of the association during the coming year.

*   *   *

Clyde R. Hoey, former Governor of the State of North Carolina, responds to an introduction in a speech before the American Bankers Association.

I count it a high privilege to come this morning to say just a few words to this great assembly. Of course I am highly indebted to my friend of the years, your distinguished president, for his most gracious presentation of me. He was so much kinder than a friend of the late Senator James of Kentucky was in presenting him that I am doubly contented. This friend of Senator James was a very plain, blunt man, and in introducing the senator he said: "Ladies and gentlemen, I am not going to bore you with a speech today, but I will present to you a man who will."

*   *   *

George H. Love, president and member of the board of Pittsburgh Consolidated Coal Company and a director of the Mellon National Bank & Trust Company, responds to an introduction.

I didn't know there were quite so many executives in Chicago. As a matter of fact, the size of this audience really worries me a little.

This audience is a sort of triple threat to me today, because in the coal business, if you're a speaker, you become a labor leader, and you don't have to bother about meeting payrolls. Unfortunately, I didn't become a labor leader.

Secondly, I see quite a few people who really know something about coal. That's going to cramp my style in telling you about coal, and I won't be able to talk as glibly about it as I had hoped.

Finally, we also have quite a few of my old classmates here, and none of those particular gentlemen ever believed anything I said. So I have three hurdles to get over, and I'll do the best I can. But I do enjoy being here, and I thank you for the opportunity of talking to you a little bit about coal.

* * *

Gen. James H. Doolittle responds to an introduction.

I am delighted to be with you today.

I am very pleased with the introduction; but that sort of introduction can't give you the "big head" if you deal with children.

I am reminded of an experience I had here while I was still in uniform, immediately after returning from Okinawa after the war was over. I was walking along Michigan Avenue when a little boy came along, recognized me and said, "May I have your autograph?" I said, "Certainly." Presently I was surrounded by boys who wanted my autograph. I was in a hurry, but continued signing autographs until one little mucous-nosed fellow came through the crowd, elbowing his way in, put a scrap of paper in my hand and said, "Sign your name here," and then turned to the kid next to him and said "Who is the old buzzard anyway?"

CHAPTER 6

INTERESTING STORIES FROM INTRODUCTIONS AND SPEECHES

OFTEN a toastmaster or speaker will find it helpful if he can refer to a humorous or otherwise interesting story which someone else has told. He may say, for example, in illustrating a point, "United States Senator Leverett Saltonstall of Massachusetts said that he once received a letter from a gentleman which read, 'I have two children. One of them has been sick, unfortunately. Now my wife is about to have twins, and what are you going to do about it?' " The speaker may then state, "Now I should like to ask a similar question: What are we going to do about this matter?" The speaker is thus able to tell a story with credit to someone else and use it to bring out a point he himself is seeking to emphasize. Any story takes on additional interest if it can be credited to someone who is well known.

This chapter contains a great many stories actually used in introductions and speeches, as well as interesting comments on various subjects.

The name of the person who told the story is given in each case at the end of the story.

* * *

A Great Spirit

A preacher in San Antonio, Texas, while ministering among the poor, stopped in front of a dilapidated shack in which resided a Mexican family with two sons, the younger of the two having been afflicted with infantile paralysis. The older of the two boys was playing on the front porch and was greeted by the minister as he went in the house. About twenty or thirty minutes later as the minister prepared to leave, he saw the older brother admiring his car, which was a long black Cadillac sedan with a full portion of bright chromium trim. And as the little tyke was caressing one of the shiny fenders, the minister said:

"How do you like it, sonny?"

The little boy answered, "Fine! Where did you get it?"

The minister then explained. "Well, sonny, I'm just a preacher and don't make very much money and, of course, could not afford to buy such an expensive automobile. But I have a brother who lives up in Dallas, Texas, who has made a fortune out of oil and my brother gave me this automobile."

Whereupon the little fellow looked up and said, "Gee, mister," (now all of you think you know what the little boy said. You think he said, "I wish I *had* a brother like that," but it is what he really said that is important and is the thing I want you to remember) the little fellow looked up and said, "Gee, mister, I wish I could *be* a brother like that." *Charles W. Wooldridge, past president of the Rotary Club of Dallas, Texas.*

Never Satisfied

I guess football coaches are a lot like the actor, Frank McGlenn, who himself attempted always to be a perfectionist. The actor spent his life doing Lincoln, both on the legitimate stage and in the movies. In his living room he assumed Lincoln postures, he walked like Lincoln, dressed like Lincoln. On this particular day he was coming out of his apartment in the habiliment of Lincoln—top hat, frock coat, striped trousers—and when he reached the sidewalk he surveyed one end of the block, and then the other, very deliberately, and then with long strides, very similar to Lincoln's, he walked up the street. A fellow standing across the street watching him said, "Look; that guy will never be satisfied until he's assassinated." *James Conzelman, well known football coach.*

It Helps

I escape as frequently as possible from the artificial and highly hectic atmosphere of Washington because if one did not I am quite sure he would lose all grasp of realities. When new arrivals come into the departments down there they say: "You don't have to be crazy to work here but it helps." *From an address by United States Senator Ralph O. Brewster of Maine.*

Married Life

A long time ago, when Mrs. Chandler and I were courting, she made me a proposition which seemed entirely all right, but, in the state that I found myself, I think I would have taken it anyway. The married men will know what I mean, and the single ones will know what to expect. She said that, during the time we lived together, if important subjects came up, I could have the say. She said if they were not very important, she wouldn't bother me with them; she would just decide them and let it go. Well, we have been married quite a while; we got two baby girls and two baby boys and a grand-baby, but no major problems have come up.

She said she was going to try to teach the children good manners—and she thought she was doing very well, until one day during her temporary absence from the house, an elderly lady came suddenly into the room. Our six-year-old put his hands on his hips and said, "Well, who are you?" "Why," she said, "honey, I am your grandmother on your father's side." He said, "Huh, you'll not be here very long until you find out you're on the wrong side." *Albert B. Chandler, former United States Senator from Kentucky and now Baseball Commissioner.*

Courage of His Convictions

Down in Mississippi we have a squirrel law, and half of the people are for it and half of them are against it. Well, during a certain campaign down there, one of the campaign fellows came in one day and was making a big speech, and after he had finished, he said, "Now, does anybody have any questions?"

One of the people in the crowd said, "Yeah, how do you stand on the squirrel law?"

Well, when we heard that, we were scared to death, because we knew he'd say the wrong thing, but he said, "Glad you asked me that question. I understand that half of my friends are for it and half are against it. I want it definitely understood that I'm for my friends!"

Economy

I want to tell you about a friend of mine, and a great many of you people knew him, too. He was a fine fellow. His name was John Pelley, head of the American Association of Railroads. He lived in Chicago for a long time, as he used to be with the Illinois Central Railroad.

Well, John left the Illinois Central and went over to the Central of Georgia, just at the time the depression hit. It was pretty bad. He got there just at the wrong time, and he began to have to make a lot of cuts.

Well, times were bad, so Pelley began to do everything. He would take the colored porters who had been on the private cars, working two days a week, and he would make them do other jobs, and they would have to go out on runs which they didn't like. In fact, he began to fire everybody, and it got very, very bad.

Pelley said he walked down to his office one morning and on his way, overheard two colored boys talking.

The first boy said, "Boy, I dreamed last night that this fellow Pelley died."

The other said, "He did?"

The first boy said, "Yes, and I went to the funeral."

"What happened then?"

"Well, they were bringing the casket down the aisle, when all at once they threw the top of the casket up and Mr. Pelley stuck his head up and said, 'How many pallbearers?' Somebody said 'Eight,' and Mr. Pelley said, 'Let two go.'"

George E. Allen, friend of Presidents Franklin D. Roosevelt and Harry S. Truman, and director of many corporations.

Beggar's Choice

Freud says that in a great deal of joking we set up a situation in which there is a joker, a hidden change of values. Something looks like something and turns out to be something else.

Freud gives a number of amusing illustrations of that. In one, two beggars meet at the door of a rich man. This rich man has taken a vow never to turn a beggar away—always to give a beggar something. Of course the beggars found this out, and it was a regular business among the beggars to go there every day.

Well, one beggar is coming out of the door when he encounters another going in. The one going in says—referring to the rich patron —"How is he today?" The one coming out says, "He's in a very bad humor today; he only gave me a dollar." The one going in stops for a moment and then says, "Oh, well, I'll go in, anyway. Why should I give him a dollar?"

Satire

The great composer, Liszt, is said to have called upon Rossini with a letter of introduction. Rossini asked him to play, listened politely, and when he was done, asked him what the piece was. Liszt said, "It is a march which I have written on the death of Meyerbeer. How do you like it?"

Rossini replied, "I like it very much, but don't you think it would have been better if you had died and Meyerbeer had written the music?"

From speeches by Professor Bergen Evans of Northwestern University, author of The Natural History of Nonsense.

Failure

I am one of these foolish fellows who believe that I can train kids to be inventors, and somebody made a study—I think it was the Brookings Institution—one time that proved that a man who had an education was less likely to make an invention than a fellow who had no education. Well, that should be just exactly the other way. So I tried to find out why that was, and I think the reason is quite elementary. That kid from the time he was six or eight years old, was examined three or four times a year in school, and, if he flunked once, he was out and it was a pretty disgraceful thing; while a research fellow fails 999 times, and if he succeeds once, he is in.

Research

The word "research" has been so glamorized that it really doesn't hold the factors at all that I think it should have. We have tried to get definitions. We tried to get a definition for research that makes it something that takes it out of the academic and very intangible phase. Most people think of research men as being either highbrows or nuts. Well, we don't like either one of them, because we think that all the research there is is trying to find out something that we don't know. So we devised this definition: "Research is a process of finding out what you are going to do when you can't keep on doing what you are doing now, or what are you going to do when you quit doing what you are doing now." One fellow said, "I don't know!" He needs research.

Imagination

Some fellows in my office one time said, "What are some of the problems that are worrying you?" "Well," I said, "one is why I can see through a pane of glass." "Well," they said, "that is simple. It is transparent." If you look into a Webster dictionary, it says that something transparent is something you can see through. What he said was, "You can see through a pane of glass because you can see through a pane of glass," but it sounded much better when he said "transparent." There is an awful lot we don't know. In fact, most everything we don't know very well. Therefore, the opportunities that are in the world are just as great as we have the imagination to create.

Charles F. Kettering, formerly vice president and director, General Motors Corporation.

Better Keep Quiet

When the microphone was being tested, I was reminded of a speaker who didn't have very good attention, which is usually true of very poor speakers, and the fellow was talking away and talking away, and he noticed that he wasn't getting attention. He stopped and said, "Can you hear me back there? I can't hear myself talk." A little fellow out in front said, "Go right ahead, brother, you're not missing a thing." *Emil Schram, president of the New York Stock Exchange.*

Surplus

An Englishman went to New York State and was told by a native, "If you say money doesn't grow on trees, buy some apples here and you'll find out money does grow on trees." "Well," the Englishman said, "What do you do with all of them?" The New Yorker said, "Well, we eat what we can, and what we can't we can." The Englishman got all mixed up, and here's what he told the folks back home about it: "They ate what they could, and what they couldn't, they could." *Harry L. Sain, superintendent, The Industrial Commission of Ohio.*

No Bad Habits

A businessman was accosted by a tramp. This particular tramp was probably the dirtiest, filthiest looking human being that anybody had ever looked at, and, when he asked the businessman for a quarter, of course, the businessman gave him that fishy eye that businessmen always dish out when they are asked for money, and he said, "I am not going to give you a quarter. If I gave you a quarter, you'd go buy a drink with it." The tramp said, "No, sir, I don't use liquor." "Well, if I gave you a quarter, you'd probably buy some tobacco or cigarettes or some cigars." "No, sir," the tramp said, "I don't use tobacco at all." "Well," the businessman continued, "you'd probably go out and shoot craps, or gamble, or get in trouble." "No," replied the tramp, "I don't gamble." Well, the businessman took another look at him, and said, "You are a most unusual fellow, for the shape you are in. I'm going to give you a quarter, and I'd like to take you home to dinner with me."

Of course, the tramp wasn't going to turn down an offer of a meal, so they went home to dinner. The man didn't let his wife know that they were coming, and, when they stepped into the front door, for once the good lady was speechless. She took a look at this exhibit, and she closed her mouth tightly, and said nothing all through dinner.

After dinner was over, the tramp left, and then she backed the old boy up in the corner, and let him have it. She said, "Now, listen, I am very glad to see that, at last, you are beginning to have a little understanding for those less fortunate. I am glad to know that you think about those who are up against it, but the next time you bring somebody home to this house for dinner, you are going to let me know that you are bringing somebody, and, second, you are going to bring somebody that is clean. Why in the world did you bring such a dirty, filthy-looking individual into my nice home?" He said, "Honey, I just wanted to convince you, once and for all, what awful shape a man can get himself into who has no bad habits!" *Rilea W. Doe, vice president, Safeway Stores, Inc., Oakland, California.*

Entirely Crazy

A professor wanted to give a rather difficult question in logic one day, so he asked this question: "The United States is bounded on the north by Canada, on the south by the Gulf of Mexico, on the east by the Atlantic Ocean, and on the west by the Pacific Ocean; how old am I?"

After a moment one of the students held up his hand, and the professor called on him and asked the answer. The student said, "Well, you're forty-four."

"Why," said the professor, "that's right. How did you reason that out so quickly?"

The student said, "Well, I have a cousin at home who is twenty-two, and he's only half crazy."

Weapon of War

Someone asked Mr. Einstein one day what kind of weapons would be used in the third world war. "Well," he answered, "I don't know. I don't know what they are developing, because things are progressing so rapidly, but I can tell you what they'll use in the fourth world war," he said. "They'll use rocks."

James W. Fulbright, United States Senator from Arkansas.

They Were Right

Everyone that goes to Mexico, or wants to go to Mexico, always asks me one question and I shall answer it so that it won't bother you. What about travel conditions in Mexico? What about the problem of food and water? The first time I went to Mexico I rode a donkey from Mexico City down south over the mountains to Guatemala, and when I told them I planned such a trip, they said, "They will bring you back in a pine box."

"Well," I said, "I am going anyway." They said to take all precautions and "you might conceivably come back to us alive. You have to get inoculated for typhoid, vaccinated for smallpox, sleep under mosquito netting every night, peel all your vegetables and boil all your drinking water." The first time I went down to Mexico, I didn't get inoculated or vaccinated for anything, and I slept in the swamps and up in the mountains with never a mosquito net. I ate enchiladas and drank water running in streams, backyard ditches and any place in Mexico—and boy, was—I—sick! *Robert Friars, travel lecturer.*

No Taxes—No Debts

A boy came home from school and asked his father, "Father, was the white man superior to the Indian?" The father thought for a minute and said, "Well, when the Indians were running things, they had no taxes, they had no debts, and the women did all the work. How can you improve on that?"

Foolish Question

A small boy was practicing his piano lessons because he had to, and a traveling salesman stuck his head in the door, and said, "Son, is your mother home?" The boy said, "What do you think?"

Don't Touch It

I heard of two moonshiners down in Kentucky who were fifty-five years of age on the same day and wanted to celebrate. They didn't know what to do. Someone who knew them well suggested that they take a train ride. Well, they thought that was a good idea so they walked ten miles across country to the little railroad station.

Someone showed them how to buy tickets so they purchased tickets and got on the train. After getting on the train someone said, "Why don't you sit down?" They didn't know they were allowed to sit down, but finally they sat down.

The moment they sat down a big, burly fellow with a blue uniform and brass buttons came along for their tickets. They had never seen a conductor or heard of a conductor. This man took the tickets away from them and that made them mad because they hadn't even read them.

Another fellow they didn't know went to the platform at the end of the car and yelled the name of the next town—something that people couldn't possibly understand—and people got up and left the train and more people got on. They didn't know where they were— they didn't know anybody lived on the other side of the mountains.

Well, a boy came by selling peanuts, popcorn, chocolate bars and soda pop. They had heard of the first three things but had never seen soda pop before. One of the other passengers said, "Boy, give me a bottle of soda pop." Well, the minute he said "bottle," these moonshiners were all attention. They watched the fellow take the bottle of pop, knock off the top, and slowly drink the contents. The moonshiners winked at each other and one of them said, "Give us a bottle of that stuff, boy." They decided to "go halvers" on the first bottle to see how they liked it.

One of them started to drink his half of the contents just as the train went into a big, black tunnel. "How is it, Lem?" asked the other. "Don't touch the stuff," said the first man, "I've been struck blind!"

Knew What to Do

A friend of mine and I went to Coney Island, and we had a wonderful time. He knew what to see and what to avoid that wasn't worthwhile. The last attraction we visited was a shooting gallery, and there they had celluloid balls propelled by jets of water. The balls rose and fell and when they fell, they fell out of sight. The idea was to hit them as you saw them. I shot all the cartridges in my rifle and didn't hit one of the balls. My friend picked up a gun took careful aim, shot once and all the balls fell.

I said, "Bill, that's the most wonderful shooting I ever saw in my life. How on earth did you do it?" Bill replied, "I shot the fellow working the pump!" It was just a matter of knowing what to do.

James E. Gheen, humorous lecturer.

Honest

The warm ocean current near Alaska has some disadvantages. It produces a lot of rain. Alaskans are not Californians. They confess freely that they have a lot of rain. Sometimes I think they overstress it. In fact, it has often occurred to me that if an Alaskan and a Californian could meet and marry, the offspring would probably be an honest person. *Ernest T. Gruening, Governor of Alaska.*

Poor Hearing

A man was very hard of hearing, and went to the doctor. The doctor examined him and said, "I think you are drinking too much." He said, cupping his ear, "How is that, Doc?" And the doctor repeated, "You are drinking too much." The man said, "Maybe I am." "Well," the doctor said, "cut it out and see if you can't hear better." Six weeks later he came to see the doctor, and he was hearing perfectly. Six weeks more and he came back and he couldn't hear a thing, and the doctor said, "I thought, when you stopped drinking, you were hearing all right." He said, "I was, Doc, but I liked what I was drinking so much better than what I was hearing that I went back to drinking again." *Mark Brown, executive vice president of the Harris Trust & Savings Bank of Chicago.*

Useless Words

Pat and Mary were in some difficulty in court. They had been fighting, and the judge said: "Pat, I understand you and Mary had some words." "Yes, I had some," said Pat, "but I didn't get to use mine." *United States Senator John W. Bricker of Ohio.*

No Handicap Desired

[Mr. Halleck had no prepared manuscript for his speech.] When it comes to a manuscript, I am kind of like the boy who wanted to join the army. They asked him if he wanted to be in the cavalry, and he said, no, when they started shooting at him, he didn't want to be bothered with any horse!

Chaplain and Congress

The young fellow said to his dad: "Dad, why do they have a chaplain in Congress?" He said, "They have a chaplain there to pray." "Well, who does he pray for? Does he pray for the Congress?" He said, "Oh, no, he stands up and takes a look at the Congress, and then prays for the country!"

Hon. Charles A. Halleck, member of House of Representatives from Indiana.

Love

Two teardrops were floating down the river of time, and one said to the other. "Why were you shed?" And the little teardrop said, "I am the tear of a young girl who loved a young man and lost him. Whose tear are you?"

And the other tear replied, "I am the tear of the girl who got him." *Ilka Chase, star of radio, stage and screen.*

Accurate

The great baseball manager, Connie Mack, had a son who married a North Carolinian, and Connie used to go up there for his vacations after the season. He liked to hunt some. Not a particularly good shot, he went out one day with a fine rifle and excellent equipment, and came back without a squirrel. He met a native mountain North Carolina boy with a bag full of squirrels, and he said, "Son, where did you get all those squirrels?" "Well," he said, "Mister, I killed them chunking rocks at them." Connie said, "I don't believe that can be done, young man." "Well, sir," he said, "come on with me and if we find one I'll show you."

So they walked on through the woods of that beautiful mountain section, and soon the leaves shook and the boy reached down with his left hand and sailed a rock into the trees and down came the squirrel. Connie then had a new interest. He said, "Son, I need you for the Athletics. You will be the greatest left-handed pitcher the world has ever known." The boy said, "Thank you Mister, but I ain't left-handed." Connie said, "Pray tell me then, if you are not left-handed, why you didn't use your right hand when you threw that rock at that squirrel?" "Well, sir, when I uses my right hand, I mangles them too bad."

Correction, Please

It is sometimes hazardous to speak without a manuscript, because you might get misquoted, but my experience has been with the press that, whenever I have been misquoted, it constitutes an improvement in what I otherwise would have said. Sometimes you get into difficulty. My distinguished predecessor in office, who is quite a courtly, handsome, magnificent gentleman, had a little incident occur in the mansion there one day. He was lifting one of those heavy windows in that old building and sustained a slight hernia while lifting this window, and the morning papers the next morning said the "Governor had sustained a slight hernia while lifting a widow in the Governor's Mansion.

Joseph Melville Broughton, Governor of North Carolina.

Can't Know Everything

I like to tell the story about a little Protestant boy who came home with a big black eye, and his mother said, "Where on earth did you get that black eye?" He said, "The O'Reilly kids hung it on me." She said, "How did they come to do that?" "Well," he said, "I was over at their house, making some cracks about the Pope." His mother said, "Didn't you know the O'Reilly's were Catholics?" "Yes," he said, "but I didn't know the Pope was."

The Boy and the Drum

I live next door to a little boy, and some misguided guy gave him a drum for his birthday. I hope none of you have ever had to endure that reprehensible combination. It almost drove me out of my wits. I didn't know the answer to it. Finally I got a fellow I know and who likes me a little bit. I said, "Joe, what are we going to do with this, before I lose what passes for my wits?" He said, "I've got a notion. We'll go and see the kid." And we called on that little guy and my neighbor pulled out his pocket knife, and he said, "Son, I am making you a present of this knife. Wouldn't you love to know what is in the middle of that drum?"

Fear

A worry, a fear of failure has often held you and me back and you know it. I've got a friend who has done very well calling on tough customers, the kind that usually say no, and I said to him, "How do you get in a frame of mind to call on a tough guy?" He said, "I say to myself: Where am I? I am out here. Where is he? He is in there in his office. Where do I have to go? I have to go in where he is. What if he says no and throws me out—where am I? Out here— that's where I am now. I've got nothing to lose."

He Knew

I have a friend who plays the 'cello—in a kind of queer fashion. He clamps his finger on the neck and saws away, and he never moves that finger. He holds the 'cello in one spot, tight. One tone is all he ever produces, and his wife said to him, "Other people don't play the 'cello the way you play it. They fiddle up and down on the neck. They don't just leave their finger in one spot the way you are doing." "Oh," he said, "they are just hunting the place to play, but me, I've found it."

Tom Collins, humorist and philosopher.

He Had to Stay

A speaker talked and talked and talked on endlessly like the proverbial brook. Finally there came an end to the patience of the audience, and gradually the crowd began to leave. On and on the speaker went until finally there remained but one man who sat right out in front of him.

The speaker leaned over and said: "I would like to say in conclusion, sir: You are a gentleman." And the fellow looked up and said: "You are still wrong, Mister. I am the next speaker." *Charles Francis Coe, executive vice president and general counsel of the Motion Picture Producers & Distributors of America, Inc.*

Modernization

The story is told of an *"Uncle Tom's Cabin"* company that was touring in Russia. They came to the place in the play where Little Eva dies and goes to heaven, but since the Russians didn't believe in heaven, they had her get well and go to work in a cement factory. *Charles Milton Newcomb, humorist and philosopher.*

Facts

I remember very distinctly an incident—which took place two years or so before I joined the Communist Party, in the days of unemployment activity. At that time I was organizing unemployed leagues, and I was speaking in front of Tombs Prison in New York, on a very cold December day.

In those days I could speak with a great deal of vigor, and all the zeal that was in me, all the energy, went into this message.

I was very much encouraged when I observed, on the outskirts of the crowd, a rather distinguished looking gentleman who seemed to agree with me. He bowed his head several times, he repeated sentences which I had uttered, and he even condescended to applaud.

That gave me a great deal of boldness. I spoke to that man. I endeavored to enter into his mind. When the meeting was over, one person from the crowd rushed up and said, "That gentleman certainly thought a great deal of you." I felt sure that he had accepted my full message, so I asked, "What did he say?" The man replied, "If I could speak like that man, I'd go home immediately and tell my wife what I thought of her."

That true story from the sidewalks of New York took a great deal of the ego out of me. It taught me that in addition to having zeal and vigor, one must have facts in giving a message to any group.

I speak today—in addition to being a Hoosier—as a Catholic layman, standing four-square insofar as I can on the encyclicals of the Pope in regard to the conditions of labor, in regard to social reform, and in regard to the question of atheistic Communism and peace. *Louis F. Budenz, professor of economics, Fordham University, who renounced Communism.*

Missed Him

Back in '32, in the depths of the depression, they invited President Hoover down to Charleston, West Virginia, to dedicate some sort of a public institution. He got there at eight o'clock in the morning, and was greeted by an appropriate committee, taken to a hotel for breakfast, and out to the scene of the ceremony about eleven o'clock.

There were about twenty thousand people assembled. They had erected a platform, and they escorted the President up on the platform. Immediately they gave him the presidential salute of twenty-one guns. They boomed out from cannons close by. Everything was deathly still while the cannons were booming and for a moment after-ward. Back in the middle of the audience an old man shaded his eyes with his hand, and peered up on the platform and saw Hoover still standing there, and he said to himself, "By Gosh! They missed him." *Alben W. Barkley, United States Senator from Kentucky.*

Not Particular

A gentleman who was slightly under the weather decided to leave the party he was attending at a hotel and go home. He went out to the front door and there, on the sidewalk, was a man dressed in a blue uniform with gold braid and brass buttons, so he said, "Call me a cab." The uniformed man said, "I'm not a doorman; I'm a United States naval officer." The drunk said, "Well, call me a boat; I've got to get home." *James E. Gheen, humorist.*

Public Speaking

Dr. Johnson—the famous Dr. Samuel Johnson—said, two hun-dred years ago, "A public speaking lady is like a dog standing on its hind legs. It never is well done; in fact, one is surprised that it is done at all." *Mrs. Katherine L. Parker, wife of the late Maj. Gen. Frank Parker.*

Better Work

A little girl was pirouetting in front of a mirror one day, wearing her first long gown. She said, "Mamma, did God make Papa?"

Mamma said, "Yes." She said it with a kind of a gulp, but she admitted that God made him.

The little girl asked, "Mamma, did God make you?"

"Well, yes," replied the mother.

After a pause, the little girl took another pirouette and looked at herself very keenly from top to bottom, then she said, "Mamma, God's doing better work lately, isn't he?" *Upton Close, radio com-mentator and lecturer.*

Cash

One time a man was introducing me to a meeting, and he said, "I've just heard this man, LeTourneau, talking about giving the Lord credit. I know a lot of folks who will give the Lord the credit, but they won't give him the cash." *Robert G. LeTourneau, president of R. G. LeTourneau, Inc., who has given substantially of his time and funds to further Christian activities.*

Time

We do not have meal times like you have meal times over here. You go by a clock for everything you do. The clock tells you when to eat, the clock tells you what to eat, when to get up, and the clock tells you when to get to bed, if you do go to bed. We never go to bed by time. We don't have clocks. You go as far as you can in the daytime. When the sun gets low down you have gone a whole day's travel, because the sun has crossed the sky. But we are not going by clock, we are not going by time.

Over here, my goodness, you don't eat by your stomachs. When it is time to eat you go by the clocks. Out there we only eat when we are hungry and no other time. Because I am hungry, that is not saying that my family is hungry, so I will eat when I am hungry, and my family eats when they are hungry, and we do not eat together. We do not feel alike. I think that is the funniest thing, the way people go by time. *Anauta, Eskimo from Baffin Island and author of* Land of the Good Shadows.

Proper Address

Soon after being elected a bishop, I happened to be out in Wichita, Kansas. In the lobby of a hotel, I noticed my friend Channing Pollock, the playwright, sitting there. It was the first time I had seen him since my election to this office. I called out—he didn't see me, but I called out so he could hear me, "There's old Channing Pollock!" He rushed over.

He was a spontaneous, effervescent type of personality. He said this —I didn't say it, for a bishop wouldn't say this. He grabbed my hand and said, "My God, Bishop, I'm glad to see you!" Then I looked at him for a moment and I said, "Mr. Pollock, you may know all about the theater, sir, but the proper way to address a bishop is Me Lord— not My God!" *Bishop G. Bromley Oxnam, noted Methodist churchman, educator and leader in public affairs.*

Sizzle

When I was just a little fellow, back in Penfield, every Sunday I put a box out in front of Grandpa's farm; an old apple box. Grandpa had built me the prettiest handpainted sign, in three colors, "Eggs— 30¢" with a beautiful white Leghorn up in the corner, and I did a fair business.

But, one time, the wind came along and destroyed my sign and I made myself a homemade one, and just being a young fellow, I couldn't spell very well and I had the "s" marked backwards and the cent mark in the wrong place. That is the day success came to me, because all the city folks driving down the highway would see the crude, homemade sign, and figured, he is just a dumb country boy and his prices will be cheap. So, they pulled up in front of my sign and the wife would always nudge her husband and say, "Charlie, go on out and get me a dozen eggs."

He would come out in front of the car and then she would stick her head out the door and say, "Ask the boy if they are fresh." Now, I could have been ordinary. I could have been trite. I could have said to the lady, "Of course, they are fresh, lady; one-day-old eggs." But, I knew all the city fellows could say the same thing.

When she asked me if they were fresh, I looked the woman smack in the eye and said, "Madam, do you mind waiting a moment while I get them fresh from the henhouse?"

She would say, "No, go right ahead."

So, I went to the henhouse. Of course, just inside the henhouse door, I had a big bushel basket of eggs that I had been saving up all week for Sunday's business. So, I would put twelve eggs in my little bag, but here was my big selling sizzle. Every Sunday, I had a hen in the henhouse. I always knew she would be there because I had her roped in. And, just before I came out of the henhouse, I used to kick the hen just enough to make her cackle. Just when she cackled the loudest, that is when I walked out of the henhouse with the eggs in my right hand.

After hearing all that cackling, did I have to tell the woman how old my eggs were? Why, some of the customers thought I went in, swept the hens off the nests that had one-second-old eggs. *Elmer Wheeler, author of* How to Sell Yourself to Others, *and president of the Tested Selling Institute of New York.*

Cooperation

Dr. Leverett S. Lyon, chief executive officer, The Chicago Association of Commerce and Industry, was acting as moderator of a discussion in which one of the participants defined marriage as a status of antagonistic cooperation. Dr. Lyon said, "This interesting and intriguing definition of marriage, in which it turns out to be a 'status of antagonistic cooperation' reminds me of the definition of 'cooperation' which one man used when he said that every time he had been asked to cooperate, he was expected to *coo* while the other fellow *operated.*"

If It Doesn't Rain

A young man had just returned from an enjoyable date with his girl friend. He immediately sat down and wrote her a letter, asserting his undying devotion.

"There is nothing I would not do to reach your side," he wrote. "I would climb the highest mountains, I would cross the trackless desert, I would swim the widest ocean to be near you, my beloved!" Then he added: "P.S. I'll see you Saturday night, if it doesn't rain."

That is the danger of public speeches! We may be so entertained, or so enthusiastic about a problem, or so enamoured of great, shining generalities that we never do get around to take appropriate action! *Edward G. Olson, director of school and community relations, Washington State Office of Public Instruction.*

Skinned

Some time ago one of my countrymen, who was engaged in the prosperous business of tailoring in Singapore, had a rather exciting idea. He was getting along very well with his men's tailoring and he thought he would extend and expand his business by entering the ladies' clothing field, and he wanted to start with fur coats. He then devoted the second story of his premises to the new enterprise, putting up a sign in big letters, "Ladies' Fur Coats Made to Order—

F

Your Skin or Mine." *Dr. V. K. Wellington Koo, Ambassador of China to the United States.*

Exercise

A man was celebrating his eightieth birthday and his fiftieth wedding anniversary. The reporters gathered around and congratulated him, and asked, "Can you tell us how you account for this?"

He said, "I never thought about it. I do know that when I got married my wife and I had an agreement that any time we saw an argument coming on, I would grab my hat and walk three times around the block, and you'd be surprised what fifty years of outdoor exercise will do for your health." *Dr. W. Ballentine Henley, president of The College of Osteopathic Physicians and Surgeons of Los Angeles.*

Bureaucrat Correspondence

I have made a rather extensive survey of the unusual phraseology used in letter writing by bureaucrats. I find it is like basic English, in that it is entirely different English than business men use. And from time to time in analyzing and interpreting that strange language I made the following notes:

The phrase, "The matter is under consideration," when used by a bureaucrat, means: "I never heard of it."

When they use the phrase, "The matter is receiving preferred consideration," they mean "I will have a shot at finding the file."

The phrase, "You will recall this matter," means, "I know darn well you have forgotten or never knew because I am sure I don't."

The phrase, "This urgent matter is hereby transmitted to you," means, "You hold the bag a while—I am tired of it."

The phrase, "My present reaction is that I approve the document in a general way," means, "I haven't even read the document and don't intend to be bound by anything I say."

"Please take appropriate action" means, "Do you know what to do with it? I don't."

And lastly, the phrase, "Kindly expedite your reply," means "For Pete's sake try and find the papers!" *Thomas R. Mulroy, Chicago attorney.*

There Are Too Many Like This Church Member

A colored parson, who was trying to arouse his membership to action and get people personally to participate in whatever matter he had at hand, told his "brethren and sistern" that "dis yere church should do things . . . dey should walk forward." And the brother in the back row called out, "Amen, let her walk, brother, let her walk."

The preacher continued, "Not only should she walk but she should run." The brother in the back said, "Amen, let her run, brother, let her run."

"But,"' said the preacher, "not only should she walk and run, but she should fly." And the brother in the back said, "Amen, brother, let her fly, let her fly."

"But," said the parson, "to fly, dat means dat every membah of dis church has got to sacrifice, he has got to give more, every Sunday to de work ob de Lawd. Dey has got to gib ob dere time and ob dere money." The same voice in the back of the room said, "Let her walk, brother, let her walk." *E. P. Hamilton, president of the Hamilton Manufacturing Company of Two Rivers, Wisconsin.*

Opposed

A New York newspaper reporter who went up to Maine to interview a centenarian quite politely approached the old gentleman, who was sitting in his chair with his cane in his hand, and said, "Sir, you must have seen a great many changes during your hundred years." The old man replied, "Yes, and I've been agin' all of 'em." *George V. Denny, Jr., founder and moderator of America's Town Meeting of the Air.*

Character

The Yankee Pilgrim Fathers landed on our shores in 1620. When they got in, the democrats were not down to the dock to meet them, and neither were the republicans. None of the unions showed up. Wasn't that funny? So, the Pilgrim fathers and mothers started out looking for a steam-heated apartment with electric lights. They wanted a radio and a telephone, and they had to be near the nearest moving picture show. Just the bare necessities of life, you know. What we take for granted nowadays, they didn't find. So they took an axe and went into the woods and chopped down some trees to build themselves homes. The first winter they were on our shores in New England, half of their number died, but the following spring when the *Mayflower* returned to England, not one of that gallant band went back. They were absolutely sold on the future of America. That is the faith that has been born in the Yankee. That is why we live in those rocky hills; that is how we raise our families; that is why we do the best we can for our neighbor. If his house burns down, we build him a house. If his cow gets killed, we buy him a cow. *Billy B. Van, musical comedy star and "Ambassador of Good Will from New England."*

Living

I enjoy living so much I want everyone else to feel as I do. There is never a day when I drive out to my home in California that I don't look up and see the beautiful sky and see the sun—and see what God put here for us to enjoy. Instead of thinking what is wrong with the other guy, or the other fellow that is driving alongside of you, the best thing for us to do is see what is good in the other person, and bring that out instead of criticizing and finding what is wrong. *Joe E. Brown, star of stage, screen and radio.*

Long-winded

One time, Irvin Cobb was listening to some speeches in which a group of government people had talked. After listening for two or three hours, he turned to the man next to him and said, "Now I know why they wrote *The Stars and Stripes Forever." Tom C. Clark, Attorney-General of the United States.*

Recognition

To the south of Two Rivers, Wisconsin, is a fine nine-hole golf course. We have an excellent greens-keeper there who has made it his life work to develop fairways and greens that are the best in the state. He was hired by the founder of our company forty-five years ago.

A few years ago the greens-keepers of the state held a convention in Madison, Wisconsin, and Chris, our good-hearted Swede, was sent at the club's expense to attend the three-day session. When he returned, the president of our club called him and said, "Well, Chris, what did you learn?"

Chris said, "I tell you dis. I learn dat I am de tird best greens-keeper in de state—and de worst paid."

Horse Colic and Patrick Henry

There was a certain college professor who was an instructor in debate. He thought it would be well for him to select some outstanding speaker, thoroughly familiarize himself with the man's life and his writings, and learn many of his speeches. He chose Patrick Henry as his patron saint, and gradually the subject of Patrick Henry became obnoxious to his friends and relatives, and particularly to the boys in his classes. He used Patrick Henry in every speech.

One evening when the debate society was in session, the professor was called to the platform. The chairman, planning to put him on the spot said, "Professor, we should like to have you make an extemporaneous speech for three minutes, and your subject is "Horse Colic." Now, to show you how thoroughly saturated the professor's mental processes had become with Patrick Henry and his works, he faced his audience without hesitation and said, "Boys, what is horse colic? Why, 'tis nothing but a ball of wind, roaming hither and thither within the abdominal confines of the horse, crying out 'Give me liberty or give me death' "—and with that the Professor was off!

E. P. Hamilton, president of the Hamilton Manufacturing Company of Two Rivers, Wisconsin.

Foresight

A boy was taking Latin, and he was not exactly the best student in the class. I observed that he had written something in the front of his Latin book. I thought it must be very important if he had written it down, so I read it. This was what it said: "In case of fire, throw this book in."

Knowledge

A man said to his friend, "You know, when I was a boy, I used to think Sodom and Gomorrah were man and wife." His friend answered, "You've got nothing on me. I thought Epistles were the wives of the Apostles."

Charles Milton Newcomb, humorist and philosopher.

No Mud-Slinging

Chauncey Depew was a very ardent republican, a great entertainer, a great after-dinner speaker. In the course of one political campaign, he was approached by a stalwart democrat, who said to him, "Chauncey, can't we conduct this campaign now without any mud-slinging?" Chauncey said, "Why, of course we can. If you will promise not to tell any lies about the republican party, then I will promise you that I will not tell the truth about the democratic party." *Dwight H. Green, Governor of Illinois.*

Hadn't Seen Anything

One of the leading citizens of a small Ohio city, the first in the community to make such a trip, went around the world. He could hardly wait to get home to go to the club and tell all the fellows about the wonders he had seen and the interesting experiences he had had in India, China, Egypt, and all around the globe. He got up to the club one evening, and had orated for two or three hours in front of the bar and, finally, a chap down at the end, about half asleep and sort of leaning over, roused himself sufficiently to address this fellow, and said to him, "As one gentleman to another, may I ask you a question?" Our friend said, "Why, certainly. What is it?" He said, "Have you ever had delirium tremens?" My friend said "No." "Well," he said, "Brother, you hain't seen nothing and you hain't been nowhere!" *James S. Kemper, chairman of the board, Lumbermen's Mutual Casualty Company of Chicago.*

God

This universe of ours hasn't any meaning, it can't have any meaning, unless somewhere there is a power or a ruler that holds it all together. You cannot explain the very world in which you live unless you begin with the thing that you call God. I am not thinking of God as he might be described in a book, as he might be given to you by a Mohammedan or a Confucian or Brahman, or any other human being. I am thinking of God as a Power, as Someone who reveals His will in the manifestations of nature.

You can't escape that. We know there is such a thing as the law of gravity, and we know if there were no law of gravity, this universe would fly apart; it couldn't hold together. Explain the law of gravity, if you will. Explain how all these spheres hold their proper relationships to each other.

Explain, if you will, so common a phenomenon—all of us know it and very few of us appreciate its significance—that the world turns on its axis once every twenty-four hours, traveling at the rate of one thousand miles an hour. What difference does it make? Suppose it traveled only one hundred miles an hour? Why not? Who made it travel a thousand miles an hour? Why didn't He make it travel a hundred miles an hour? If that thing were sheer accident, if there were no will, no God who determined that, why one thousand miles an hour? Why not five hundred? Why not two thousand? Why not one hundred? And what a difference it would make! If this world traveled at the rate of one hundred miles an hour, your days and nights would be ten times as long as they now are. For what amounts to five full days now, ten times as long, you would be in night, without the warmth of the sun, and the world would freeze up, freeze up so solidly that everything would be dead before dawn came. And that which was still alive would roast during the day that was ten times as long as it is now. Suppose your noon-hour, which is already threatening in some places in the world to burn things up sometimes—suppose it lasted ten times as long.

The world couldn't exist if it didn't turn at that rate of one thousand miles an hour.

Or take so simple a thing as the freezing of water. When water freezes, it gets lighter. Why should it get lighter? Why should water, as it turns into ice, weigh less than it weighed before? Who did that? Who ordered that, and made it that way? What are the conveniences of it? As it becomes lighter, as it freezes, the ice floats on top of the water, and the water that is underneath can never freeze, but remains above the freezing point, and the life that is in the water lives. But if the water as it froze became heavier, or remained just as heavy as it was, it would go down to the bottom—this ice—and the lake and the ocean and the river would freeze solid. There wouldn't be any life there when the spring came, and when the summer came the solid ice at the bottom would never be reached by the rays of the sun. You could not have life on the earth if it weren't for the simple fact that ice is lighter than water.

Who ordered it that way? All through the manifestations of nature you will find a will, a sense of orderliness, a sense of relationship. What some of us call accepting or following God, the things that the Communist shrinks from in horror, in the last analysis mean nothing more difficult than accepting the laws of nature as they are manifested all about us every day. *Dr. Alfred P. Haake, economist and consultant for General Motors Corporation.*

Tradition

Man has not only forgotten his purpose; he has also been uprooted from tradition. The modern man is anti-traditional. That, in part, comes from the revolutionary tempo of our times. We are not very much concerned in basing ourselves upon the wisdom of the fathers. We feel that we must break with everything that has gone before us as antiquated and passé.

You and I certainly cannot think unless we go back into the storehouse of our memory and bring out from it the deposit of the past and use it as the foundation of future thinking. And so, too, if any civilization is to progress, man must go back to the past, to the storehouse of his traditions and bring out from that granary all the fine ideas that are hidden there, and use them as the basis of constructive thinking for the future.

Man today has broken with all that. Not only has man become dehumanized by having lost his purpose, by divorcing himself from tradition, but finally his dehumanization has reached a point where he has broken with his fellow man.

The great unities of the world are lost. First of all, the natural unity, that we are all human beings endowed with an intellect and will, with a common purpose—that unity which Christianity gives: that we have all been redeemed by the Son of God sent to this earth.

The tendency today is to break up unities. A man who has once considered himself one with his fellow man has broken that up into the unity, first of all, of the political order, the national order.

And today what is the basic unity among men? *Classes.* The laboring class set against capital; capital against labor—and simply because any unity which is founded upon class is necessarily *antagonistic.* It is the enemy of the other class.

That, incidentally, is why patriotism is on the decline. Patriotism assumes a greater unity, the unity of a common culture, and a common language under a common flag. And because the great interest of man today is in the class to which he belongs, patriotism has suffered and has become almost a lost virtue. *Rev. Monsignor Fulton J. Sheen, author and noted Catholic clergyman.*

Is the Young Man, Absalom, Safe?

Revolt was in the air. Anybody could feel it, though it was not easy to find the source of it. David was growing old and it seemed obvious to some of the enlightened members of the younger generation that the nation needed a change. The king still believed in the old fashioned virtues of the "good old days," and the older he grew, the more cautious he became. Absalom did the best he could to enlighten his aged father, but it seemed to him that David simply had lived too long. It was time for a younger hand to take over the leadership of the nation, Absalom thought, but he was depressed by the realization that old though his father was, he was disgustingly healthy and vigorous.

Absalom covered his trail well and few suspected his intrigues. He knew how to use his attractive personality for all it was worth and his ingratiating ways made him popular everywhere. The fact that he was David's son gave him access to the "right people" and enabled him to sidetrack the suspicion that might have fallen upon him. All in all, Absalom cut no mean figure in his father's kingdom.

F*

When Absalom finally showed his hand, much to his father's amazement, it was almost too late to save the kingdom. David and his servants fled from Jerusalem while his captains rallied the loyal remnants of the army. Perhaps it was overconfidence or an excessive estimate of his military genius that led to Absalom's disaster, but in any event, his armies were defeated and he lost his life.

Then there follows one of the most dramatic incidents in the Old Testament. Joab, the king's captain, sent Ahimaaz, a runner, from the battlefield to the king to inform him that Absalom was dead. David was watching for the messenger, who, when he arrived, was startled by the king's first question: "Is the young man, Absalom, safe?" The question was so eager, so anguished, that Ahimaaz had not the courage to tell the truth. He retreated behind a halfhearted evasion. A second runner, however, broke the old man's heart with the callous and exultant announcement that Absalom was dead. Weeping, David cried out: "O Absalom, my son, my son, would I had died for thee."

"Is the young man, Absalom, safe?" The question should have occurred to David long before it did. Absalom had been playing with fire for years and anybody should have been able to see that he was riding for a fall. Pride, self-will, ruthless ambition, lack of integrity —these were forerunners of disaster and David should have known it. The valiant faith and the striking idealism that had made David great had made no claim upon his son. The stirring traditions of Israel and the spiritual heritage of the nation meant nothing to Absalom; he could sweep away the glory of the past without a qualm. *From a sermon by Dr. Harold Blake Walker of The First Presbyterian Church of Evanston.*

Three Stories

In an ancient literature, which I happen to teach at the University of Chicago, is to be found this little story: Three men were in a boat, none of whom could swim. When they got out to midstream, one man took out an augur and started to bore a hole in the bottom of the boat. The other two shouted, "What are you doing?"

"Tend to your own business," said he, "I am boring a hole beneath my seat only, and not beneath yours."

"But," shouted the other two, "we are *all* in the same boat."

That story is two thousand years old. It is as true, if not truer, than when it was written. We are all in the same boat.

* *

Whittier tells how two rabbis, on the day of atonement, prayed the whole day long, each for his sins to be forgiven. Just before nightfall each still felt the burden of sin on his conscience. Finally, one rabbi prayed, "Oh, Lord God, if it be Thy will not to forgive my sins, do Thou forgive the sins of my brother who writhes in the agony of his soul."

And just then he felt that he, himself, had been forgiven. The great climax of that poem reads:

"Heaven's gate is not opened to him who comes alone;
    Save another's soul, and thus tho'lt save thine own."
We are all in the same boat! Are we not?

* *

In the sixteenth century, John Donne wrote a little poem that Hemingway has resurrected in his novel, *For Whom the Bell Tolls*. Listen to these lines:

"No man is an island in himself; he is part of the main land.
If a clod be washed away, Europe is less.
Any man's death diminishes me.
Never send to know for whom the bell tolls;
    It tolls for thee."

What did John Donne mean? *We live in and through every man's life. We die in and through every man's death.* Evidently, even our souls are in the same boat.

Dr. Louis L. Mann, Rabbi, Sinai Temple, Chicago.

Collective Security—Collective Suicide

If by collective we mean "gathered in a mass" or "individuals within a group following a common course of action" and even "pooling their interests," I would say amen, and then suggest that we seek our security that way. For that is the way of insurance companies, banks, corporations, partnerships. It is the way of churches, societies and finally, even government itself, under constitutional safeguards which protect individual rights to property and freedom of action. In these it is the individual who takes the initiative, sharing both the responsibility and the benefits. In that way I can provide my security through insurance policies, savings and investments, even though I do it, and must do it, in cooperation with other individuals. We pool our individual risks and benefits and do it voluntarily.

Note this very significant characteristic of *this* kind of collective security: it invests funds productively, in response to the profit motive, and results in the creation of wealth which can and will pay the benefits sought. The collectivism lies in sharing risks and benefits, not in substituting govenment coercion and control for individual initiative and control.

However, this is not what the term "collective security" usually means. The term normally implies government control and administration. It carries with it the subtle suggestion that the government owes me a living. Voluntary incentive for work disappears, and then we suffer a severe reduction in our standard of living or the government is forced to compel production. With that culmination liberty is gone, security soon follows and finally the nation itself dies. Thus it is that collective security *becomes* collective suicide. *Dr. Alfred P. Haake, economic consultant.*

Using Pronouns

Pronouns are interesting in value. A little girl used a number of them recently when she was writing an essay on Benjamin Franklin. She said, "He was born in Boston; he traveled to Philadelphia; he met a lady on the street; she laughed at him; he married her and he discovered electricity." *Philip Lovejoy, secretary of Rotary International.*

Insomnia

I was talking to a friend who was complaining of his inability to sleep. He finally went to a doctor about it. The doctor suggested that he try counting sheep. He did so that night, and returned to the doctor the next day more exhausted than before, stating that he didn't sleep at all.

He said: "For four, maybe five, hours, I count sheep. I count up to 20,000. Then I begin thinking—20,000 sheep would produce 80,000 pounds of wool—that would be 30,000 yards of cloth—that would make 12,000 overcoats! And, man, who can sleep with an inventory like that?" *Edwin B. Moran, manager of the Central Division of the National Association of Credit Men.*

Free Enterprise and Liberty

My definition of democracy is opportunity for excellence in performance and a fitting reward therefor.

Can it be that the critics of free enterprise consciously or unconsciously compare the realities of our system with some other system imagined to be perfect which has been worked out on paper?

In foreign lands where other types of economic systems have been worked out, do the people gladly and voluntarily accept these systems or must they be maintained by abridging freedom of speech, of assembly, of press and of action?

The sheeplike trust of people in the omniscience of government is an incredible and tragic phenomenon of our times.

Why do people believe, as F. A. Harper points out, "that if a person enslaves himself voluntarily or if his liberty is taken from him piece by piece through the mechanism of government, he has not lost his liberty at all"?

Under the spell of this great illusion, liberty *is* lost and its loss is not discovered until too late!

Listen to the testimony of a great English thinker, Charles Morgan. "In England, there is no incentive to bold undertakings—today it is safer to be a bureaucrat than a maker and young men know it—Socialism is competition without prizes, boredom without hope, war without victory and statistics without end. It takes the heart out of young men—It is not only politically false, but morally destructive."

You and I have known that for a long time. Down through history every attempt to solve human problems through Big Government has produced the same unfortunate result. *Clem D. Johnston, president of Roanoke Public Warehouse, Roanoke, Virginia, and past chairman, committee on international political and social problems of the Chamber of Commerce of the United States.*

An Open Mind

We are on the verge of getting into the rut of becoming "experts" who know what can't be done. Let us cultivate some new ideas. Let us cultivate some "foolish" ideas. Let us have some smart youngsters around us that don't know enough to know that certain things can't be done, and maybe they'll do them.

I want to tell you about an experience which Max Mason had in World War I. Our nation was in dire straits because of the activities of enemy submarines, and we didn't know what to do about it. We finally went to the National Research Council and asked for a committee that would work on the problem of discovering a submarine detector, and Max Mason, who was then a research professor of mathematics, astronomy and physics at the University of Wisconsin, was named chairman of that committee. He then went to visit a great ichthyologist—that means fish—asked him how fish heard, and he got the answer. He then planned his submarine detector accordingly. He invented the process which is still in use, and it was largely instrumental in turning the tide in the last war. It has been used ever since, and Max Mason has since been called back to Washington to improve his invention.

In making the machine there was one step that bothered him. He just couldn't do it. He had to have a certain process developed, and he didn't know how to do it. He asked three or four other topnotchers who were working with him about it, but not one of them was able to help him solve this minute technical problem, something which had to be done in order to make the submarine detector work properly.

So one night he put it up to a smart young assistant whom he had in his office, a young fellow about twenty-eight years of age who had been assigned to him. He didn't tell this chap that the problem was a hard one. He simply informed that chap that it was eight o'clock, that he had to rush home for dinner or his wife would be worried about him, and that he had to have this particular job by nine o'clock the next morning. Here was a chap who didn't know that it couldn't be done—and so he did it!

Just as an interesting comment, I might tell you that it later developed that fish didn't hear the way the ichthyologist had described to him, but the submarine detector worked successfully. The only moral to that story is that it was just too bad for the fish, because they worked out theoretically the proper technique and probably the fish would be better off if they heard that way!

Speaking of ichthyologists reminds me of David Starr Jordan, who was quite noted in that line. He was the president of Indiana State University before he became president of Leland Stanford. While at Indiana he knew the name of every student who was there, and when he went to Leland Stanford he definitely decided not to remember the names of any of them. One day somebody asked him why that was, and he answered that it was because he had arrived at the conclusion that every time he remembered the name of a student he forgot the name of a fish. *Harold H. Swift, vice chairman of the board of directors of Swift & Company.*

Form Letters

A man found bedbugs in his bed and complained to the hotel. He got a very nice letter back explaining that those things would happen once in a while. They were very careful and so forth, and they thanked him for writing the letter. But somebody had forgotten to detach a little slip that said, "Send this customer the bedbug letter."

I think our form letters need overhauling every once in a while. I know after I have read mine for a while I say to myself, "How could anybody think this is anything but a form letter?" It isn't personal any more, after several months. You might look over your own, however, and see how they sound. *Paul A. Mertz, director of company*

*training of Sears, Roebuck & Company and past president of the In-
dustrial Relations Association of Chicago.*

Horse Sense

Somebody once said that horse sense is the quality you never find
in a jackass. American people have a lot of that horse sense.

Another definition of horse sense is "stable" thinking.

The one I like best of all—and this is very typical of the American
people—horse sense is what keeps a horse from betting on a man.

Yes or No

A gentleman in Texas some years back wrote in and inquired if we
would take a survey on what the public thinks about the whole subject of gold and the gold standard for our dollar. He also took the
trouble to write out the question which he wanted us to put on the
ballot. I want to read you the question as he suggested it because it
illustrates the problem we are up against in the matter of wording
the inquiries that we put on our ballots.

This man said, "Kindly poll the American people on this question: Do you believe that instead of allowing a free open market with
bidding for gold unavoidably determining its value and production
in keeping with the law of supply and demand, automatically maintaining the gold supply properly apace growing industry's needs for
financing unrestricted production of desired goods, employment,
wages, profits, and consumption of goods—answer yes or no."

William A. Lydgate, editor of the Gallup Poll.

Doing Something Worthwhile

People who do not believe in anything never accomplish anything
worthwhile in the world. You can build a railroad across a desert if
you believe that the job can be done, but not if you take the position
that there are so many obstacles in the way of its being done that
there is no use attempting it. You can make a better world if you believe that the conditions of the world can be improved, but not if you
take the position that, human nature being what it is, there is nothing
that anyone can do about them. If you want to do something worthwhile with your life, you will have to believe that whatever needs to

be done can be done, if only someone is brave enough to undertake it. And you will yourself have to be brave enough to undertake it, whether anyone else does so or not.

This, of course, is also to say that you must become devoted to something that is truly great and significant. You must find a great cause and give to it the best you have as long as you live. Today, there are many great causes that are bidding for your support: world peace, desperately; and the abolition of poverty of a kind that denies to human beings the necessities of life and of personal development; intellectual freedom, and the preservation of those civil liberties that are all-essential to the existence of a democracy. You will have no difficulty in finding a great cause. You may have difficulty in supporting it. People who support great causes are not always understood or approved by their contemporaries. It is only when a great cause has finally triumphed and the worth of it can no longer be doubted or denied that most people begin to understand and appreciate the faithful few who, during the years, have valiantly supported it. But unless you have the courage to support great causes in the days of their unpopularity, you will not accomplish anything worthwhile in the world. Far from contributing to the solution of any human problem, you will yourself become a part of the problem that braver men and women have to solve. *From a sermon by Dr. Ernest Fremont Tittle, pastor of the First Methodist Church of Evanston, Illinois.*

Meeting Nice People

I came to this bankers convention feeling somewhat like a fellow named Joe, who was fond of dogs. He was going to a dog show in Chicago one day when he chanced to meet a lanky countryman leading a moth-eaten hound on a leash. Joe fell in with him and said, "Are you going to the dog show?" and he said he was. Joe said, "Are you going to take that dog?" "O, yes, I am going to take the dog." "You don't mean you are going to exhibit that dog?" said Joe, and the fellow answered yes again. "Well, you don't expect him to take a prize do you?" said Joe, and the countryman said, "No, I don't expect him to take a prize, but he is going to meet an awful lot of nice dogs"

So, while I didn't expect I could come to this convention and instruct you very much in the banking business, I thought I would meet an awful lot of nice people, and I certainly feel recompensed already. *United States Senator Ralph O. Brewster of Maine addressing the Iowa Bankers Association.*

Modern Medicine

My little daughter was sent to the store supposedly to get a thermometer because her daddy was quite ill. She forgot what she went after and got the thing mixed up. When she got home, my wife supposedly put the thing in my mouth, and when she took it out after waiting the proper period for the reading, she discovered it was a barometer instead of a thermometer and the reading was Dry and Windy. *Jans J. Vander Graff, formerly Protestant Chaplain of Vaughn General Hospital, Hines, Illinois, tells this story which others are said to have originated about him.*

Conditions Change

Things are going to keep on changing and we have got to be flexible in our thinking. A man called up the doctor in the middle of the night and said, "Doctor, come over here right away! My wife is awfully sick. I think she is going to need an operation for appendicitis."

The doctor said, "Man! You're crazy! Your wife couldn't have appendicitis. I took her appendix out myself six or seven years ago." He said, "Did you ever hear of a woman having a second appendix?"

The fellow said, "No, Doc, but didn't you ever hear of a man with a second wife?"

So, things do change. *Arthur H. Brayton of Des Moines, Iowa.*

Little Journeys Into Famous Lives

Very few persons know the name of George Matheson, but millions have sung the hymn he wrote. Mr. Matheson decided to study for the ministry. He was a brilliant scholar with a promising career, but suddenly lost his sight. All the bright prospects of life seemed closed to him. His career appeared ended, but he would not have it so. He became a great preacher and wrote many books. In that period of terrible disaster, when the darkness first fell on him, he wrote that immortal hymn, a part of which follows:

> O Light that followest all my way
> I yield my flickering torch to Thee;
> My heart restores its borrowed ray,
> That in Thy sunshine's blaze its day
> May brighter, fairer be.
>
> O Joy that seekest me through pain,
> I cannot close my heart to Thee;
> I trace the rainbow through the rain,
> And feel the promise is not vain
> That morn shall tearless be.

This hymn takes rank with Cardinal Newman's *Lead Kindly Light,* as one of the greatest hymns of the Christian church. It is notable for its beauty, its freshness, its devotional appeal; it is even more conspicuous as a hymn of courage. But its beauty is infinitely magnified when one understands that suffering out of which it came. Trials and hardships frequently unlock men's greatest virtues.

* * *

Two of the three greatest epic poets of the world were blind— Homer and Milton. Dante was in his later years almost blind. Beethoven was almost deaf when he produced his greatest works.

* * *

When Sir George Stephenson was working on the invention of the railroad engine, people said he was crazy. They said, "Smoke will pollute the air," and "Carriage makers and coachmen will starve for want of work." A House of Commons committee asked many questions. This was one of them: "If a cow gets on the track of the engine traveling ten miles an hour, will it not be an awkward situation?" "Yes, very awkward, indeed, for the cow," replied Stephenson. A government inspector said that if an engine ever went ten miles an hour, he would attempt to eat a stewed locomotive for breakfast. "What can be more palpably absurd than the prospect held out of locomotives traveling twice as fast as horses?" asked a writer in the English *Quarterly Review* for March, 1825.

* * *

One of the greatest writers and novelists in American history, Nathaniel Hawthorne, owed his success as a writer and the composition of his masterpiece to the loss of his job and the inspiration of his wife. One day he came home brokenhearted because of the loss of his job. He told his wife he was a failure. She replied, to his surprise, that the loss of his job had given him a wonderful opportunity to write a book. When he remarked that they had nothing on which to live in the meantime, she showed him that she had saved, out of her allowance and without his knowledge, enough so they could live for a year. She had implicit confidence in the fact that Hawthorne was a man of great ability. Hawthorne began work and wrote an exceptionally good book, *The Scarlet Letter.*

* * *

Alexander Hamilton said, "Men give me credit for genius. All the genius I have lies just in this: when I have a subject in hand I study it profoundly. Day and night it is before me. I explore it in all its bearings. My mind becomes pervaded with it. Then the effort which I make the people are pleased to call the fruit of genius; it is the fruit of labor and thought." The law of labor is equally binding on genius and mediocrity.

The American Idea

What are your privileges and responsibilities as American citizens? As the world hums with the rising clamor of confusing opinion and propaganda, ever more positively, skillfully, dominantly presented, it is imperative that you and I understand the significance of our citizenship and the American idea upon which it is firmly based.

For there is an American idea.

It came with the Pilgrim Fathers and the William Tells of many races, who found homes here.

It took as its emblem the freedom of the eagle and the independence of the pioneer.

It overleapt the hurdles that had blocked human progress in many other lands for centuries.

It blew through the sordid runways of outworn civilizations with the sweetness of mountain winds.

It amazed the world with the rich outpourings of its untrammeled spirit.

It made men cry: "Give me liberty or give me death."

It dedicated itself in strength, humility and tolerance, to the care of the needy and sick in this land and in all others.

It brought forth a beneficent downpouring of free thought, free speech, a free press, and a free pulpit.

It proclaimed the dignity of labor and the right to the profits of personal effort.

It erected the little white church and the little red schoolhouse in 250 thousand communities.

It created a nation of men with free bodies, free minds, free opinions and free souls.

It brought forth in only 150 years, the greatest wealth and the highest standard of living any people in history have ever known.

That is the American idea.

The Responsibilities of Citizenship

If a citizen demands wise government, he must recognize that wise government is the product of an intelligent citizenry, and nothing else.

If a citizen demands that crime be in the cell and not in the saddle, he must support honest law enforcement without any personal reservations whatsoever.

If a citizen demands unfair advantages for his industry, union, or geographical section, he must remember that the price of class and sectional selfishness is national destruction.

If a citizen demands sound fiscal policies, he must not advocate expenditures for his own community, which, when demanded by all communities, bring the crushing burden of national insolvency; and he must realize that every dollar which a government expends must eventually be repaid by the toil of its citizens in the creation of wealth.

If a citizen demands that his country protect him, he must co-operate unselfishly in giving his time and money to maintain the institutions which afford that protection.

If a citizen demands freedom of worship for himself, he must be tolerant of all creeds.

If a citizen demands freedom of speech, he must not encourage its suppression in those who disagree with him, nor must he use it maliciously to destroy the government from which that privilege flows.

If a citizen demands a paternalistic government to assume responsibilities which he himself rightfully should discharge, he must not forget that a nation's strength comes largely from each citizen standing on his own feet, and that the paths of benevolent despotism and personal decadence lead eventually to the destruction of the privileges of free citizens.

If a citizen demands of his fellow citizens that they work increasingly for a great nation by

Building homes,

Rearing families,

Caring for the sick, needy and suffering,

Giving children and adults more education,

Eliminating disease, accident and disaster, and

Developing communities in which men may have pride,

let him as a citizen, grateful for the priceless privileges which are his, dedicate himself in a spirit of humility to those responsibilities.

Achieving Greatness

Great achievement demands giving life itself. See Webster working thirty-six years on his dictionary; Bancroft writing twenty-six years on his *History of the United States*. Gibbon devoted twenty years to his *Decline and Fall of the Roman Empire* and rewrote his autobiography nine times. Vergil spent twelve years writing the *Aeneid*.

* * *

The publishers of the *Atlantic Monthly* returned Louisa Alcott's writing with the suggestion that she had better stick to school-teaching. A leading magazine ridiculed young Tennyson's first poems. Only one of Emerson's books had a profitable sale. Thackeray's *Vanity Fair* was turned down by a dozen publishers. Milton worked on *Paradise Lost* when he could not see.

* * *

When young Disraeli was ridiculed and hissed from the House of Commons, he said, "The time will come when you will hear me." And the time did come when this boy, with no opportunity, furnished England with her leadership for a quarter of a century.

* * *

Morse, the inventor of the telegraph, wrote: "So straitened were my circumstances that, in order to save time to carry out my invention and to economize my scanty means, I had for some months lodged and eaten in my studio, procuring my food in small quantities from some grocery, and preparing it myself. To conceal from my friends the stinted manner in which I lived, I was in the habit of bringing my food to my room in the evenings, and this was my mode of life for many years."

* * *

Daniel Webster, the youngest of ten children, as a child was so feeble in health he could not work. He developed physically and helped to earn his way through college, later becoming the leading lawyer in New England. He served in Congress, both as a representative and a senator, later becoming secretary of state under President Harrison.

The foregoing are excerpts from speeches by Herbert V. Prochnow, vice president of The First National Bank of Chicago.

Redemption or Conversion

Bill Michaels, vice president of the First National Bank of Tulsa, told the story about the woman who telephoned the bank to arrange for the disposal of a thousand-dollar bond.

"Is the bond for redemption or conversion?" she was asked.

There was a long pause, then the woman demanded: "Am I talk-ing to the First National Bank or the First Baptist Church?" *Finance*

Nine Famous Irishmen

Thomas H. Cannon, for fifty years High Chief Ranger of the Catholic Order of Foresters, has been a militant Irishman for every one of his 84 years. He has told the following story of "Nine Famous Irishmen." It goes like this:

In the Young Irish Disorders, in Ireland in 1848, the following nine men were captured, tried and convicted of treason against Her Majesty, The Queen, and were sentenced to death: John Mitchell, Morris Lyene, Pat Donahue, Thomas McGee, Charles Duffy, Thomas Meagher, Richard O'Gorman, Terrence McManus, Michael Ireland.

Before passing sentence, the judge asked if there was anything that anyone wished to say. Meagher, speaking for all, said:

"My lord, this is our first offense but not our last. If you will be easy with us this once, we promise, on our word as gentlemen to try and do better next time. And next time—sure we won't be fools enough to get caught."

Thereupon, the indignant judge sentenced them all to be hanged by the neck until dead, and drawn and quartered. Passionate protest from all the world forced Queen Victoria to commute the sentence to transportation for life to far wild Australia.

In 1874, word reached the astounded Queen Victoria that the Sir Charles Duffy who had been elected Prime Minister of Australia was the same Charles Duffy who had been transported twenty-five years before. On the Queen's demand, the records of the rest of the trans-ported men were revealed and this is what was uncovered:

Thomas Francis Meagher, Governor of Montana.

Terrence McManus, Brigadier General, United States Army.

Patrick Donahue, Brigadier General, United States Army.

Richard O'Gorman, Governor General of Newfoundland.

Morris Lyene, Attorney General of Australia, in which office Michael Ireland succeeded him.

Thomas D'Arcy McGee, Member of Parliament, Montreal, Minister of Agriculture and President of Council, Dominion of Canada.

John Mitchel, prominent New York politician. This man was the father of John Purroy Mitchel, mayor of New York, at the outbreak of World War I.

> "O, Ireland, must we leave you,
> Driven by a tyrant hand,
> Must we seek a mother's blessing
> In a strange and distant land?" *Finance*

Medicine and Law

I well remember a young legal friend of mine who went to a great gathering of the medical profession, trying to curry favor with them, which is a fault of some members of the legal profession. He tried to draw an analogy between the medical profession and the legal profession, and said: "I know not why I was invited here unless it be, there is some affinity between your great profession and mine, because I know that whenever I finish a case I say to myself, 'Now, have I left anything out?' whereas the medical profession, at the end of a case, say, 'Have I left anything in?' " *Sir Norman Birkett, judge of King's Bench, England.*

Difficult Question

In a class on Americanism the teacher of the class, just before turning his students over to the official who was there to give them the oath of allegiance to complete their papers on Americanism, wanted to impress the official with what the men had learned. The teacher said to them: "What is it, gentlemen, that flies over the City Hall on the Fourth of July?" Well, that stumped the boys. They could not get the answer.

As the teacher looked upon the class in despair, one fellow held up a hand rather reluctantly. The teacher said: "All right, Ole, what is it that flies over the City Hall on the Fourth of July?" What do you suppose Ole's answer was? "Pigeons." *George McCarty, head of speech department, South Dakota State College.*

One of the Group

I live out in the northeastern section of Pennsylvania, in the anthracite fields, and forty or fifty miles above my home is an insane asylum in which they lodge the criminal insane, and about forty or fifty miles below they lodge those who recuperate to some extent. In order to transport them from one town to the other they have got to go on a railroad that passes through my home town of Plymouth.

So they were bringing about twenty of the convicts from the upper insane asylum down, and I got on that train at Plymouth, and inadvertently got into the same car in which these twenty members of the insane asylum were lodged. The conductor went through the train checking up on his passengers.

He was going down the line counting them: "One, two, three, four, five, six, seven, eight—" and he stopped at the seat in which I was sitting and said: "Who are you?" I said: "I am the Governor of Pennsylvania." "Nine, ten, eleven." *Arthur H. James, former Governor of Pennsylvania.*

Legal Ethics

After I was graduated from Harvard, I went out to Wyoming to practice law. The Attorney-General of Wyoming at that time was an old cowpuncher. He was a salty old character and loved to give advice. I went around to see him. He asked me: "Did you ever have a course in legal ethics?"

I said: "No, they don't consider it necessary to teach that at Harvard."

He said: "I am very happy to hear that, because I can in one sentence tell you all the legal ethics that any lawyer needs to know."

I said: "Go ahead, General."

He replied: "Remember this. Whenever you are involved in any litigation and it becomes apparent that someone has got to go to jail, be sure it is your client." *Thurman W. Arnold, former Assistant At-torney-General of the United States.*

Do Your Best

Some years ago a colored defendant was convicted before the late Judge David on a charge of arson on ten separate counts of 99 years each, a total of 990 years. "Judge, yo honor," said the defendant, "that's gonna be moughty hard for me to do!"

"Well," replied Judge David, "Just do the best you can!" *Thomas R. Mulroy, Chicago attorney.*

Quoting the Bible

Justice Chase was a very famous justice of the supreme court of Ohio. He was a republican.

Before assuming the bench he was governor, and in his position as governor issued a Thanksgiving proclamation. To make it very realis-tic he decided that he could do no better than go to the source of Thanksgiving, the Bible. So he studded the entire proclamation with Biblical phrases, thinking that surely the people of Ohio, who read it, would know where it came from and would not accuse him of plagiarism. He never put the quotation marks in it.

The next day a democratic newspaper came forth with a statement as follows: "The Editor wishes to state that these statements made by Governor Chase sound suspiciously familiar; he has read them somewhere but he cannot recall where, and he is inclined to believe that they are rank plagiarism."

Now, that would have been enough but the following day the republican newspaper came out in defense of their governor and said:

"The statement of the democratic editor is a lie. These are original statements and I challenge anybody to show where they were ever used before." *Rabbi Charles E. Shulman.*

The Importance of Boys and Girls

In a homely but dramatic fashion Elbert Hubbard characterizes the significance and the importance of boys and girls as follows:

"Boys and girls are men and women in the cocoon. You do not know what they are going to become. Their lives are big with many possibilities. They may make or unmake kings, change boundary lines between nations, write books that will mold character, or invent machines that will revolutionize the world. Yesterday I rode horseback past a field where a boy was plowing. The lad's hair stuck out through the top of his hat. His form was bony and awkward—one suspender only held his trousers in place. His bare legs and arms were brown and sunburned and briar-scarred. He swung his horses around just as I passed by and from under the flapping brim of his hat he cast a quick glance out of dark, half-bashful eyes, and modestly returned my salute. His back turned. I took off my hat and sent a 'God bless you' down the furrows after him. Who knows? I may yet go to that boy as a banker and borrow money; or to hear him preach; or to beg him to defend me in a lawsuit; or he may stand with pulse unhastened, in white apron ready to do his duty while the cone is placed over my face and night and death come creeping into my veins. So I beg you be patient and generous with the boys and girls. You are dealing with soul-stuff." *Harold O. McLain, president of the Railways Ice Company, Chicago.*

Correct

There were a couple of fellows in a nut college or pecan university who got together in a two-man huddle and decided unanimously without a dissenting voice that they were now sane; it was an outrage to confine them longer in this abode of crackpots. So they decided to go to the superintendent of the institution and demand their instantaneous release on the ground that they were now fully recovered mentally. But on the way to the boss's office one of them stopped and said: "Now, just a minute. About you. I am not half as sure of you as I am of me about this recovery business. Suppose, for instance, we got into the boss's office and you did some crazy thing and spoiled it all. Would you mind much if I gave you a little test before we go in there, just to check up?" He said: "Mind if you give me a test! I welcome any test as to my sanity. Go ahead, do anything you want to." So he shut up his fist and put it behind his back and said: "What have I got in my hand?" The fellow looked at the ceiling thoughtfully for a while, a good while, and he said: "A Greyhound bus." His friend said: "Wait a minute. Somebody told you." *Strickland Gillilan, humorist.*

A Few Kind Words

There was a Britisher visiting the United States for the first time, and he was going up and down the country. He arrived in a little junction-town out west in the morning and wanted some breakfast. So he went into one of these greasy-spoon affairs that you find about those places and sat down. The waitress came to him and he said: "If you don't mind, you know, I should like some three-minute eggs, please, and some buttered toast, a little bacon, a pot of coffee, and a few kind words." In a moment the coffee was back and the eggs were back and the bacon was back, and they were all placed in front of this Britisher, all very lovely and fine. He looked up and said: "It is very nice, you know, and now for the few kind words." She leaned over to him and said: "If I were you, I wouldn't eat the eggs." *Dr. Preston Bradley, pastor, People's Church of Chicago.*

Active

A colored gentleman had been a preacher for some little time.

Someone said: "Uncle Amos, how many members have you got in your church?" And he replied: "I got sixteen."

"Are they all active?"

And the old preacher answered: "Yes, eight of them fur me and eight of them agin' me."

Difficult Question

A little fellow asked his mother: "Do you know what makes the Tower of Pisa lean?" And she said: "No, if I did, I would take some."

Greatness

I think I am a great man. I will tell you why. In claiming greatness for myself I am claiming greatness for every one of you. I can think; I can love; I can purpose; I can dream; I can hope; I can aspire; I can grow. I can peer through the telescope and see the skies and understand the stars. I am bigger than the stars themselves. I am great. You are.

California

I come from Los Angeles. I always like to make that plain. A little schoolboy was asked by his teacher to define California, and he said: "It is Los Angeles and outlying territory." The teacher said: "That cannot be; there is no territory that can outlie Los Angeles."

Dr. Roy L. Smith, editor, author and well known preacher.

Sports Events

There is a little town in deepest Texas where they are raising their community money by putting on some kind of a show. One year they had a field and sports day. They made some money out of their concessions, and out of the tickets for admission, and it promised to be quite a going concern. They had the women's sports events in the forenoon and the men's sports events in the afternoon.

In the morning the woman who won the long-distance rolling-pin throw threw this rolling pin $87\frac{1}{2}$ feet. Somebody standing by her with a stop watch—though time was not a factor in this—timed her shot and it was four seconds and a quarter from the time the rolling pin left the woman's hand until it landed in the sandpit.

Now, I should say about this lady that she was the president of this, and general secretary of that, and a delegate to all the conventions, and was pretty much on the go, and she was one of the most eminent gavel-swingers in all that part of the state. Her husband, who was a mild-mannered, hollow-chested, meek little thing, in the afternoon won the 100-yard dash. He did this in twelve seconds flat, which is by no means a world's record, but fairly good going for a layman.

Interested neighbors who knew something about the circumstances of his life got out their lead-pencils and figured he could do $87\frac{1}{2}$ feet in three and seven-eighth seconds, which left him in the clear.

I know these mathematical sharks, and people who work in the upper brackets of physics will probably be reminded that there is a trajectory, and a lot of fussing around with the upper flights of figures in connection with this event, but I have investigated this, too, or had the research done for me by somebody who knew something about mathematics, which I do not, and he tells me the man was still in the clear.

Thunder and Dawn

There is a fine old fellow named Dean Chandler who is the head of English at Maudlin College, Oxford, who every summer takes an undergraduate student with him on a hiking trip. Last summer the old man and one of his boys went on a trip down in the Pyrenees.

One afternoon they got caught out on one of the stiffest, steepest, ruggedest slopes of the Pyrenees before they had a chance to get to shelter. They camped out there for the night, and before light there was a terrific storm. This boy had never heard such thunder and he had never seen such lightning. There was an avalanche that swept down the slope a few feet from them carrying great, big boulders. And this boy was thoroughly terrified. He grasped the old man's sleeve, and above the fury of the storm he shouted: "Doctor, I believe this is the end of the world." And the old man said: "No, my son, this is not the end of the world. This is the way dawn comes in the Pyrenees."

Dr. Lloyd C. Douglas, author.

CHAPTER 7

EPIGRAMS AND WITTICISMS

THIS chapter contains several hundred epigrams and concise humorous comments which frequently may be more effective than anecdotes in introductions. Brevity may be imperative in an introduction, and the epigram meets this requirement perfectly. A humorous story followed later in an introduction by an epigram provides a "change of pace" that is not made possible by telling two or three humorous stories. A chairman who plans his introductions carefully will find many occasions to use epigrams.

*　　*　　*

If a man has more personality than brains, he soon gets to the point where he is overpaid.

When the census taker asked how old she was, she couldn't remember whether she was thirty-eight or thirty-nine, so she said twenty-five.

A doctor will order you to stop working and rest. Then he will give you a bill that will keep your nose to the grindstone for six months.

All a good executive needs for an office is a room that's big enough for his brains.

Most of us are broadminded; in an argument we see both points of view, the one that is wrong and our own.

When in doubt (also when not), do the friendliest thing.

He wasn't exactly a sculptor, just a chiseler.

Advice—The cheapest commodity in all the world. "What older

men offer to younger men when they no longer can set them a bad example." *Irvin S. Cobb.*

A small town businessman is one who conducts a business so small he doesn't have to bribe a government official to let him alone.

Short Book Review—Little girl describing a book: "This book tells more about birds than I am interested in knowing."

If a person has no education he just has to use his brains.

Grapefruit—A California lemon.

A mother may hope that her daughter will get a better husband than she did, but she knows her son will never get as good a wife as his father did.

April showers bring May double-headers.

Rotarian—A person who is sober when he sings at luncheon.

The world is divided into people who do things and people who get the credit. Try, if you can, to belong to the first class. There's far less competition. *Dwight Morrow.*

James McNeill Whistler was invariably tart of tongue. To a man who remarked, "I passed your house last night," Whistler retorted, "Thanks!"

Every executive knows there is nothing common about common sense.

Professor—"If the young man in the back row will remove his hat, I shall continue and point out a concrete example."

Seven Ages of Woman—Baby, infant, miss, young woman, young woman, young woman, young woman.

Bubble gum has certainly made this a country of the wide open faces.

Death and taxes may always be with us, but death at least doesn't get any worse.

No man enjoys life like the man who doesn't think, but thinks he does.

Socialism becomes popular whenever hard working, thrifty people build something worth owning which other people want.

G

If the world is too much with you, put a nickel in a telephone booth slot and you will be cut off from everything.

What the world needs is a diplomat who can satisfy the Communists without giving them what they want.

Economics Simplified—Prosperity is the period when it is easy to borrow money to buy things which you should be able to pay for out of your own income.

In a budget of billions it ought to be possible to set aside enough money to teach the Internal Revenue Department the basic English necessary to write a readable income tax form.

Statistics show great increases in marriages. Life seems to be just a marry chase.

The five B's of middle age—Baldness, bridgework, bifocals, bay-windows and bunions.

Something ought to be done to improve sandwiches sold in depots. A coat of clear shellac would make them more attractive and easier to dust.

A conference is a gathering of important people who singly can do nothing, but together can decide that nothing can be done. *Fred Allen.*

A man said he was glad he didn't like olives, because he knew if he did, he'd eat a lot of them, and he hated the things. *Charles Milton Newcomb, humorist and philosopher.*

Nobody ever listened himself out of a job. *Calvin Coolidge.*

The mystery to a married man is what a bachelor does with his money.

The worst telegram we ever saw was the one the father received reading: "Twins arrived tonight. More by mail."

Love starts when she sinks in your arms and ends with her arms in the sink.

Life—A span of time, of which the first half is ruined by our parents and the second half by our children. *The Phoenix Flame.*

A man is as old as he feels; a woman as old as she feels—like admitting.

An army rifle weighs 8.69 pounds. After it has been carried a few miles, the decimal point drops out. *Banking*.

A cynic defined professional courtesy as a lawyer swimming through shark-infested waters.

Do the best you can. The forests would be very quiet if all the birds were quiet except the best singers.

Boids is on the wing--I hoid; but that's absoid, 'cause wings is on the boid—I hoid.

Sign on a store which went bankrupt after two weeks' business: "Opened by mistake."

"As the earth is round," remarked a lecturer the other day, "it is obvious that we could go east by going far enough west." That's the sort of thing that puts ideas into taxi-drivers' heads.

Advice is what a person asks for when he wants you to agree with him.

No person who has to ask the price of a mink coat should think of buying one.

Marriage is somewhat like a cafeteria. You look the possibilities over carefully, select what you like best and pay later.

When the average man says he loves greens, he is speaking of a golf course.

A modest pat on the back develops character—if given young enough, often enough and low enough.

It's an ill wind that blows a saxophone.

We have often wondered what it is about windshield glass that makes a pedestrian look like a fly and a forty-ton locomotive like a toy train.

If you win at either love or war, it doesn't mean the expense has ended.

Progress is slow. Four thousand years of civilization and not more than ten good shortstops in the country.

Truth is not only stranger than modern fiction but more decent.

It might be a good idea to put some of our crossword puzzle experts at work on our unsolved crimes.

There is never any traffic congestion on the straight and narrow path.

Nothing helps a person's complexion like putting it to bed before 1:00 A.M.

It pays to be honest even though you may be a long time collecting.

Prizefighting rules now prevail in many European nations. When one side leads with the Right, the other counters with the Left.

If the number of automobiles shows a big increase in the next two or three years, we may have to adopt the lily as our national flower.

Some author is going to make a fortune not in writing a book on building your vocabulary, but on giving it a rest.

The income tax payment in June keeps many a bride from getting the thirty gravy bowls or compotes.

Hope springs eternal in the suburban gardener.

Apparently the same persons write the seed catalogs and the resort folders.

The most wonderful thing about a popular song is that it can't last.

Many persons seem to think that when the Declaration of Independence says they are entitled to the pursuit of happiness it means at sixty miles per hour.

A parking place is where you leave your car to have the wheelbase shortened and the trunk caved in.

No matter how many new translations of the Bible come out, the people still sin the same way.

A man is happily married if his wife is boss but doesn't know it.

It's a comfort to know that the wars the world fought in the eleventh and twelfth centuries are paid for.

We often wonder what became of the old eighth grade copy books with their maxims on economy.

Out in the country life is what you make it, but in the city it too often is what you make.

Despite what the cartoonists make him look like, Uncle Sam is a gentleman with a very large waste.

Almost all businesses have strikes but not the Internal Revenue Department.

Just because a man passes you with his car is no sign that he isn't behind with his payments.

Famous last words—"Go right ahead, don't let that big truck crowd you off the road."

One improvement we would like to see on automobiles is a device to make the brakes get tight when the driver does.

If you lend a friend ten dollars, you lose either a friend or ten dollars.

We never knew who wrote the descriptions in the seed catalogs until we read *Jack and the Beanstalk*.

Green seems to be the color that gives the eyes the most rest—especially the long green.

What we like about spring is that you can call plain laziness spring fever.

When a politician says that the nation is due for a reawakening, it means he is running for office.

It's a good thing that Moses didn't have to submit the Ten Commandments to a council of foreign ministers for approval.

We suggest to some enterprising young American who is looking for a business opportunity that he establish a junk shop near an important railroad crossing.

Publishers ought to take the description of promissory notes out of the banking books and put it in the books on international relations.

With 40,000,000 automobiles this is going to be a tough world for a horsefly.

We have sometimes wondered whether those automobile-type trolley cars that can go from one side of the road to the other were meant to catch dodging pedestrians.

Let him who doesn't wish to die yet diet.

The average man knows as much about an atomic bomb as he does about his income tax form.

If a man can remember what he worried about last week, he has a very good memory.

Of the sounds the human ear cannot hear it is a sad fact that none are made by the human tongue.

The poor house is always the last house on Easy Street.

What this country needs is a pair of shoestrings that will last as long as a pair of shoes.

Even chaos has almost become normal now.

What Latin-Americans need is a way to satisfy their longing to be generals without starting revolutions.

If one marries in haste, there is sometimes no leisure for repentance.

For most of us ice-skating is a sedentary sport.

The trouble with opportunity is that it generally comes disguised as hard work.

Whenever you get disgusted with a movie, think how utterly idiotic the rejected movie scenarios must be.

The lost chord in the harmony of nations is accord.

The only person we know who beats time is a drum player.

There is a vast difference between realism and reelism in the movies.

A lame duck is never so lame he can't waddle as far as a new government job.

American Indians used to eat pine bark. We still do, only we call it breakfast food.

They say every worm finally turns, but if he does he probably meets either a chicken or a fisherman.

Newspaper advertisement: "Farmhouse, barn and garden for rent. Room to keep animals: suitable for summer boarders." We think we stayed there.

When they award the Pulitzer book prizes for the best definitive biography, we should like to submit our last income tax report.

The millennium will be here when the pedestrians keep inside the traffic safety zones and the automobiles stay outside of them.

A newspaper reported a certain well known man had no friends except his wife. In Hollywood that wouldn't be a bad showing.

When a man opposes change, he probably has his.

When you try to define a living wage, it depends on whether you are giving or getting it.

The chances are that the American who criticizes India for judging a man by his caste judges his own neighbor by his cash.

There is just a faint possibility that a kangaroo is nature's evolutionary process of developing a safe pedestrian.

An attorney said, "Moses was a great lawgiver. But the way he was satisfied to keep the Ten Commandments short an' to the point shows he wasn't a regular lawyer."

It's almost reached the point where if a person takes a day off he falls behind in his income tax payments.

What a banker calls unsecured paper, a politician calls an election pledge and a diplomat calls a treaty.

We have often wondered why men lie about each other. The plain truth would be bad enough.

Many a driver runs a dead heat trying to beat a streamliner to a railroad crossing.

An intelligent businessman not only knows how to take advice but also how to reject it.

A street lamp never hits an automobile except in self-defense.

No government ever cuts off an expense that is capable of voting.

If you want to teach history realistically, print a picture of a tax receipt on the front of each book.

The doctors are trying to find out what makes men tall or short. We'll gladly explain why we're short.

Technical progress has been great. But we'll bet on the locomotive against an automobile at a railroad crossing.

There is some relationship between stable government and horse sense.

After you watch the crowd at a hockey game when the referee

makes a close decision against the home team, you have some idea of the problem of world peace.

To a young boy there is no such period as "between meals."

For most businessmen success not only brings poise but avoirdupois.

Let's not be unreasonable. People went crazy before there were any double feature movies or singing radio commercials.

Any time you think a college freshman is a dumbbell, we suggest you try a college entrance examination.

Convention speaker: "These are not my own figures I'm quoting. They're the figures of someone who knows what he's talking about."

There's no secret about "Button, button, who's got the button?" The laundries have.

An economist says women are lovely. When economists eliminate theory and get down to fact, they are easier to understand.

We suggest to the ladies of Hollywood that less interest in permanent waves and more interest in permanent wives would be a stimulating example for the rest of the country.

We think the fellow ought to go to the foot of the class who said, "A dog's lungs are the seat of his pants."

A diplomat is a man who knows what it isn't safe to laugh at.

The fellow who saves knows there is nothing like cash down to feather a nest.

The dove of peace after a war brings not only an olive branch in her bill, but an olive branch and the bill.

Washington made the cherry tree popular, but the plum is more common in politics now.

Oil may be a lubricant, but it never is in international affairs.

The greatest general to emerge from any war is General Taxation.

From the size of the tips you have to leave to get any service in a restaurant, you realize the truth of the old saying that all things come to him who waits.

A penny saved is a penny taxed.

Unlike a tree, a salesman who stays rooted to a spot never branches out.

Women wear funny things, but a hard collar isn't one of them.

Sometimes we think the world is growing worse, but it may be that the news and radio coverage is better.

The records of the history of nations are merely scrap books.

Being a senator isn't so difficult. All you have to do is satisfy the farmers, labor unions, businessmen and a few other groups.

The one thing we have never been able to save for a rainy day is an umbrella.

Governments trim their expenditures when there is nothing else left to trim.

The ambitious folks who are always trying to introduce simplified spelling might read some of the papers written by our recent high school graduates.

Most men never get so pessimistic they can't see the bright side of the other fellow's misfortune.

Advertisement: "After 30 washings, how do your undies look?" How do you get undies back from the laundry 30 times?

As a reward in life, popularity is small change.

The trouble with modern civilization is that we so often mistake respectability for character.

The one advantage of a dictatorship over a republic is that you have one particular individual to criticize when things go wrong—that is, if you have the right to criticize.

A successful marriage is one in which two persons learn to get along happily without the things they have no right to expect anyway.

When you are completely satisfied, remember what happens to a fat turkey.

The lines and wrinkles in a person's face are generally trademarks.

Want ad in a Kansas newspaper: "For sale—a full-blooded cow, giving milk, three tons of hay, a dozen chickens, and four turkeys." What a cow!

G*

A visitor from Mars could easily pick out the civilized nations. They have the best implements of war.

It takes a good auditor to keep records that satisfy the stockholders, the income tax authorities, and the management.

All you have to do in business is to stand and watch the world go by—and, brother, it sure will.

He was unbearable and a bore, but otherwise a great guy.

The thirst for truth is seldom a passion of nations.

Hard times are those periods when the right to strike seems less important than the right to work.

Spring is the period of the annual race between the bugs, weeds and vegetables in the garden.

An optimist is a fellow who believes that after he pays his taxes he can live on top of the world and put away a nice nestegg of savings.

Socialism is Communism with a bath, a clean shirt and a shave.

There may be a closer relationship between the unread and the Red than we think.

In the old days at receptions for the President everybody had to approach him with empty hands. The Internal Revenue Department has made it easy now for us to meet that requirement.

A fool and his money may part, but they were lucky to get together in the first place.

Guests of a nightclub were held up on the way home. After all, these are days of keen competition.

We wish the SEC would investigate to see if the button industry is the holding company which owns the laundries.

It's a short step from being in love with a dimple to marrying the whole girl.

When a wife really loves her husband, he can make her do anything she wants to do.

Every automobile should have a small compartment in which to keep the installment loan contract.

No married man ever pokes fun at a woman for shopping all day and buying nothing.

The public has the idea that no banker is a yes-man.

Capital and labor should pull together. We don't mean on the public's leg.

At election time political candidates are more candied than candid.

A man doesn't have to live as long as Methuselah to learn there is nothing common about common sense.

When a person has no more illusions, he is suffering from old age.

An ignorant person is one who doesn't know anything about what you know, and knows things you don't know anything about.

A diplomat leads a terrible life. When he isn't straddling an issue, he is dodging one.

We're inclined to think American wild life isn't disappearing. It's just merging with domestic life.

You can't say much for the average father's skin, but he certainly has a pocketbook they love to touch.

What Lord Macaulay apparently tried to say years ago was that a democracy may be ushered in by a Liberty Bell and ushered out by the dumbbells.

We wonder whether the University of Chicago includes a passbook in its list of 100 great books.

Judging from our experience we would say that a summer resort is a place where the mosquitoes start work when the flies quit.

The difference between a man and a woman buying a hat is about four hours.

The politician who keeps his ear to the ground may limit his vision.

A magazine featured a story about a Colorado rooster living without his head. What's so unusual about that? All kinds of human beings seem to get along without using their heads.

We have always envied the fellow who can tell whether the violinist in the symphony orchestra is tuning up or playing.

A banker recently caught a sixty-pound fish off the coast of Florida and in describing the feat dislocated both shoulders.

A friend is a person who dislikes the same people you do.

With these modern beauty shops many a young girl is as old as her mother looks.

This generation can fly, talk by wireless radio and harness atomic power. It can do about everything but bring up children.

Millions of Americans may have only the mentality of children. But if you have tried to work your child's arithmetic you may think that's not so bad.

What our engineers should concentrate on is an automobile that will get over a railroad crossing after the gates are down.

Being bald on the outside of one's head is not so bad. What is serious is when the baldness is on the inside.

About the only difference between history and hysteria is the spelling.

It is almost getting so a respectable person is ashamed to carry a modern book.

You can say one thing at least for the United States. It's about the only country where the people don't want to move to another country.

If all the pedestrians were laid end to end, it would greatly simplify the task for some automobile drivers.

We have often wondered what would happen with the numbers if telephone operators worked in shoe stores.

One thing we learn each summer is that what this country needs is a lawn grass that will grow an inch high and quit.

The fellow who puts up the billboards on country roads must have some sense of beauty because he always picks out the best views to obstruct.

A farmer is a fellow who gets up at 5:00 A.M. and hurries through his work by 9:30 P.M. so he can read a farm paper about how to make money by farming more intensively.

Why not arrange loans to European nations so payments would be made to us after each tourist season?

In the old days spirited chargers carried noble knights on their backs. Nowadays spirited chargers run the winter and summer vacation resorts.

The easiest thing for anyone to run into is debt.

When a diplomat comes to the parting of the ways, he goes both ways.

They now say that we will live fifteen years longer than our grandfathers, but they don't say why.

The great trouble in government is that the men who have wisdom enough to run it have wisdom enough to stay away from the job.

After our experience at picnics each summer we still think Noah had more than two ants in the Ark.

American highways are filled with tourists and detourists.

Classical music is music that threatens every other bar to develop a tune and then disappoints you.

The Life of Man—School tablet; aspirin tablet; stone tablet.

The greatest undeveloped resources of any nation are its people.

An egotist is a person of questionable taste more interested in himself than in me.

Nothing recedes like success.

If it's a sin to die rich, few businessmen will have to bear that reproach in the future.

A conservative statesman is one who wishes to continue existing evils whereas a liberal wishes to replace them with others.

 When some women shop, it looks like they were taking an inventory of the stock.

It is easy to be in favor of government ownership of something that belongs to somebody else.

It has been said that if you take an average group of 100 men, 1 will later become rich, 4 well-to-do, 30 independent, and 65 will be supported by relatives. Apparently, they all will have it easy.

We wonder whether it ever occurred to the archeologists that some of the deserted cities they have discovered over the world may represent communities where people paid the taxes as long as they could and then moved.

Satisfaction is a state of mind produced when you witness another person's discomfort.

A statesman thinks he belongs to the nation, but a politician thinks the nation belongs to him.

Hunger is an instinct placed in man to make certain that he will work.

Only three things are found in sand—petroleum, gold and spinach.

A prudent man today is one who never asks the waitress what a Salisbury steak is.

If we had had today's taxes a generation ago, the world would never have heard of a guy named Horatio Alger. His books would now read *From Riches to Rags*.

The best thing you can do for spring fever is absolutely nothing.

A conviction is that commendable quality in ourselves that we call bullheadedness in others.

We understand some savage tribes in Africa pay no taxes. Then what makes them savage?

The fellow who traces his ancestors way back admits he has been descending for centuries.

There may be, as a professor has said, over 10,000 useless words in the dictionary, but a great many come in handy in framing the political platforms.

The difficulty of a cocktail "hour" is that it generally stretches into four or five.

A traffic safety committee has announced most automobile accidents are avoidable. We wish pedestrians were also.

The modern American is a fellow who can answer the $64 question on a radio program, but can't tell you the name of his congressman.

Tolerance is the patience shown by a wise man when he listens to an ignoramus.

Political leaders seldom look for the biggest man for the job. Experience has shown them you can win without that kind.

A dentist says it takes over fifty pounds' pressure to chew a steak. What we want to know is where he buys those tender cuts.

It takes the old family album to convince some people that the truth is a terrible thing.

The average American woman is not old at forty. In fact, she isn't even forty.

Newspaper headline: "Farmers to Hear Pest Talk." We believe we have heard the same fellow.

The country is really in bad shape when you think that 140,000,000 people wake up every morning with halitosis, B.O. and athlete's foot.

When a diplomat puts his cards on the table, he still has a deck up each sleeve.

About the only class of downtrodden people America has ever had are those in the aisle seats at the movies.

Mr. Kettering of the Research Department of General Motors wants to know why grass is green and glass is transparent. We would like to know why a fly invariably picks out a bald head on which to land.

The way to avert another war is to have peace long enough now to learn the lessons of the last war.

The test of whether any government can survive is its ability to ring the dinner bell.

What the average woman wants is a great big strong he-man who can be wrapped around her finger.

There is no one so narrow-minded as the fellow who disagrees with you.

Summer is the time when the weather gets too hot to cook and the relatives come to visit you.

The only place a woman's intuition doesn't work is when she is trying to decide which way to turn the car at a corner.

The elephant and the donkey were probably chosen as political party emblems because they are beasts of burden. If a new party is started, a taxpayer might suitably be used as the emblem.

Any earthquake shocks the world may feel in the years ahead will probably not be due to the fact that the nations are settling.

There are some scientists who believe the height of intelligence is reached at sixteen. Well, at that age one generally feels sure of it.

Egotism is a drug that enables some people to live with themselves.

It isn't the $100,000 a mile that a good road costs which is so ex pensive; it's the wrecked cars and funeral expenses that follow.

Federal aid is simply a system of taking money from the people and making it look like a gift when you hand it back.

Foreign missionaries will be more successful when they can show civilization to the heathens and not merely tell them about it.

We never could quite understand why children are too young to work under eighteen, but are old enough to drive an $1,800 car seventy miles an hour.

Some of the big guns are silenced when a war ends; others begin work on their memoirs.

There is an old story about an ass being disguised with a lion's skin. Every now and then some college does it with a sheepskin.

Economics Lesson—Even when a debt is cancelled, somebody pays it.

An army travels on its stomach, but some individuals travel on their gall.

No politician is ever as bad as he is painted by his enemies or as good as he is whitewashed by his friends.

We wonder if nations experience declining birth rates because the stork is a bird with a big bill.

Americans will have to learn that for every export there must be an import, or we shall continually be sending out relief ships to the world to keep peace.

When a woman demands equal rights, she is simply indulging in flattery.

You can get a government bulletin on almost every subject except curbing government expenditures.

When God made man he didn't arrange the joints of his bones so he could pat himself on the back.

It is reported by scientists that man's jaw has dropped half an inch in several thousand years. That's not so bad when you consider the government budgets he has faced.

The pessimist says when a diplomat lays his cards on the table it's a good idea to count 'em.

A government bureau often turns out to be a group of people organized to keep the taxpayers worried.

Several million people in this country cannot read or write. They devote themselves to writing our popular songs.

The market reports often say, "Hogs are little changed." Well, what is new about that?

A good politician is a fellow who has prejudices enough to suit the needs of all his constituents.

It won't be long now until American tourists will see Europe's poverty and will bring it back with them.

If a man wants to borrow trouble, he never needs collateral.

A wise husband remembers his wife's birthday but forgets which one it is.

Ulcers are said to be the occupational disease of radio announcers. We wonder what affliction is reserved for the news commentators.

The modern city consists of a large number of persons striving to avoid being hit by an automobile.

America may spend more money on chewing gum than on books, but judging from some best-sellers that doesn't necessarily mean we have bad judgment.

Sometimes when we look at the headlines, we're not sure the fellow who can't read is missing so much.

A cynic has defined a politician as a man who keeps his ear to the ground and his hand in the taxpayer's pocket.

A false alarm may cost a city fire department $100. In business one costs even more.

Convictions are what an employee has after he knows what the boss thinks.

How far a little scandal throws its beams.

Mud thrown is ground lost.

" 'Too many husbands being shot,' " says worried judge (*Chicago Daily News*). Judge, would you mind telling us just how many would be the right number?

A man who owns a summer cottage on a lake may not have a good time during the summer season, but the chances are dozens of his friends who visit him do.

The bone of contention in most quarrels is generally just a little above the ears of those doing the arguing.

It's not a bad idea for a politician to remember that no newspaper can misquote silence.

In the concert of nations too many nations want to beat the drum and few want to play second fiddle.

He was the kind of fellow who would rather blow his own horn than listen to the marine band.

The fellow who laughs last may laugh best, but he gets the reputation of being a dumbbell.

Some oldtimer spoke of the political pot boiling. That never happens. The old applesauce is just warmed over.

You can't fool all the people all the time, but that doesn't keep some persons from trying.

We didn't think it would go this far, but our laundry has just sent back some buttons with no shirt on them.

There, little luxury, don't you cry—you'll be a necessity by and by.

The big problem on the average home reading table is to keep those old next month's magazines from cluttering up the place.

You may fear that much of the world is going to destruction. But after you read the tabloids and the confession magazines you don't much care.

If a woman can be a sweetheart, valet, audience, cook and nurse, she is qualified for marriage.

If you want to know how much a man can't remember, call him as a witness to an automobile accident.

Some day a progressive newspaper is going to develop a comic feature for grownups.

Every once in a while you find a police department that seems to work on the theory that if you leave the burglars alone they will soon become rich enough to quit.

The modern teacher believes that spanking misses its aim. If so, the method must be different than it was in the days when we were on the receiving end.

Did you ever meet anyone who said he couldn't sleep last night because of his conscience?

Life is often a battle of the wits, but some folks are unarmed.

This is the day of youth and they can have it. They'll age rapidly when the taxpaying starts.

It often takes a speaker twice as long to tell what he thinks as to tell what he knows.

An Illustration of Financial Illiteracy—The young woman who said the bank had sent back all the checks she used to pay bills with last month and so she hadn't spent a cent.

Wars may come and wars may go, but a politician never forgets the new sources of revenue that are discovered.

First you have to teach a child to talk; then you have to teach it to keep quiet.

An excavating archeologist at least proves that you can't keep a good man down.

A landlord is a fellow who pays for a house once and then quits. Write your own definition of a renter.

No one thinks faster on his feet than a pedestrian—if he wants to live.

It looks like eventually we will all make our living by collecting taxes from each other.

A radical is a person who feels he might get a little more if he howled a little louder.

The disgusted professor: "Class is dismissed. Please don't flop your ears as you pass out."

The world's worst: Are airmail stamps fly paper?

It's remarkable when you think that under the American system a man can have a savings account and an automobile at the same time.

Intelligence tests may be a means of grading intelligence, but there is nothing that equals a grade crossing for effectiveness.

With the increasing output of new automobiles now, some enterprising manufacturer ought to start making spare parts for pedestrians.

Secret diplomacy is never secret long and seldom diplomatic.

Someone says love is a solvent; but whoever saw a solvent lover?

We can't think of anything so urgent to any man that he can't wait until the train gets past the crossing.

The genius of another world war will be the fellow who figures out how to run it on a cash instead of an accounts-payable basis.

When the average man looks at what he has left after paying his taxes, he realizes social security may have some real meaning for him.

A man who is not in need certainly is a friend.

The higher taxes go, the sharper the voter grinds his ax.

Question for Experts: Is the zebra a white animal with black stripes or a black animal with white stripes?

Why is it that a man will always marry the woman who sweeps him off his feet rather than the one who keeps him on them.

When we look at the price tags on some articles, we don't know whether they represent value or nerve.

He was in his salad days—very particular about his dressing.

Author: "She dropped her eyes and her face fell." Total collapse we'd call it.

The kind of reference book that ought to sell in Hollywood is a "Who's Whose."

We don't wish the folks who have some $100 bills hoarded any bad luck, but we remember once upon a time there were some counterfeits out of this denomination.

Communists seem to labor under the impression that everybody wants to die poor.

In September most of the folks return from the summer resorts for a greatly needed rest.

Many a member of a union has an eight-hour day for himself but sixteen for his wife.

The easiest way to remain poor is to pretend to be rich.

If they ever start making paper suits, we're going to need a little better service from the weather man.

The average American is an incurable optimist. He admits the necessity for saving for his old age, but puts it off with the expectation that a miracle will come along and do it for him.

A man never knows how careful he can be until he wears white flannel pants and white shoes.

> What is a Communist? One who hath yearnings
> For equal division of unequal earnings.
> Idler or bungler, or both, he is willing,
> To fork out his copper and pocket your shilling.

The old-fashioned pioneer woman who crossed the plains and the Rocky Mountains in a skirt now has a granddaughter who puts on slacks to shop at the A & P.

We'll bet it irritates the tax collector to see a man buy a necktie and realize there goes two bucks the government didn't get.

The American youngster's three R's now are, readin', 'ritin' and radio.

To get collective bargaining men engage in collective loafing.

If a woman is good-looking, higher education is unnecessary. If she isn't, it is inadequate.

Business efficiency is the art of working hard to write reports someone thinks he will read but never does.

Whenever a businessman wastes time, he ought to remember that Father Time never makes round trips.

Statues are so often erected for the dead that we're surprised none has been put up for Municipal Virtue.

Daylight saving just makes some people tired an hour earlier.

There seems to be a juvenile problem of children running away from home. It is entirely possible they may be looking for their mothers.

When we have Utopia and everyone has work to fit his brains, some people are going to be unemployed.

We wish some bright economist would tell us the difference between nuisance taxes and just ordinary taxes.

Sedentary work lessens a businessman's endurance. To put it an other way—the more you sit, the less you can stand.

Solomon said, "There is no new thing under the sun," but he didn't say it over a coast-to-coast radio network.

A public speaking instructor says, "Not one person in ten thinks on his feet." Why add "on his feet"?

The fellow who says he would go through anything for his girl friend doesn't necessarily mean his bank account.

A politician is a person who keeps the people loyal to him by keeping them angry at someone else.

Someone has said nothing is done as well as it might be done. Well, what about the American taxpayer?

The modern girl has accepted the advertising motto, "Save the surface and you save all."

Never cling to a liberal idea too long unless you want to be called a reactionary five years from now.

Some people are bent with work; others get crooked trying to avoid it.

A conservative is a fellow who thinks a rich man should have a square deal.

When the folks who have something to sell are courteous, it's a buyer's market.

Sometimes a nation abolishes God, but fortunately God is more tolerant.

After listening to some commencement speeches, we gather that the world is in such terrible shape that nothing can save it except the graduating class.

Many caddies become good golfers. Unlike businessmen they never read one of those books on how to play golf.

"Chickens," said the colored philosopher, "is de usefulest animal dere is. You kin eat 'em fo' dey is born an' after dey is dead."

Some animals can understand but can't talk, whereas it's just the other way with some human beings.

Perhaps we should say that freedom of speech is for those who know the speech of freedom.

From newspaper: "Henry Jones has bought a cow and will now

supply his neighbors with milk and fresh eggs." Apparently an advance model.

Civilization is a slow process of adopting the ideas of minorities.

We think the juvenile problem is not so much one of ruling youngsters with a firm hand as using a firm hand with a ruler.

When the people aren't sure of what they want in democracy, they vote for something different from what they have.

In the future the world will need guns of smaller and men of larger caliber.

Supreme Example of Conceit—The father who tries for twenty years to make his child just what he is.

Someone wants to know where the population is most dense. Well, one answer might be—from the neck up.

It's remarkable how large a part ignorance plays in making a man satisfied with himself.

Our idea of Utopia would be a nation in which principles would win the battles with expediency in politics.

There is no assurance that wealthy parents will not make poor parents.

Money may talk, but it doesn't talk as loud as it used to when we pay the bills.

It is never the initial outlay that floors you; it's the running expenses that keep you out of breath.

When a man thinks he is important, he should ask what the world would miss if he were gone.

The inventive genius who first makes a good combination small car and cigarette lighter will make a fortune.

Every time I see a bald-headed man sporting a mustache, I keep wondering whether it is a case of overproduction or just poor distribution.

The only thing wrong with the world is the people.

What we would like is an alarm clock that goes off when we are ready to get up.

A joint checking account is one in which the wife writes the checks and the husband makes the deposits.

CHAPTER 8

QUOTATIONS FOR MANY DIFFERENT OCCASIONS

THE toastmaster will frequently find it necessary to refer to the speeches or speechmaking ability of those whom he is called upon to introduce. Consequently, any quotation, epigram or proverb that deals with such subjects as speeches, speechmaking, eloquence, discussions or oratory may on some occasion be helpful to him in preparing an introduction for a speaker. There are included in this chapter a number of short items of this character which the toastmaster may adapt for various uses and various situations. They will help to make introductions more colorful and sparkling.

In addition, the toastmaster may find it very helpful to have quotations, epigrams and proverbs on different occupations and professions. For example, if he is called upon to introduce a businessman, lawyer, teacher or musician, some pertinent quotation may assist him greatly in preparing an introduction that will be interesting and directly to the point. Many quotations of this type are also included in the following pages.

Sometimes a toastmaster will be called upon to introduce young people; at other times some reference may be necessary to those who have reached old age. Quotations have therefore been included on both youth and age. All of the quotations in this chapter are arranged alphabetically by groups such as actors, age, authors, doctors, lawyers, musicians, speeches and speechmaking, teachers, wedding anniversaries and youth.

*   *   *

Actors

An actor is a sculptor who carves in snow. *Lawrence Barrett.*

The profession of the player, like that of the painter, is one of the imitative arts, whose means are pleasure, and whose end should be virtue. *Shenstone.*

> Let him who plays the monarch be a king;
> Who plays the rogue, be perfect in his part.
> > *Erskine.*

Actors are the only honest hypocrites. Their life is a voluntary dream; and the height of their ambition is to be beside themselves. They wear the livery of other men's fortunes: their very thoughts are not their own. *Hazlitt.*

The actor who took the role of King Lear played the king as though he expected someone to play the ace. *Eugene Field.*

All the world's a stage, and all the men and women in it merely players. They have their exits and their entrances; and one man in his time plays many parts. *Shakespeare.*

> Our Garrick's a salad; for in him we see
> Oil, vinegar, sugar and saltiness agree.
> > *Goldsmith.*

It is with some violence to the imagination that we conceive of an actor belonging to the relations of private life, so closely do we identify these persons in our mind with the characters they assume upon the stage. *Lamb.*

> On the stage he was natural, simple, affecting,
> 'Twas only when he was off, he was acting.
> > *Goldsmith.*

At the Academy Award dinners all the actors and actresses in Hollywood gather around to see what someone else thinks about their acting besides their press agents. *Bob Hope.*

The most difficult character in comedy is that of the fool, and he must be no simpleton that plays that part. *Cervantes.*

Some of the greatest love affairs I've known have involved one actor—unassisted. *Wilson Mizner.*

Aside from the moral contamination incident to the average theater, the influence intellectually is degrading. Its lessons are morbid, distorted, and superficial; they do not mirror life. *T. T. Munger.*

* * *

Advertisers

There is too much culture in the advertising business. *C. F. Kettering.*

The advertising man is a liaison between the products of business and the mind of the nation. He must know both before he can serve either. *Glenn Frank.*

Advertising is the mouthpiece of business. *James R. Adams.*

You can tell the ideals of a nation by its advertisements. *Norman Douglas.*

One-third of the people in the United States promote, while the other two-thirds provide. *Will Rogers.*

* * *

Age

It is not by the gray of the hair that one knows the age of the heart. *Bulwer.*

A graceful and honorable old age is the childhood of immortality. *Pindar.*

How beautiful can time with goodness make an old man look. *Jerrold.*

A person is always startled when he hears himself seriously called old for the first time. *O. W. Holmes.*

We do not count a man's years until he has nothing else to count. *Emerson.*

One of the many things nobody ever tells you about middle age is that it's such a nice change from being young. *Dorothy Canfield Fisher.*

Some fall into their "anecdotage." *Disraeli.*

Let us respect gray hairs, especially our own. *J. P. Senn.*

When we are young, we are slavishly employed in procuring something whereby we may live comfortably when we grow old; and when we grow old, we perceive it is too late to live as we proposed. *Pope.*

They say music and women should never be dated. *Goldsmith.*

To be seventy years young is sometimes far more cheerful and hopeful than to be forty years old. *O. W. Holmes.*

> The best of friends fall out, and so
> His teeth had done some years ago.
> *Thomas Hood.*

No wise man ever wished to be younger. *Swift.*

Years do not make sages; they only make old men. *Mme. Swetchine.*

Forty is the old age of youth; fifty is the youth of old age. *Victor Hugo.*

Every one desires to live long, but no one would be old. *Swift.*

How many fancy they have experience simply because they have grown old. *Stanislaus.*

Whenever a man's friends begin to compliment him about looking young, he may be sure that they think he is growing old. *Washington Irving.*

Men of age object too much, consult too long, adventure too little, repent too soon, and seldom drive business home to the full period, but content themselves with a mediocrity of success. *Bacon.*

As we grow old we become both more foolish and more wise. *La Rochefoucauld.*

Childhood itself is scarcely more lovely than a cheerful, kindly, sunshiny old age. *L. M. Child.*

Age is the most terrible misfortune that can happen to any man; other evils will mend, this is every day getting worse. *George James.*

Old age is a tyrant, which forbids the pleasures of youth on pain of death. *La Rochefoucauld.*

When a noble life has prepared old age, it is not decline that it reveals, but the first days of immortality. *Mme. de Staël.*

The old forget, the young don't know. *German proverb.*

The evening of a well-spent life brings its lamps with it. *Joubert.*

No man is so old but thinks he may yet live another year. *St. Jerome.*

Age does not make us childish, as some say; it finds us true children. *Goethe.*

As winter strips the leaves from around us, so that we may see the distant regions they formerly concealed, so old age takes away our enjoyments only to enlarge the prospect of the coming eternity. *Richter.*

In old age life's shadows are meeting eternity's day. *Clarke.*

Nobody loves life like an old man. *Sophocles.*

I venerate old age; and I love not the man who can look without emotion upon the sunset of life, when the dusk of evening begins to gather over the watery eye, and the shadows of twilight grow broader and deeper upon the understanding. *Longfellow.*

It is only necessary to grow old to become more charitable and even indulgent. I see no fault committed by others that I have not committed myself. *Goethe.*

Gray hairs seem to my fancy like the soft light of the moon, silvering over the evening of life. *Richter.*

It is often the case with fine natures, that when the fire of the spirit dies out with increasing age, the power of intellect is unaltered or increased, and an originally educated judgment grows broader and gentler as the river of life widens out to the everlasting sea. *Mrs. Gatty.*

The young man who has not wept is a savage, and the old man who will not laugh is a fool. *Santayana.*

*   *   *

Architects

Architecture is the printing press of all ages, and gives a history of the state of society in which the structure was erected, from the cromlechs of the Druids to the toyshops of bad taste. The Tower and Westminster Abbey are glorious pages in the history of time, and tell the story of an iron despotism, and of the cowardice of an unlimited power. *Lady Morgan.*

> Old houses mended,
> Cost little less than new before they're ended.
> *Colley Cibber.*

The architecture of a nation is great only when it is as universal and established as its language, and when provincial differences are nothing more than so many dialects. *Ruskin.*

Architecture is frozen music. *Mme. de Staël.*

Greek architecture is the flowering of geometry. *Emerson.*

Architecture is a handmaid of devotion. A beautiful church is a sermon in stone, and its spire a finger pointing to heaven. *Schaff.*

A gothic church is a petrified religion. *Coleridge.*

Architecture is the art which so disposes and adorns the edifices raised by man, that the sight of them may contribute to his mental health, power, and pleasure. *Ruskin.*

* * *

Artists

True art is reverent imitation of God. *Tryon Edwards.*

All great art is the expression of man's delight in God's work, not his own. *Ruskin.*

The highest art is always the most religious, and the greatest artist is always a devout man.—A scoffing Raphael, or an irreverent Michael Angelo, is not conceivable. *Blaikie.*

Artists are nearest God. Into their souls He breathes His life, and from their hands it comes in fair, articulate forms to bless the world. *J. G. Holland.*

The little dissatisfaction which every artist feels at the completion of a work forms the germ of a new work. *Auerbach.*

When a work of art appears to be in advance of its period, it is really the period that has lagged behind the work of art. *Jean Cocteau.*

A photograph is a portrait painted by the sun. *Dupins.*

> In the vaunted works of Art,
> The master-stroke is Nature's part.
>
> *Emerson.*

Art is the surest and safest civilizer. *Charles B. Fairbanks.*

A highbrow is the kind of person who looks at a sausage and thinks of Picasso. *A. P. Herbert.*

Only God Almighty makes painters. *Sir Godfrey Kneller.*

The true work of art is but a shadow of the divine perfection. *Michelangelo.*

A room hung with pictures is a room hung with thoughts. *Joshua Reynolds.*

When love and skill work together expect a masterpiece. *Ruskin.*

What garlic is to salad, insanity is to art. *Homer Saint-Gaudens.*

Every time I paint a portrait I lose a friend. *John Sargent.*

Painting is silent poetry, and poetry is painting with the gift of speech. *Simonides.*

To sit for one's portrait is like being present at one's own creation. *Alexander Smith.*

Every artist writes his own autobiography. *H. Ellis.*

Nothing can come out of the artist that is not in the man. *Proverb*

*   *   *

Astronomers

No one can contemplate the great facts of astronomy without feeling his own littleness and the wonderful sweep of the power and providence of God. *Tryon Edwards.*

An undevout astronomer is mad. *Young.*

The contemplation of celestial things will make a man both speak and think more sublimely and magnificently when he comes down to human affairs. *Cicero.*

He that looks for a star puts out his candle. *Proverb.*

He that strives to touch the stars
Oft stumbles at a straw.

Spenser.

Hitch your wagon to a star. *Emerson.*

Too low they build, who build beneath the stars. *Young.*

*   *   *

Authors

Clear writers, like clear fountains, do not seem so deep as they are; the turbid seem the most profound. *Landor.*

No fathers or mothers think their own children ugly; and this self-deceit is yet stronger with respect to the offspring of the mind. *Cervantes.*

The most original authors are not so because they advance what is new, but because they put what they have to say as if it had never been said before. *Goethe.*

For people who like that kind of a book—that is the kind of book they will like. *Lincoln (on being asked for an opinion).*

The chief glory of a country, says Johnson, arises from its authors. But this is only when they are oracles of wisdom. Unless they teach virtue they are more worthy of a halter than of the laurel. *Jane Porter.*

Next to doing things that deserve to be written, nothing gets a man more credit, or gives him more pleasure than to write things that deserve to be read. *Chesterfield.*

There are three difficulties in authorship: to write anything worth publishing, to find honest men to publish it, and to get sensible men to read it. *Colton.*

Talent alone cannot make a writer; there must be a man behind the book. *Emerson*

Every author in some degree portrays himself in his works, even if it be against his will. *Goethe.*

Man builds no structure which outlives a book. *E. F. Ware.*

Writers are the main landmarks of the past. *Bulwer.*

Authorship is a royal priesthood; but woe to him who rashly lays unhallowed hands on the ark or altar, professing a zeal for the welfare of the race, only to secure his own selfish ends. *Horace Greeley.*

Books are sepulchers of thought. *Longfellow.*

Some books are to be tasted; others swallowed; and some few to be chewed and digested. *Bacon.*

> Shakespeare was a dramatist of note;
> He lived by writing things to quote.
> *H. C. Bunner.*

No man but a blockhead ever wrote except for money. *Johnson.*

Books are the legacies that genius leaves to mankind, to be delivered down from generation to generation, as presents to those that are yet unborn. *Addison.*

In composing, as a general rule, run your pen through every other word you have written; you have no idea what vigor it will give your style. *Sydney Smith.*

When I get a little money, I buy books; and if any is left, I buy food and clothes. *Erasmus.*

When a book raises your spirit, and inspires you with noble and manly thoughts, seek for no other test of its excellence. It is good, and made by a good workman. *Bruyère.*

If religious books are not widely circulated among the masses in this country, and the people do not become religious, I do not know what is to become of us as a nation. And the thought is one to cause solemn reflection on the part of every patriot and Christian. If truth be not diffused, error will be; if God and His word are not known and received, the devil and his works will gain the ascendancy; if the evangelical volume does not reach every hamlet, the pages of a corrupt and licentious literature will; if the power of the gospel is not felt through the length and breadth of the land, anarchy and misrule, degradation and misery, corruption and darkness, will reign without mitigation or end. *Daniel Webster.*

Only presidents, editors and people with tapeworm have the right to use the editorial "we." *Anon.*

A house without books is like a room without windows. No man has a right to bring up his children without surrounding them with books, if he has the means to buy them. It is a wrong to his family. Children learn to read by being in the presence of books. The love of knowledge comes with reading and grows upon it. And the love of knowledge, in a young mind, is almost a warrant against the inferior excitement of passions and vices. *H. Mann.*

Books are men of higher stature; the only men that speak aloud for future times to hear. *Barrett.*

After all manner of professors have done their best for us, the place we are to get knowledge is in books. The true university of these days is a collection of books. *Carlyle.*

Upon books the collective education of the race depends; they are the sole instruments of registering, perpetuating, and transmitting thought. *H. Rogers.*

A good book is the precious life-blood of a master spirit . . . *Milton.*

Books are ships which pass through the vast seas of time. *Bacon.*

Books, the children of the brain. *Proverb.*

*   *   *

Bankers

Neither a borrower nor a lender be; for loan oft loses both itself and friend. *Shakespeare.*

Put not your trust in money, but put your money in trust. *O. W. Holmes.*

The use of money is all the advantage there is in having it. *Franklin.*

H

If money be not thy servant, it will be thy master. *Italian Proverb.*

When money represents so many things, not to love it would be to love nearly nothing. To forget true needs can be only a weak moderation; but to know the value of money and to sacrifice it always, maybe to duty, maybe even to delicacy—that is real virtue. *Senancour.*

Money and time are the heaviest burdens of life, and the unhappiest of all mortals are those who have more of either than they know how to use. *Johnson.*

He that wants money, means, and content, is without three good friends. *Shakespeare.*

He who has no money in his purse, should have honey on his tongue. *French Proverb.*

Men are seldom more innocently employed than when they are honestly making money. *Johnson.*

Who steals my purse steals trash. *Shakespeare.*

No man will take counsel, but every man will take money. Therefore, money is better than counsel. *Swift.*

A person who can't pay, gets another person who can't pay, to guarantee that he can pay. *Dickens.*

However gradual may be the growth of confidence, that of credit requires still more time to arrive at maturity. *Disraeli.*

The covetous man never has money; the prodigal will have none shortly. *Ben Jonson.*

But for money and the need of it, there would not be half the friendship in the world. It is powerful for good if divinely used. Give it plenty of air and it is sweet as the hawthorn; shut it up and it cankers and breeds worms. *G. Macdonald.*

Ready money is Aladdin's lamp. *Byron.*

Money is the life blood of the nation. *Swift.*

Creditors have better memories than debtors; they are a superstitious sect, great observers of set days and times. *Franklin.*

Credit is like a looking-glass, which when once sullied by a breath, may be wiped clear again; but if once cracked can never be repaired. *Scott.*

Give me money, not advice. *Portuguese Proverb.*

A small debt produces a debtor; a large one, an enemy. *Publilius Syrus.*

You know it is not my Interest to pay the Principal; nor is it my Principle to pay the Interest. *Sheridan.*

The holy passion of Friendship is of so sweet and steady and loyal and enduring a nature that it will last through a whole lifetime, if not asked to lend money. *Mark Twain.*

When some men discharge an obligation you can hear the report for miles around. *Mark Twain.*

* * *

Book Reviews and Dramatic Critics

Critics are sentinels in the grand army of letters, stationed at the corners of newspapers and reviews, to challenge every new author. *Longfellow.*

It is ridiculous for any man to criticize the works of another if he has not distinguished himself by his own performances. *Addison.*

There is scarcely a good critic of books born in our age, and yet every fool thinks himself justified in criticizing persons. *Bulwer.*

Silence is sometimes the severest criticism. *Charles Buxton.*

Some critics are like chimney-sweepers; they put out the fire below, and frighten the swallows from their nests above; they scrape a long time in the chimney, cover themselves with soot, and bring nothing away but a bag of cinders, and then sing out from the top of the house, as if they had built it. *Longfellow.*

It is much easier to be critical than to be correct. *Disraeli.*

The critical faculty has its value in correcting errors, reforming abuses, and demolishing superstitions. But the constructive faculty is much nobler in itself, and immeasurably more valuable in its results, for the obvious reason that it is a much nobler and better thing to build up than to pull down. It requires skill and labor to erect a building, but any idle tramp can burn it down. Only God can form and paint a flower, but any foolish child can pull it to pieces. *J. M. Gibson.*

The most noble criticism is that in which the critic is not the antagonist so much as the rival of the author. *Disraeli.*

It behooves the minor critic, who hunts for blemishes, to be a little distrustful of his own sagacity. *Junius.*

> The stones that critics hurl with harsh intent
> A man may use to build his monument.
> > *Arthur Guiterman.*

Criticism, as it was first instituted by Aristotle, was meant as a standard of judging well. *Johnson.*

To be a mere verbal critic is what no man of genius would be if he could; but to be a critic of true taste and feeling, is what no man without genius could be if he would. *Colton.*

Critics are a kind of freebooters in the republic of letters, who, like deer, goats, and diverse other graminivorous animals, gain subsistence by gorging upon buds and leaves of the young shrubs of the forest, thereby robbing them of their verdure and retarding their progress to maturity. *Washington Irving.*

He, whose first emotion on the view of an excellent production is to undervalue it, will never have one of his own to show. *Aikin.*

The severest critics are always those who have either never attempted, or who have failed in original composition. *Hazlitt.*

Of all mortals a critic is the silliest; for, inuring himself to examine all things, whether they are of consequence or not, he never looks upon anything but with a design of passing sentence upon it by which means he is never a companion, but always a censor. *Steele.*

Few persons have sufficient wisdom to prefer censure, which is useful to them, to praise, which deceives them. *La Rochefoucauld.*

The proper function of a critic is to save the tale from the artist who created it. *D. H. Lawrence.*

The strength of criticism lies only in the weakness of the thing criticized. *Longfellow.*

Criticism often takes from the tree caterpillars and blossoms together. *J. P. Richter.*

Pay no attention to what critics say. There has never been set up a statue in honor of a critic. *Sibelius.*

Censure is the tax a man pays to the public for being eminent. *Swift.*

The sting of reproof is the truth of it. *Proverb.*

* * *

Breakfasts, Luncheons and Dinners

For the sake of health, medicines are taken by weight and measure; so ought food to be, or by some similar rule. *Skelton.*

To eat is human; to digest, divine. *C. T. Copeland.*

One should eat to live, not live to eat. *Franklin.*

A man once asked Diogenes what was the proper time for supper, and he made answer, "If you are a rich man, whenever you please; and if you are a poor man, whenever you can." *Diogenes Laertius.*

They are as sick that surfeit with too much, as they that starve with nothing. *Shakespeare.*

A full belly makes a dull brain. *Franklin.*

It isn't so much what's on the table that matters, as what's on the chairs. *W. S. Gilbert.*

At table it becomes no one to be bashful. *Latin Proverb.*

By suppers more have been killed than Galen ever cured. *George Herbert.*

When the crowd of your admirers is shouting, "Bravo! Hear, hear!" it is not you, Pomponius, but your dinner that is eloquent. *Martial.*

To pamper the body is a miserable expression of kindness and courtesy; the most sumptuous repast is "the feast of reason and the flow of soul"—an intellectual and moral treat. *C. Simmons.*

Their sole reason for living lies in their palate. *Latin Proverb.*

The more the merrier; the fewer, the better fare. *John Palgrave.*

When I behold a fashionable table set out in all its magnificence, I fancy that I see gouts and dropsies, fevers and lethargies, with other innumerable distempers, lying in ambuscade among the dishes. Nature delights in the most plain and simple diet. Every animal, but man, keeps to one dish. Herbs are the food of this species, fish of that, and flesh of a third. Man falls upon everything that comes in his way; not the smallest fruit or excrescence of the earth, scarce a berry or a mushroom can escape him. *Addison.*

The difference between a rich man and a poor man, is this—the former eats when he pleases, and the latter when he can get it.—*Sir Walter Raleigh.*

A dinner lubricates business. *William Scott.*

* * *

Business and Businessmen

In business, three things are necessary, knowledge, temper, and time. *Feltham.*

The playthings of our elders are called business. *St. Augustine.*

Business will be either better or worse. *Calvin Coolidge.*

A man who cannot mind his own business, is not to be trusted with that of the King. *Saville.*

It is a wise man who knows his own business; and it is a wiser man who thoroughly attends to it. *H. L. Wayland.*

A business, like an automobile, has to be driven, in order to get results. *B. C. Forbes.*

Rare almost as great poets, rarer perhaps than veritable saints and martyrs are consummate men of business. *Helps.*

To business that we love, we rise betimes, and go to it with delight. *Shakespeare.*

No nation was ever ruined by trade. *Franklin.*

Men of great parts are often unfortunate in the management of public business, because they are apt to go out of the common road by the quickness of their imagination. *Swift.*

Big business makes its money out of by-products. *Elbert Hubbard.*

Call on a business man only at business times, and on business; transact your business, and go about your business, in order to give him time to finish his business. *Wellington.*

The merchant has no country. *Jefferson.*

It was a beautiful truth which our forefathers symbolized when in the old market towns they erected a market-cross, as if to teach both buyers and sellers to rule their actions and sanctify their gains by the remembrance of the cross. *Bowes.*

When two men in a business always agree, one of them is unnecessary. *William Wrigley, Jr.*

The Christian must not only mind heaven, but attend diligently to his daily calling, like the pilot, who, while his eye is fixed on the star, keeps his hand upon the helm. *T. Watson.*

It is not the crook in modern business that we fear, but the honest man who doesn't know what he is doing. *Owen D. Young.*

The secret of success in life is for a man to be ready for his opportunity when it comes. *Disraeli.*

> Seek not for fresher founts afar,
> Just drop your bucket where you are.
> *S. W. Foss.*

Everyone lives by selling something. *Proverb.*

*   *   *

Clergymen

The Christian ministry is the worst of all trades, but the best of all professions. *John Newton.*

"Three things," says Luther, "make a Divine—prayer, meditation, and trials." These make a Christian; but a Christian minister needs three more—talent, application, and acquirements. *C. Simmons.*

If a minister takes one step into the world, his hearers will take two. *Cecil.*

The preaching that comes from the soul, most works on the soul. *Fuller.*

"I have heard many great orators," said Louis XIV to Massillon, "and have been highly pleased with them; but whenever I hear you, I go away displeased with myself." This is the highest encomium that could be bestowed on a preacher. *C. Simmons.*

It is bad preaching to deaf ears. *German Proverb.*

The minister is to be a real man, a live man, a true man, a simple man, great in his love, in his life, in his work, in his simplicity, in his gentleness. *John Hall.*

The proud he tamed; the penitent he cheered; nor to rebuke the rich offender, feared; his preaching much, but more his practice wrought, a living sermon of the truths he taught. *Dryden.*

The life of a pious minister is visible rhetoric. *Hooker.*

Men of God have always, from time to time, walked among men, and made their commission felt in the heart and soul of the commonest hearer. *Emerson.*

Actors speak of things imaginary as if they were real, while you preachers too often speak of things real as if they were imaginary. *Thomas Betterton.*

The body of our prayer is the sum of our duty; and as we must ask of God whatsoever we need, so we must watch and labor for all that we ask. *Jeremy Taylor.*

Certain thoughts are prayers. There are moments when, whatever be the attitude of the body, the soul is on its knees. *Victor Hugo.*

Let not him who prays, suffer his tongue to outstrip his heart; nor presume to carry a message to the throne of grace, while that stays behind. *South.*

Prayer is not eloquence, but earnestness; not the definition of helplessness, but the feeling of it; not figures of speech, but earnestness of soul. *H. More.*

I have been driven many times to my knees by the overwhelming conviction that I had nowhere else to go. My own wisdom, and that of all about me, seemed insufficient for the day. *Abraham Lincoln.*

A prayer in its simplest definition is merely a wish turned Godward. *Phillips Brooks.*

God's way of answering the Christian's prayer for more patience, experience, hope, and love, often is to put him into the furnace of affliction. *Cecil.*

It is no use walking anywhere to preach unless we preach as we walk. *St. Francis of Assisi.*

Our prayers should be for blessings in general, for God knows best what is good for us. *Socrates.*

Whatsoever we beg of God, let us also work for it. *Jeremy Taylor.*

He who runs from God in the morning will scarcely find Him the rest of the day. *Bunyan.*

Trouble and perplexity drive me to prayer, and prayer drives away perplexity and trouble. *Melanchthon.*

Practice in life whatever you pray for, and God will give it to you more abundantly. *Pusey.*

Any heart turned Godward, feels more joy in one short hour of prayer, than e'er was raised by all the beasts on earth since its foundation. *Bailey.*

Improve your style, monsieur! You have disgusted me with the joys of heaven! *François de Malherbe.*

The simple heart that freely asks in love, obtains. *Whittier.*

The Lord's Prayer is not, as some fancy, the easiest, the most nat-

H*

ural of all devout utterances. It may be committed to memory quickly, but it is slowly learned by heart. *Maurice.*

In prayer it is better to have a heart without words, than words without a heart. *Bunyan.*

He who prays as he ought will endeavor to live as he prays. *Owen.*

The best and sweetest flowers of paradise God gives to his people when they are on their knees. Prayer is the gate of heaven—the key to let us into paradise. *T. Brooks.*

The Christian will find his parentheses for prayer even in the busiest hours of life. *Cecil.*

A strong, a faithful pulpit is no mean safeguard of a nation's life. *John Hall.*

The half-baked sermon causes spiritual indigestion. *Austin O'Malley.*

I don't like those mighty fine preachers who round off their sentences so beautifully that they are sure to roll off the sinner's conscience. *Rowland Hill.*

As the great test of medical practice is that it heals the patient, so the great test of preaching is that it converts and builds up the hearers. *H. L. Wayland.*

That is not the best sermon which makes the hearers go away talking to one another, and praising the speaker, but which makes them go away thoughtful and serious, and hastening to be alone. *Bishop Burnet.*

Many a meandering discourse one hears, in which the preacher aims at nothing, and—hits it. *Whately.*

The world looks at ministers out of the pulpit to know what they mean when in it. *Cecil.*

The defects of a preacher are soon spied. Let him be endued with ten virtues, and have but one fault, and that one fault will eclipse and darken all his virtues and gifts, so evil is the world in these times. *Luther.*

I preached as never sure to preach again, and as a dying man to dying men. *Baxter.*

My grand point in preaching is to break the hard heart, and to heal the broken one. *John Newton.*

To love to preach is one thing—to love those to whom we preach, quite another. *Cecil.*

The world is dying for want, not of good preaching, but of good hearing. *G. D. Boardman.*

*   *   *

Death

It is impossible that anything so natural, so necessary, and so universal as death, should ever have been designed by Providence as an evil to mankind. *Swift.*

We understand death for the first time when he puts his hand upon one whom we love. *Mme. de Staël.*

Death to a good man, is but passing through a dark entry, out of one little dusky room of his father's house, into another that is fair and large, lightsome and glorious, and divinely entertaining. *Clarke.*

We picture death as coming to destroy; let us rather picture Christ as coming to save. We think of death as ending; let us rather think of life as beginning, and that more abundantly. We think of losing; let us think of gaining. We think of parting; let us think of meeting. We think of going away; let us think of arriving. And as the voice of death whispers "You must go from earth," let us hear the voice of Christ saying, "You are but coming to Me!" *N. Macleod.*

The sole equality on earth is death. *Philip J. Bailey.*

The gods conceal from men the happiness of death, that they may endure life. *Lucan.*

No man who is fit to live need fear to die. To us here, death is the most terrible thing we know. But when we have tasted its reality it will mean to us birth, deliverance, a new creation of ourselves. It will be what health is to the sick man; what home is to the exile;

what the loved one given back is to the bereaved. As we draw near to it a solemn gladness should fill our hearts. It is God's great morning lighting up the sky. Our fears are the terror of children in the night. The night with its terrors, its darkness, its feverish dreams, is passing away; and when we awake it will be into the sunlight of God. *Fuller.*

Death is the golden key that opens the palace of eternity. *Milton.*

One may live as a conqueror, a king, or a magistrate; but he must die a man. The bed of death brings every human being to his pure individuality, to the intense contemplation of that deepest and most solemn of all relations—the relation between the creature and his Creator. *Daniel Webster.*

> Much talking man, in earth thou soon wilt lie;
> Be still, and living think what 'tis to die.
>
> *Palladas.*

Be still prepared for death: and death or life shall thereby be the sweeter. *Shakespeare.*

To neglect, at any time, preparation for death, is to sleep on our post at a siege; to omit it in old age, is to sleep at an attack. *Johnson.*

Is death the last sleep? No, it is the last and final awakening. *Walter Scott.*

> Death,
> The undiscover'd country, from whose bourne
> No traveller returns.
>
> *Shakespeare.*

Cullen, in his last moments, whispered, "I wish I had the power of writing or speaking, for then I would describe to you how pleasant a thing it is to die." *Derby.*

The darkness of death is like the evening twilight; it makes all objects appear more lovely to the dying. *Richter.*

Death is the liberator of him whom freedom cannot release; the physician of him whom medicine cannot cure; the comforter of him whom time cannot console. *Colton.*

Let death be daily before your eyes, and you will never entertain any abject thought, nor too eagerly covet anything. *Epictetus.*

On death and judgment, heaven and hell, who oft doth think, must needs die well. *Sir W. Raleigh.*

It matters not at what hour the righteous fall asleep. Death cannot come untimely to him who is fit to die. The less of this cold world, the more of heaven; the briefer life, the earlier immortality. *Milman.*

God's fingers touch'd him, and he slept. *Tennyson.*

There is no better armor against the shafts of death than to be busied in God's service. *Fuller.*

He who always waits upon God, is ready whensoever he calls. He is a happy man who so lives that death at all times may find him at leisure to die. *Feltham.*

Let dissolution come when it will, it can do the Christian no harm, for it will be but a passage out of a prison into a palace; out of a sea of troubles into a haven of rest; out of a crowd of enemies, to an innumerable company of true, loving, and faithful friends; out of shame, reproach, and contempt, into exceeding great and eternal glory. *Bunyan.*

We sometimes congratulate ourselves at the moment of waking from a troubled dream; it may be so the moment after death. *Hawthorne.*

Death and love are the two wings that bear the good man to heaven. *Michelangelo.*

If Socrates died like a philosopher, Jesus Christ died like a God. *Rousseau.*

Each departed friend is a magnet that attracts us to the next world. *Richter.*

Living is death; dying is life. On this side of the grave we are exiles, on that, citizens; on this side, orphans; on that, children; on this side, captives; on that, freemen; on this side disguised, unknown; on that, disclosed and proclaimed as the sons of God. *H. W. Beecher.*

There is no death! What seems so is transition; this life of mortal breath is but a suburb of the life elysian, whose portal we call death. *Longfellow*.

> No life that breathes with human breath
> Has ever truly longed for death.
>
> *Tennyson*.

When the sun goes below the horizon, he is not set; the heavens glow for a full hour after his departure. And when a great and good man sets, the sky of this world is luminous long after he is out of sight. Such a man cannot die out of this world. When he goes he leaves behind much of himself. Being dead he speaks. *H. W. Beecher*.

Not by lamentations and mournful chants ought we to celebrate the funeral of a good man, but by hymns, for in ceasing to be numbered with mortals he enters upon the heritage of a diviner life. *Plutarch*.

I know of but one remedy against the fear of death that is effectual and that will stand the test either of a sick-bed or of a sound mind—that is, a good life, a clear conscience, an honest heart, and a well-ordered conversation; to carry the thoughts of dying men about us, and so to live before we die as we shall wish we had when we come to it. *Norris*.

*   *   *

Diplomats

An ambassador is an honest man sent to lie and intrigue abroad for the benefit of his country. *Sir H. Wotton*.

A court is an assemblage of noble and distinguished beggars. *Talleyrand*.

Falsehood and dissimulation are certainly to be found at courts; but where are they not to be found? Cottages have them, as well as courts, only with worse manners. *Chesterfield*.

The court is a golden, but fatal circle, upon whose magic skirts a thousand devils sit tempting innocence, and beckon early virtue from its center. *N. Lee*.

The two maxims of any great man at court are, always to keep his countenance and never to keep his word. *Swift*.

The court is like a palace built of marble—made up of very hard, and very polished materials. *Bruyère*.

The chief requisites for a courtier are a flexible conscience and an inflexible politeness. *Lady Blessington*.

See how he sets his countenance for deceit, and promises a lie before he speaks. *Dryden*.

International arbitration may be defined as the substitution of many burning questions for a smouldering one. *Ambrose Bierce*.

> Diplomacy is to do and say
> The nastiest thing in the nicest way.
> > *Isaac Goldberg*.

Men, like bullets, go farthest when they are smoothest. *J. P. Richter*.

Ambassadors are the eye and ear of the state. *Italian Proverb*.

*   *   *

Doctors

The building of a perfect body crowned by a perfect brain, is at once the greatest earthly problem and grandest hope of the race. *Dio Lewis*.

Half the spiritual difficulties that men and women suffer arise from a morbid state of health. *H. W. Beecher*.

> Physicians mend or end us,
> Secundum artem; but although we sneer
> In health—when ill we call them to attend us,
> Without the least propensity to jeer.
> > *Byron*.

If the mind, that rules the body, ever so far forgets itself as to trample on its slave, the slave is never generous enough to forgive the injury, but will rise and smite the oppressor. *Longfellow*.

Dyspepsia is the remorse of a guilty stomach. *A. Kerr*.

Happy the doctor who is called in at the end of the disease. *French Proverb.*

A good surgeon operates with his hand, not with his heart. *Dumas.*

Health is certainly more valuable than money, because it is by health that money is procured; but thousands and millions are of small avail to alleviate the tortures of the gout, to repair the broken organs of sense, or resuscitate the powers of digestion. Poverty is, indeed, an evil from which we naturally fly; but let us not run from one enemy to another, nor take shelter in the arms of sickness. *Johnson.*

Every doctor thinks his pills the best. *German Proverb.*

There is this difference between the two temporal blessings—health and money; money is the most envied, but the least enjoyed; health is the most enjoyed, but the least envied; and this superiority of the latter is still more obvious when we reflect that the poorest man would not part with health for money, but that the richest would gladly part with all his money for health. *Colton.*

The only way for a rich man to be healthy is by exercise and abstinence, to live as if he were poor. *Sir W. Temple.*

With stupidity and sound digestion man may fret much; but what in these dull unimaginative days are the terrors of conscience to the diseases of the liver. *Carlyle.*

It's no trifle at her time of life to part with a doctor who knows her constitution. *George Eliot.*

From the physician and lawyer keep not the truth hidden. *Italian Proverb.*

Anguish of mind has driven thousands to suicide; anguish of body, none. This proves that the health of the mind is of far more consequence to our happiness than the health of the body, although both are deserving of much more attention than either receives. *Colton.*

People who are always taking care of their health are like misers, who are hoarding up a treasure which they have never spirit enough to enjoy. *Sterne.*

Health is the greatest of all possessions; a pale cobbler is better than a sick king. *Bickerstaff*.

> The alienist is not a joke:
> He finds you cracked, and leaves you broke.
> *Keith Preston*.

Look to your health; and if you have it, praise God and value it next to a good conscience; for health is the second blessing that we mortals are capable of—a blessing that money cannot buy; therefore value it, and be thankful for it. *Izaak Walton*.

It is part of the cure to wish to be cured. *Latin Proverb*.

The best doctors in the world are Doctor Diet, Doctor Quiet, and Doctor Merryman. *Swift*.

Joy, temperance, and repose, slam the door on the doctor's nose. *Longfellow*.

No one tries desperate remedies at first. *Latin Proverb*.

Medicine, the only profession that labors incessantly to destroy the reason for its own existence. *Lord Bryce*.

He who has health, has hope; and he who has hope, has everything. *Arabian Proverb*.

The desire to take medicine is perhaps the greatest feature which distinguishes man from animals. *Sir William Osler*.

The best of all medicines are rest and fasting. *Franklin*.

* * *

Farmers

Let the farmer forevermore be honored in his calling, for they who labor in the earth are the chosen people of God. *Jefferson*.

Agriculture for an honorable and high-minded man, is the best of all occupations or arts by which men procure the means of living. *Xenophon*.

Trade increases the wealth and glory of a country; but its real strength and stamina are to be looked for among the cultivators of the land. *Lord Chatham*.

The farmers are the founders of civilization and prosperity. *Daniel Webster.*

He that would look with contempt on the pursuits of the farmer, is not worthy the name of a man. *H. W. Beecher.*

> Tools were made, and born were hands,
> Every farmer understands.
>
> *Blake.*

Whoever makes two ears of corn, or two blades of grass, to grow where only one grew before, deserves better of mankind, and does more essential service to his country than the whole race of politicians put together. *Swift.*

We may talk as we please of lilies, and lions rampant, and spread eagles in fields of *d'or* or *d'argent,* but if heraldry were guided by reason, a plough in the field arable would be the most noble and ancient arms. *Cowley.*

Farmers fatten most when famine reigns. *Proverb.*

To plow is to pray—to plant is to prophesy . . . *Proverb.*

*   *   *

Florists

What a desolate place would be a world without flowers! It would be a face without a smile; a feast without a welcome. Are not flowers the stars of the earth? And are not our stars the flowers of heaven? *Mrs. Balfour.*

To me the meanest flower that blows can give thoughts that do often lie too deep for tears. *Wordsworth.*

What a pity flowers can utter no sound! A singing rose, a whispering violet, a murmuring honeysuckle—oh, what a rare and exquisite miracle would these be! *H. W. Beecher.*

The flowers are nature's jewels, **with whose wealth** she decks her summer beauty. *Croly.*

The instinctive and universal taste of mankind selects flowers for the expression of its finest sympathies, their beauty and fleetingness serving to make them the most fitting symbols of those delicate sentiments for which language seems almost too gross a medium. *Hillard.*

Flowers are love's truest language. *P. Benjamin.*

To analyze the charms of flowers is like dissecting music; it is one of those things which it is far better to enjoy, than to attempt fully to understand. *Tuckerman.*

How the universal heart of man blesses flowers! They are wreathed round the cradle, the marriage altar, and the tomb. They should deck the brow of the youthful bride, for they are in themselves a lovely type of marriage. They should twine round the tomb, for their perpetually renewed beauty is a symbol of the resurrection. They should festoon the altar, for their fragrance and beauty ascend in perpetual worship before the most high. *Mrs. L. M. Child.*

Stars of earth, these golden flowers; emblems of our own great resurrection; emblems of the bright and better land. *Longfellow.*

Every rose is an autograph from the hand of God on His world about us. He has inscribed His thoughts in these marvellous hieroglyphics which sense and science have, these many thousand years, been seeking to understand. *Theodore Parker.*

To cultivate a garden is to walk with God. *Bovee.*

There is not the least flower but seems to hold up its head and to look pleasantly, in the secret sense of the goodness of its heavenly Maker. *South.*

*   *   *

Fourth of July

We hold these truths to be self-evident, that all men are created equal, that they are endowed by their Creator with certain inalienable Rights, that among these are Life, Liberty, and the pursuit of Happiness. *Jefferson.*

Is life so dear, or peace so sweet, as to be purchased at the price of chains and slavery? Forbid it, Almighty God! I know not what course others may take, but as for me, give me liberty, or give me death! *Patrick Henry.*

There is no liberty worth anything which is not a liberty under law. *N. J. Burton.*

Freedom is not worth having if it does not connote freedom to err. *Mahatma Gandhi.*

Liberty has restraints but no frontiers. *Lloyd George.*

Personal liberty is the paramount essential to human dignity and human happiness. *Bulwer.*

Give me the liberty to know, to think, to believe, and to utter freely, according to conscience, above all other liberties. *Milton.*

Easier were it to hurl the rooted mountain from its base, than force the yoke of slavery upon men determined to be free. *Southey.*

The liberty of a people consists in being governed by laws which they have made themselves, under whatsoever form it be of government; the liberty of a private man is being master of his own time and actions, as far as may consist with the laws of God, and of his country. *Cowley.*

No free government, or the blessings of liberty can be preserved to any people but by a firm adherence to justice, moderation, temperance, frugality, and virtue, and by a frequent recurrence to fundamental principles. *Patrick Henry.*

Personal liberty is the right to act without interference within the limits of the law. *J. Oerter.*

Safe popular freedom consists of four things, the diffusion of liberty, of intelligence, of property, and of conscientiousness, and cannot be compounded of any three out of the four. *Joseph Cook.*

Christianity is the companion of liberty in all its conflicts, the cradle of its infancy, and the divine source of its claims. *de Tocqueville.*

The principle of liberty and equality if coupled with mere selfishness, will make men only devils, each trying to be independent that he may fight only for his own interest. And here is the need of religion and its power, to bring in the principle of benevolence and love to men. *John Randolph.*

Where the press is free, and every man able to read, all is safe. *Jefferson.*

Liberty is the right to do what the laws allow; and if a citizen could do what they forbid, it would be no longer liberty, because others would have the same powers.

A nation may lose its liberties in a day, and not miss them in a century. *Montesquieu.*

Men are qualified for civil liberty in exact proportion to their disposition to put chains upon their own appetites; in proportion as their love of justice is above their rapacity; in proportion as their soundness and sobriety of understanding is above their vanity and presumption; in proportion as they are more disposed to listen to the counsels of the wise and good, in preference to the flattery of knaves. Society cannot exist unless a controlling power upon the will and appetite is placed somewhere; and the less of it there is within, the more there must be of it without. It is ordained in the eternal constitution of things, that men of intemperate habits cannot be free. Their passions forge their fetters. *Burke.*

Liberty will not descend to a people; a people must raise themselves to liberty; it is a blessing that must be earned before it can be enjoyed. *Colton.*

Liberty may make mistakes but tyranny is the death of a nation. *Matteotti.*

Where liberty dwells, there is my country. *Milton.*

A country cannot subsist well without liberty, nor liberty without virtue. *Rousseau.*

The human race is in the best condition when it has the greatest degree of liberty. *Dante.*

Liberty and union, one and inseparable, now and forever. *Daniel Webster.*

A Bible and a newspaper in every house, a good school in every district—all studied and appreciated as they merit—are the principal support of virtue. morality, and civil liberty. *Franklin.*

The people never give up their liberties but under some delusion. *Burke*.

The spirit of liberty is not, as multitudes imagine, a jealousy of our own particular rights, but a respect for the rights of others, and an unwillingness that anyone, whether high or low, should be wronged or trampled underfoot. *Channing*.

A day, an hour of virtuous liberty is worth a whole eternity of bondage. *Addison*.

The true danger is, when liberty is nibbled away, for expedients and by parts. *Burke*.

Lean liberty is better than fat slavery. *Ray*.

Many politicians lay it down as a self-evident proposition, that no people ought to be free till they are fit to use their freedom. The maxim is worthy of the fool in the old story, who resolved not to go into the water till he had learned to swim. *Macaulay*.

Freedom of religion, freedom of the press, and freedom of person under the protection of the *habeas corpus,* these are principles that have guided our steps through an age of revolution and reformation. *Jefferson*.

*   *   *

Historians

History is philosophy teaching by example, and also by warning; its two eyes are geography and chronology. *Dionysius*.

History is but the unrolled scroll of prophecy. *Garfield*.

History is a voice forever sounding across the centuries the laws of right and wrong. Opinions alter, manners change, creeds rise and fall, but the moral law is written on the tablets of eternity. *Froude*.

Sin writes histories, goodness is silent. *Goethe*.

History is little more than the register of the crimes, follies, and misfortunes of mankind. *Gibbon*.

History is but a kind of Newgate calendar, a register of the crimes and miseries that man has inflicted on his fellow-man. *Washington Irving.*

All the historical books which contain no lies are extremely tedious. *Anatole France.*

We read history through our prejudices. *Wendell Phillips.*

What is history but a fable agreed upon? *Napoleon.*

What are all histories but God manifesting himself, shaking down and trampling under foot whatsoever he hath not planted. *Cromwell.*

History is neither more nor less than biography on a large scale. *Lamartine.*

It is not deeds or acts that last: it is the written record of those deeds and acts. *Elbert Hubbard.*

The best thing which we derive from history is the enthusiasm that it raises in us. *Goethe.*

If men could learn from history, what lessons it might teach us! But passion and party blind our eyes, and the light which experience gives is a lantern on the stern which shines only on the waves behind us. *Coleridge.*

History is merely gossip. *Oscar Wilde.*

The men who make history, have not time to write it. *Metternich.*

History makes us some amends for the shortness of life. *Skelton.*

We must consider how very little history there is; I mean real, authentic history. That certain kings reigned, and certain battles were fought, we can depend on as true; but all the coloring, all the philosophy of history is conjecture. *Johnson.*

The impartiality of history is not that of the mirror, which merely reflects objects, but of the judge who sees, listens, and decides. *Lamartine.*

Out of monuments, names, words, proverbs, traditions, private records and evidences, fragments of stories, passages of books, and the like, we do save and recover somewhat from the deluge of time. *Bacon.*

What is public history but a register of the successes and disappointments, the vices, the follies and the quarrels of those who engage in contention for power. *Paley.*

There is nothing that solidifies and strengthens a nation like reading the nation's history, whether that history is recorded in books, or embodied in customs, institutions, and monuments. *J. Anderson.*

Many historians take pleasure in putting into the mouths of princes what they have neither said nor ought to have said. *Voltaire.*

We find but few historians who have been diligent enough in their search for truth. It is their common method to take on trust what they distribute to the public; by which means, a falsehood, once received from a famed writer, becomes traditional to posterity. *Dryden.*

Not to know what has been transacted in former times is to be always a child. If no use is made of the labors of past ages, the world must remain always in the infancy of knowledge. *Cicero.*

History maketh a young man to be old, without wrinkles or gray hairs, privileging him with the experience of age, without either the infirmities or inconveniences thereof. *Fuller.*

*   *   *

Housewives—Wives

Nothing lovelier can be found in woman than to study household good, and good works in her husband to promote. *Milton.*

She was a woman of a stirring life, whose heart was in her house; two wheels she had, the large for spinning wool, the small for flax; and if one wheel had rest, it was because the other was at work. *Wordsworth.*

A house is no home unless it contain food and fire for the mind as well as for the body. *Margaret Fuller.*

Our home joys are the most delightful earth affords, and the joy of parents in their children is the most holy joy of humanity. It makes their hearts pure and good, it lifts men up to their Father in heaven. *Pestalozzi.*

A hundred men may make an encampment, but it takes a woman to make a home. *Chinese Proverb.*

Households there may be, well-ordered and abounding in comfort —families there may be, whose various members live in harmony and love—but homes, in their true sense, there cannot be where there is not one whom manly choice has made a wife and infant lips have learned to honor with the name of mother. *Dudley A. Tyng.*

The strength of a nation, especially of a republican nation, is in the intelligent and well-ordered homes of the people. *Mrs. Sigourney.*

Try praising your wife, even if it does frighten her at first. *Billy Sunday.*

The fingers of the housewife do more than a yoke of oxen. *German Proverb.*

The homes of a nation are the bulwarks of personal and national safety and thrift. *J. G. Holland.*

A good wife is heaven's last, best gift to man—his gem of many virtues, his casket of jewels; her voice is sweet music, her smiles his brightest day, her kiss the guardian of his innocence, her arms the pale of his safety, her industry his surest wealth, her economy his safest steward, her lips his faithful counsellors, her bosom the softest pillow of his cares. *Jeremy Taylor.*

Her pleasures are in the happiness of her family. *Rousseau.*

A wife is essential to great longevity; she is the receptacle of half a man's cares, and two-thirds of his ill-humor. *Chas. Reade.*

An ideal wife is any woman who has an ideal husband. *Booth Tarkington.*

A good wife makes the cares of the world sit easy, and adds a sweetness to its pleasures: she is a man's best companion in prosperity, and his best if not only friend in adversity; the most careful preserver of his health, and the kindest attendant on his sickness; a faithful adviser in distress, a comforter in affliction, and a discreet manager of all his domestic affairs. *L. M. Stretch.*

The sum of all that makes a just man happy consists in the well choosing of his wife. *Massinger.*

The way to fight a woman is with your hat. Grab it and run. *John Barrymore.*

The three virtues of a woman: Obey the father, obey the husband, obey the son. *Chinese Proverb.*

Kind words and few are a woman's ornament. *Danish Proverb.*

No man can live piously or die righteously without a wife. *Richter.*

Woman would be more charming if one could fall into her arms without falling into her hands. *Ambrose Bierce.*

A woman who looks much in the glass spins but little. *French Proverb.*

Women have more strength in their looks, than we have in our laws; and more power by their tears, than we have by our arguments. *Saville.*

There is one in the world who feels for him who is sad a keener pang than he feels for himself; there is one to whom reflected joy is better than that which comes direct; there is one who rejoices in another's honor, more than in any which is one's own; there is one on whom another's transcendent excellence sheds no beam but that of delight; there is one who hides another's infirmities more faithfully than one's own; there is one who loses all sense of self in the sentiment of kindness, tenderness, and devotion to another; that one is woman. *Washington Irving.*

A handsome woman is always right. *German Proverb.*

Silence gives grace to a woman. *Sophocles.*

I'm not denying the women are foolish: God Almighty made 'em to match the men. *George Eliot.*

There can be no higher ambition for a Christian woman than to be a faithful wife and a happy and influential mother. It is the place which God has given woman, and she who fills it well, is as honorable and honored as the most illustrious man can be. *C. A. Stoddard.*

Woman once made equal to man becomes his superior. *Socrates.*

Woman—last at the cross, and earliest at the grave. *E. S. Barrett.*

It is a sad house where the hen crows louder than the cock. *Italian Proverb.*

A woman of charm is as rare as a man of genius. *de Madariaga.*

All the reasonings of men are not worth one sentiment of women. *Voltaire.*

Men have sight; women insight. *Victor Hugo.*

* * *

Journalists

Great is journalism. Is not every able editor a ruler of the world, being the persuader of it? *Carlyle.*

Get your facts first, and then you can distort 'em as you please. *Mark Twain.*

Burke said there were Three Estates in Parliament; but, in the Reporters' Gallery yonder, there sat a fourth estate more important far than they all. *Carlyle.*

We live under a government of men and morning newspapers. *Wendell Phillips.*

I fear three newspapers more than a hundred thousand bayonets. *Napoleon.*

A newspaper is the history for one day of the world in which we live, and with which we are consequently more concerned than with those which have passed away, and exist only in remembrance. *Bishop Horne.*

A newspaper should be the maximum of information, and the minimum of comment. *Cobden.*

Newspapers are the schoolmasters of the common people—a greater treasure to them than uncounted millions of gold. *H. W. Beecher.*

Journalism is organized gossip. *Edward Eggleston.*

The press is good or evil according to the character of those who direct it. It is a mill that grinds all that is put into its hopper. Fill the hopper with poisoned grain and it will grind it to meal, but there is death in the bread. *Bryant.*

In these times we fight for ideas, and newspapers are our fortresses. *Heine.*

The newspaper press is the people's university. Half the readers of Christendom read little else. *J. Parton.*

Do not read newspapers column by column; remember they are made for everybody, and don't try to get what isn't meant for you. *Emerson.*

Before this century shall run out, journalism will be the whole press. Mankind will write their book day by day, hour by hour, page by page. Thought will spread abroad with the rapidity of light, instantly conceived, instantly written, instantly understood at the extremities of the earth; it will spread from pole to pole, suddenly burning with the fervor of soul which made it burst forth; it will be the reign of the human mind in all its plenitude; it will not have time to ripen, to accumulate in the form of a book; the book will arrive too late; the only book possible from day to day is a newspaper. *Lamartine.*

Let it be impressed upon your minds, let it be instilled into your children, that the liberty of the press is the palladium of all the civil, political, and religious rights. *Junius.*

The press is not only free, it is powerful. That power is ours. It is the proudest that man can enjoy. It was not granted by monarchs; it was not gained for us by aristocracies; but it sprang from the people, and, with an immortal instinct, it has always worked for the people. *Disraeli.*

The most truthful part of a newspaper is the advertisements. *Jefferson.*

*   *   *

Judges

To be perfectly just is an attribute of the divine nature; to be so to the utmost of our abilities, is the glory of man. *Addison.*

Judges ought to be more learned than witty, more reverent than plausible, and more advised than confident. Above all things, integrity is their portion and proper virtue. *Bacon.*

> Justice while she winks at crimes,
> Stumbles on innocence sometimes.
> > *Samuel Butler.*

If judges would make their decisions just, they should behold neither plaintiff, defendant, nor pleader, but only the cause itself. *B. Livingston.*

Justice is truth in action. *Disraeli.*

Justice discards party, friendship, and kindred, and is therefore represented as blind. *Addison.*

One man's word is no man's word; we should quietly hear both sides. *Goethe.*

Justice is the constant desire and effort to render to every man his due. *Justinian.*

Justice is itself the great standing policy of civil society; and any departure from it, under any circumstance, lies under the suspicion of being no policy at all. *Burke.*

> A just man is not one who does no ill,
> But he, who with the power, has not the will.
> > *Philemon.*

Justice without wisdom is impossible. *Froude.*

How can a people be free that has not learned to be just? *Sieyès.*

Justice is the great and simple principle which is the secret of success in all government, as essential to the training of an infant, as to the control of a mighty nation. *Simms.*

Justice is the first virtue of those who command, and stops the complaints of those who obey. *Diderot.*

Justice is the idea of God; the ideal of men; the rule of conduct writ in the nature of mankind. *Theodore Parker.*

Justice is the great interest of man on earth. It is the ligament which holds civilized beings and civilized nations together. Wherever her temple stands, and so long as it is duly honored, there is a foundation for social security, general happiness, and the improvement and progress of our race. And whoever labors on this edifice with usefulness and distinction, whoever clears its foundations, strengthens its pillars, adorns its entablatures, or contributes to raise its august dome still higher in the skies, connects himself, in name, and fame, and character, with that which is and must be as durable as the frame of human society. *Daniel Webster.*

The *judgment* of man is fallible. *Latin Proverb.*

If all men were just, there would be no need of valor. *Greek Proverb.*

There should be no sword in the hand of justice. *Latin Proverb.*

Justice is half religion. *Turkish Proverb.*

*   *   *

Labor

Next to faith in God, is faith in labor. *Bovee.*

Labor is the divine law of our existence; repose is desertion and suicide. *Mazzini.*

Labor is one of the great elements of society—the great substantial interest on which we all stand. Not feudal service, or predial toil, or the irksome drudgery by one race of mankind subjected, on account of their color, to another; but labor, intelligent, manly, independent, thinking and acting for itself, earning its own wages, accumulating those wages into capital, educating childhood, maintaining worship, claiming the right of the elective franchise, and helping to uphold the great fabric of the State—that is American labor; and all my sympathies are with it, and my voice, till I am dumb, will be for it. *Daniel Webster.*

Industry cannot flourish if labor languish. *Calvin Coolidge.*

There is a perennial nobleness and even sacredness in work. Were he ever so benighted and forgetful of his high calling, there is always hope in a man who actually and earnestly works. *Carlyle.*

Labor disgraces no man; unfortunately you occasionally find men disgrace labor. *Ulysses S. Grant.*

The labor and sweat of our brows is so far from being a curse, that without it our very bread would not be so great a blessing. If it were not for labor, men could neither eat so much, nor relish so pleasantly, nor sleep so soundly, nor be so healthful, so useful, so strong, so patient, so noble, nor so untempted. *Jeremy Taylor.*

Alexander the Great, reflecting on his friends degenerating into sloth and luxury, told them that it was a most slavish thing to luxuriate, and a most royal thing to labor. *Barrow.*

Blessed is he who has found his work; let him ask no other blessedness. *Carlyle.*

Labor is life; from the inmost heart of the worker rises his God-given force, the sacred celestial life-essence breathed into him by Almighty God! *Carlyle.*

Toil, says the proverb, is the sire of fame. *Euripides.*

Work is the meat of life, pleasure the dessert. *B. C. Forbes.*

Whatever there is of greatness in the United States, or indeed in any other country, is due to labor. The laborer is the author of all greatness and wealth. Without labor there would be no government, and no leading class, and nothing to preserve. *U. S. Grant.*

The workman still is greater than his work. *Menander.*

It is to labor and to labor only, that man owes everything of exchangeable value. Labor is the talisman that has raised him from the condition of the savage; that has changed the desert and the forest into cultivated fields; that has covered the earth with cities, and the ocean with ships; that has given us plenty, comfort, and elegance, instead of want, misery, and barbarism. *J. Macculloch.*

Can anything be sadder than work left unfinished? Yes; work never begun. *Christina Rossetti.*

Labor is the great producer of wealth; it moves all other causes. *Daniel Webster.*

There is a great difference between a young man looking for a situation and one looking for work. *Leslie M. Shaw.*

Nothing is impossible to the man who can will, and then do; this is the only law of success. *Mirabeau.*

Work consists of whatever a body is *obliged* to do, and play consists of whatever a body is not obliged to do. *Mark Twain.*

Be the first in the field and the last to the couch. *Chinese Proverb.*

A carpenter is known by his chips. *Proverb.*

Labor is the law of happiness. *Proverb.*

The gods will sell us all good things at the price of labor. *Greek Proverb.*

He who would eat the kernel must crack the shell. *Latin Proverb.*

*   *   *

Lawyers

No man can be a sound lawyer who is not well read in the laws of Moses. *Fisher Ames.*

There is too much reason to apprehend, that the custom of pleading for any client, without discrimination of right or wrong, must lessen the regard due to those important distinctions, and deaden the moral sensibility of the heart. *Percival.*

The law is the last result of human wisdom acting upon human experience for the benefit of the public. *Johnson.*

Accuracy and diligence are much more necessary to a lawyer than great comprehension of mind, or brilliancy of talent. His business is to refine, define, split hairs, look into authorities, and compare cases

A man can never gallop over the fields of law on Pegasus, nor fly across them on the wing of oratory. If he would stand on *terra firma,* he must descend. If he would be a great lawyer, he must first consent to become a great drudge. *Daniel Webster.*

A lawyer is a learned gentleman who rescues your estate from your enemies and keeps it himself. *Lord Brougham.*

Adversaries in law strive mightily, but eat and drink as friends. *Shakespeare.*

Why, gentlemen, you cannot live without the lawyers, and certainly you cannot die without them. *Joseph H. Choate.*

> This house where once a lawyer dwelt,
> Is now a smith's. Alas!
> How rapidly the iron age
> Succeeds the age of brass!
>   *Erskine.*

By birth and interest lawyers belong to the people; by habit and taste to the aristocracy; and they may be looked upon as the natural bond and connecting link of the two great classes of society. They are attached to public order beyond every other consideration, and the best security of public order is authority. If they prize the free institutions of their country much, they value the legality of these institutions far more. They are less afraid of tyranny than of arbitrary power. *de Tocqueville.*

A countryman between two lawyers is like a fish between two cats. *Franklin.*

When there is no will, there is a way for the lawyers. *Austin O'Malley.*

There is a great deal of law learning that is dry, dark, cold, revolting—but it is an old feudal castle, in perfect preservation, which the legal architect, who aspires to the first honors of his profession, will delight to explore, and learn all the uses to which its various parts used to be put; and he will the better understand, enjoy and relish the progressive improvements of the science in modern times. *W. Wirt.*

As well open an oyster without a knife, as a lawyer's mouth without a fee. *Proverb.*

He that is his own lawyer has a fool for his client. *Proverb.*

If there were no bad people there would be no good lawyers. *Proverb.*

Agree, for the law is costly. *Proverb.*

*   *   *

Librarians

Libraries are as the shrines where all the relics of saints, full of true virtue, and that without delusion or imposture, are preserved and reposed. *Bacon.*

> Through and through the inspired leaves,
> Ye maggots make your windings;
> But, oh, respect his lordship's taste,
> And spare the golden bindings!
>
> *Burns.*

Libraries are the wardrobes of literature, whence men, properly informed, may bring forth something for ornament, much for curiosity, and more for use. *Dyer.*

There are books of which the backs and covers are by far the best parts. *Dickens.*

My library was dukedom large enough. *Shakespeare.*

I would define a book as a work of magic whence escape all kinds of images to trouble the souls and change the hearts of men. *Anatole France.*

> Camerado, this is no book,
> Who touches this touches a man.
>
> *Whitman.*

Consider what you have in the smallest chosen library. A company of the wisest and wittiest men that could be picked out of all civil countries, in a thousand years, have set in best order the results of their learning and wisdom. The men themselves were hid and inaccessible, solitary, impatient of interruption, fenced by etiquette; but the thought which they did not uncover to their bosom friend is here written out in transparent words to us, the strangers of another age. *Emerson.*

A great library contains the diary of the human race. The great consulting room of a wise man is a library. *G. Dawson.*

The true university of these days is a collection of books. *Carlyle.*

From this slender beginning I have gradually formed a numerous and select library, the foundation of all my works, and the best comfort of my life, both at home and abroad. *Gibbon.*

No possession can surpass, or even equal a good library, to the lover of books. Here are treasured up for his daily use and delectation, riches which increase by being consumed, and pleasures which never cloy. *J. A. Langford.*

A library may be regarded as the solemn chamber in which a man may take counsel with all who have been wise, and great, and good, and glorious among the men that have gone before him. *G. Dawson.*

We enter our studies, and enjoy a society which we alone can bring together. We raise no jealousy by conversing with one in preference to another: we give no offense to the most illustrious by questioning him as long as we will, and leaving him as abruptly. Diversity of opinion raises no tumult in our presence; each interlocutor stands before us, speaks or is silent, and we adjourn or decide the business at our leisure. *Landor.*

* * *

Men—Husbands

Men are but children, too, though they have gray hairs; they are only of a larger size. *Seneca.*

> But, oh! ye lords of ladies intellectual,
> Inform us truly—have they not henpeck'd you all?
> *Byron.*

The real difference between men is energy. A strong will, a settled purpose, an invincible determination, can accomplish almost any-thing; and in this lies the distinction between great men and little men. *Fuller.*

A husband is always a sensible man; he never thinks of marrying *Dumas.*

All great men are in some degree inspired. *Cicero.*

Men, by associating in large masses, as in camps and cities, im-prove their talents but impair their virtues; and strengthen their minds, but weaken their morals; thus a retrocession in the one, is too often the price they pay for a refinement of the other. *Colton.*

> A master of a house, as I have read,
> Must be the first man up, and the last in bed.
> *Robert Herrick.*

A man's ledger does not tell what he is, or what he is worth. Count what is *in* man, not what is *on* him, if you would know what he is worth—whether rich or poor. *H. W. Beecher.*

What a piece of work is man! How noble in reason! How infinite in faculties! In form and moving, how express and admirable! In ac-tion, how like an angel! In apprehension, how like a god! *Shake-speare.*

The only time that most women give their orating husbands un-divided attention is when the old boys mumble in their sleep. *Walter Mizner.*

What a chimera . . . is man! . . . what a chaos, what a subject o contradiction! . . . A judge of all things, feeble worm of the earth, depositary of the truth, cloaca of uncertainty . . . the glory and the shame of the universe! *Pascal.*

How little man is; yet, in his own mind, how great! He is lord and master of all things, yet scarce can command anything. He is given a freedom of his will; but wherefore? Was it but to torment and perplex him the more? How little avails this freedom, if the objects he is to act upon be not as much disposed to obey as he is to com-mand! *Burke.*

Men, in general, are but great children. *Napoleon.*

Man is an animal that cooks his victuals. *Burke.*

He is of the earth, but his thoughts are with the stars. Mean and petty his wants and desires; yet they serve a soul exalted with grand, glorious aims, with immortal longings, with thoughts which sweep the heavens, and wander through eternity. A pigmy standing on the outward crest of this small planet, his far-reaching spirit stretches outward to the infinite, and there alone finds rest. *Carlyle.*

Man is to man all kinds of beasts; a fawning dog, a roaring lion, a thieving fox, a robbing wolf, a dissembling crocodile, a treacherous decoy, and a rapacious vulture. *Cowley.*

An institution is the lengthened shadow of one man. *Emerson.*

It is not what he has, or even what he does which expresses the worth of a man, but what he is. *Amiel.*

How poor, how rich, how abject, how august, how complicate, how wonderful is man! distinguished link in being's endless chain! midway from nothing to the Deity! dim miniature of greatness absolute! an heir of glory! a frail child of dust! helpless immortal! insect infinite! a worm! a God! *Young.*

Man is the highest product of his own history. The discoverer finds nothing so grand or tall as himself, nothing so valuable to him. The greatest start is at the small end of the telescope, the star that is looking, not looked after nor looked at. *Theodore Parker.*

Man is an animal that makes bargains; no other animal does this— one dog does not change a bone with another. *Adam Smith.*

Man is a reasoning rather than a reasonable animal. *Alexander Hamilton.*

The record of life runs thus: Man creeps into childhood, bounds into youth, sobers into manhood, softens into age, totters into second childhood, and slumbers into the cradle prepared for him—thence to be watched and cared for. *Henry Giles.*

There is no fact more observable in literature than how many beautiful things have been said about man in the abstract, and how few about men in particular. *Mme. l'Estrange.*

In my youth I thought of writing a satire on mankind; but now in my age I think I should write an apology for them. *Walpole.*

Every man is a divinity in disguise, a god playing the fool. It seems as if heaven had sent its insane angels into our world as to an asylum. And here they will break out into their native music, and utter at intervals the words they have heard in heaven; then the mad fit returns, and they mope and wallow like dogs! *Emerson.*

Man is but a reed, the weakest in nature, but he is a thinking reed. *Pascal.*

Man at his birth is content with a little milk and a piece of flannel: so we begin, that presently find kingdoms not enough for us. *Seneca.*

Show me the man you honor, and I will show what kind of a man you are, for it shows me what your ideal of manhood is, and what kind of a man you long to be. *Carlyle.*

An acorn is not an oak when it is sprouted. It must go through long summers and fierce winters, and endure all that frost, and snow, and thunder, and storms, and side-striking winds can bring, before it is a full grown oak. So a man is not a man when he is created; he is only begun. His manhood must come with years. He that goes through life prosperous, and comes to his grave without a wrinkle, is not half a man. Difficulties are God's errands and trainers, and only through them can one come to the fullness of manhood. *H. W. Beecher.*

Man! thou pendulum betwixt a smile and tear. *Byron.*

All that I care to know is that a man is a human being—that is enough for me; he can't be any worse. *Mark Twain.*

Contemporaries appreciate the man rather than the merit; but posterity will regard the merit rather than the man. *Colton.*

The older I grow—and I now stand on the brink of eternity—the more comes back to me that sentence in the Catechism which I learned when a child, and the fuller and deeper its meaning becomes: "What is the chief end of man? To glorify God and enjoy him forever." *Carlyle*.

Every man is a volume, if you know how to read him. *Channing*.

An honest man is the noblest work of God. *Pope*.

When faith is lost, when honor dies, the man is dead! *Whittier*.

*   *   *

Musicians

There is something marvelous in music. I might almost say it is, in itself, a marvel. Its position is somewhere between the region of thought and that of phenomena; a glimmering medium between mind and matter, related to both and yet differing from either. Spiritual, and yet requiring rhythm; material, and yet independent of space. *H. Heine*.

Swans sing before they die; 'twere no bad thing
Should certain persons die before they sing.
Coleridge.

All musical people seem to be happy; it is to them the engrossing pursuit; almost the only innocent and unpunished passion. *Sydney Smith*.

Music can noble hints impart, engender fury, kindle love, with unsuspected eloquence can move and manage all the man with secret art. *Addison*.

The man that hath not music in himself, and is not moved with concord of sweet sounds, is fit for treasons, stratagems, and spoils; let no man trust him. *Shakespeare*.

Music is the fourth great material want of our nature—first food, then raiment, then shelter, then music. *Bovee*.

And music pours on mortals
Her magnificent disdain.
Emerson.

Music is the art of the prophets, the only art that can calm the agitations of the soul; it is one of the most magnificent and delightful presents God has given us. *Luther.*

Music is the only language in which you cannot say a mean or sarcastic thing. *John Erskine.*

Music, of all the liberal arts, has the greatest influence over the passions, and is that to which the legislator ought to give the greatest encouragement. *Napoleon.*

Next to theology I give to music the highest place and honor. And we see how David and all the saints have wrought their godly thoughts into verse, rhyme, and song. *Luther.*

> A squeak's heard in the orchestra,
> The leader draws across
> The intestines of the agile cat
> The tail of the noble hoss.
>
> *Lanigan.*

We love music for the buried hopes, the garnered memories, the tender feelings it can summon at a touch. *L. E. Landon.*

Music washes away from the soul the dust of every-day life. *Auerbach.*

Music is the universal language of mankind. *Longfellow.*

Both music and painting add a spirit to devotion, and elevate the ardor. *Sterne.*

Lord, what music hast thou provided for the saints in heaven, when thou affordest bad men such music on earth! *Izaak Walton.*

Music moves us, and we know not why; we feel the tears, but cannot trace their source. Is it the language of some other state, born of its memory? For what can wake the soul's strong instinct of another world like music? *L. E. Landon.*

Music is well said to be the speech of angels. *Carlyle.*

There is no feeling, except the extremes of fear and grief, that does not find relief in music. *George Eliot.*

The meaning of song goes deep. Who is there that, in logical words, can express the effect music has on us? A kind of inarticulate, unfathomable speech, which leads us to the edge of the infinite, and lets us for moments gaze into that! *Carlyle.*

Music—the only universal tongue. *Proverb.*

* * *

Naturalists

This is the forest primeval. The murmuring pines and the hemlocks, bearded with moss and in garments green, indistinct in the twilight, stand like Druids of eld, with voices sad and prophetic, stand like harpers hoar, with beards that rest on their bosoms. *Longfellow.*

> I think that I shall never see
> A poem lovely as a tree.

* * *

> Poems are made by fools like me,
> But only God can make a tree.
> > *Joyce Kilmer.*

Nature is the art of God. *Sir Thomas Browne.*

The groves were God's first temples. Ere man learned to hew the shaft, and lay the architrave, and spread the roof above them—ere he framed the lofty vault, to gather and roll back the sound of anthems; in the darkling wood, amidst the cool and silence, he knelt down and offered to the Mightiest solemn thanks and supplication. *Bryant.*

Drive away nature, it comes back apace. *French Proverb.*

Stranger, if thou hast learned a truth which needs no school of long experience, that the world is full of guilt and misery, and hast seen enough of all its sorrows, crimes and cares to tire thee of it, enter this wild wood and view the haunts of Nature. The calm shade shall bring a kindred calm, and the sweet breeze that makes the green leaves dance shall waft a balm to thy sick heart. *Bryant.*

We talk of our mastery of Nature, which sounds very grand; but the fact is we respectfully adapt ourselves, first, to her ways. *Clarence Day.*

Study Nature as the countenance of God. *Charles Kingsley.*

There is no trifling with Nature; it is always true, grave, and severe; it is always in the right, and the faults and errors fall to our share. It defies incompetency, but reveals its secrets to the competent, the truthful, and the pure. *Goethe.*

Nature does not proceed by leaps. *Latin Proverb.*

Nature is the time-vesture of God that reveals him to the wise, and hides him from the foolish. *Carlyle.*

Nature does nothing in vain. *Latin Proverb.*

What profusion is there in His work! When trees blossom there is not a single breastpin, but a whole bosom-full of gems; and of leaves they have so many suits that they can throw them away to the winds all summer long. What unnumbered cathedrals has He reared in the forest shades, vast and grand, full of curious carvings, and haunted evermore by tremulous music; and in the heavens above, how do stars seem to have flown out of His hand faster than sparks out of a mighty forge! *H. W. Beecher.*

> All are but parts of one stupendous whole,
> Whose body Nature is, and God the soul.
>
> *Pope.*

Nature is the living, visible garment of God. *Goethe.*

Never does Nature say one thing and Wisdom another. *Latin Proverb.*

Surely there is something in the unruffled calm of Nature that over-awes our little anxieties and doubts: the sight of the deep-blue sky, and the clustering stars above, seem to impart a quiet to the mind. *Jonathan Edwards.*

Nature is too thin a screen; the glory of the One breaks in everywhere. *Emerson.*

So, naturalists observe, a flea
Hath smaller fleas that on him prey;
And these have smaller still to bite 'em;
And so proceed *ad infinitum*.

Swift.

*   *   *

Philosophers

To be a philosopher is not merely to have subtle thoughts; but so to love wisdom as to live according to its dictates. *Thoreau.*

To be a husbandman, is but a retreat from the city; to be a philosopher, from the world; or rather a retreat from the world as it is man's, into the world as it is God's. *Cowley.*

The modern skeptical philosophy consists in believing everything but the truth, and exactly in proportion to the want of evidence; in making windows that shut out the light, and passages that lead to nothing. *Nisbet.*

True philosophy invents nothing; it merely establishes and describes what is. *Cousin.*

Philosophy can add to our happiness in no other manner but by diminishing our misery; it should not pretend to increase our present stock, but make us economists of what we are possessed of. Happy were we all born philosophers; all born with a talent of thus dissipating our own cares by spreading them upon all mankind. *Goldsmith.*

There are more things in heaven and earth, Horatio,
Than are dreamt of in your philosophy.

Shakespeare.

Philosophy did not find Plato already a nobleman, it made him one. *Seneca.*

The discovery of what is true, and the practice of that which is good, are the two most important objects of philosophy. *Voltaire.*

To philosophize in a just sense, is but to carry good breeding a step higher. For the accomplishment of breeding is, to learn what is decent in company or beautiful in arts; and the sum of philosophy is to learn what is just in society, and beautiful in nature and the order of the world. *Shaftesbury.*

Philosophy is the art of living. *Plutarch.*

Philosophy consists not in airy schemes or idle speculations; the rule and conduct of all social life is her great province. *Thomson.*

Philosophy is a bully that talks very loud, when the danger is at a distance; but the moment she is hard pressed by the enemy, she is not to be found at her post, but leaves the brunt of the battle to be borne by her humbler but steadier comrade, religion. *Colton.*

Adversity's sweet milk, philosophy. *Shakespeare.*

Philosophy is the science which considers truth. *Aristotle.*

A man gazing on the stars is proverbially at the mercy of the puddles on the road. *Alexander Smith.*

Philosophy is to poetry, what old age is to youth; and the stern truths of philosophy are as fatal to the fictions of the one, as the chilling testimonies of experience are to the hopes of the other. *Colton.*

The idea of philosophy is truth; the idea of religion is life. *Peter Bayne.*

Philosophy is one thing, and Christianity quite another. The former seeks to cure the vices of human nature by educating the heart Both endeavor to lead men to what is right; but philosophy only explains what it is right to do, while Christianity undertakes to make men disposed to do it. *Ecce Homo.*

To study philosophy is nothing but to prepare one's self to die. *Cicero.*

Philosophy does the going, and wisdom is the goal. *Latin Proverb.*

The first business of a philosopher is, to part with self-conceit. *Epictetus.*

Philosophy, when superficially studied, excites doubt; when thoroughly explored. it dispels it. *Bacon.*

Philosophy, if rightly defined, is nothing but the love of wisdom. *Cicero.*

It is easy for men to write and talk like philosophers, but to act with wisdom, there is the rub! *Rivarol.*

To enjoy freedom, be the slave of philosophy. *Latin Proverb.*

Philosophy is of two kinds: that which relates to conduct, and that which relates to knowledge. The first teaches us to value all things at their real worth, to be contented with little, modest in prosperity, patient in trouble, equal-minded at all times. It teaches us our duty to our neighbor and ourselves. But it is he who possesses both that is the true philosopher. The more he knows, the more he is desirous of knowing; and yet the farther he advances in knowledge, the better he understands how little he can attain, and the more deeply he feels that God alone can satisfy the infinite desires of an immortal soul. To understand this is the height and perfection of philosophy. *Southey.*

*   *   *

Poets

Poetry is the art of substantiating shadows, and of lending existence to nothing. *Burke.*

Poetry is music in words: and music is poetry in sound: both excellent sauce, but those have lived and died poor who made them their meat. *Fuller.*

Words become luminous when the poet's finger has passed over them its phosphorescence. *Joubert.*

A poet must needs be before his own age, to be even with posterity. *J. R. Lowell.*

Sad is his lot who, once at least in his life, has not been a poet. *Lamartine.*

Poetry is not made out of the understanding. The question of common sense is always: "What is it good for?" a question which would abolish the rose, and be triumphantly answered by the cabbage. *J. R. Lowell.*

By poetry we mean the art of employing words in such a manner as to produce an illusion on the imagination; the art of doing by means of words, what the painter does by means of colors. *Macaulay.*

Poetry is truth in its Sunday clothes. *French Proverb.*

> Sir, I admit your general rule,
> That every poet is a fool;
> But you yourself may serve to show it,
> That every fool is not a poet.
>
> *Pope.*

Poetry reveals to us the loveliness of nature, brings back the freshness of youthful feeling, revives the relish of simple pleasures, keeps unquenched the enthusiasm which warmed the springtime of our being, refines youthful love, strengthens our interest in human nature, by vivid delineations of its tenderest and softest feelings, and, through the brightness of its prophetic visions, helps faith to lay hold on the future life. *Channing.*

> Would you have your songs endure?
> Build on the human heart.
>
> *Browning.*

Poetry is the sister of sorrow; every man that suffers and weeps, is a poet; every tear is a verse; and every heart a poem. *André.*

Poets utter great and wise things which they do not themselves understand. *Plato.*

> Seven wealthy towns contend for Homer dead,
> Through which the living Homer begged his bread.
>
> *Dryden.*

Poetry is the record of the best and happiest moments of the happiest and best minds. *Shelley.*

Publishing a volume of verse is like dropping a rose-petal down the Grand Canyon and waiting for the echo. *Don Marquis.*

All that is best in the great poets of all countries is not what is national in them, but what is universal. *Longfellow.*

Poetry comes nearer to vital truth than history. *Plato.*

One merit of poetry few persons will deny; it says more, and in fewer words, than prose. *Voltaire.*

* * *

Politicians and Statesmen

If ever this free people—if this government itself is ever utterly demoralized, it will come from this incessant human wriggle and struggle for office, which is but a way to live without work. *Abraham Lincoln.*

When connected with morality and the character and interest of a country, politics is a subject second only to religion in importance. *Charles Hodge.*

Nothing is politically right which is morally wrong. *Daniel O'Connell.*

How little do politics affect the life, the moral life of a nation. One single good book influences the people a vast deal more. *Gladstone.*

An honest politician is one who, when he is bought, will stay bought. *Simon Cameron.*

Responsibility educates, and politics is but another name for God's way of teaching the masses ethics, under the responsibility of great present interests. *Wendell Phillips.*

There is an infinity of political errors which, being once adopted, become principles. *Abbé Raynal.*

All political parties die at last by swallowing their own lies. *Arbuthnot.*

To be a chemist you must study chemistry; to be a lawyer or a physician you must study law or medicine; but to be a politician you need only to study your own interests. *Max O'Rell.*

Any party which takes credit for the rain must not be surprised if its opponents blame it for the drought. *Morrow.*

People vote their resentment, not their appreciation. The average man does not vote for anything, but against something. *Munro.*

I hate all bungling as I do sin, but particularly bungling in politics, which leads to the misery and ruin of many thousands and millions of people. *Goethe.*

All politics is Apple Sauce. *Will Rogers.*

Politics is the science of exigencies. *Theodore Parker.*

Some have said that it is not the business of private men to meddle with government—a bold and dishonest saying, which is fit to come from no mouth but that of a tyrant or a slave. To say that private men have nothing to do with government is to say that private men have nothing to do with their own happiness or misery; that people ought not to concern themselves whether they be naked or clothed, fed or starved, deceived or instructed, protected or destroyed. *Cato.*

Politics—a rotten egg; if broken open, it stinks. *Russian Proverb.*

Every political question is becoming a social question, and every social question is becoming a religious question. *R. T. Ely.*

A politician thinks of the next election; a statesman of the next generation. A politician looks for the success of his party; a statesman for that of his country. The statesman wishes to steer, while the politician is satisfied to drift. *J. F. Clarke.*

In politics, merit is rewarded by the possessor being raised, like a target, to a position to be fired at. *Bovee.*

Republics end through luxury; monarchies through poverty. *Montesquieu.*

True statesmanship is the art of changing a nation from what it is into what it ought to be. *W. R. Alger.*

The great difference between the real statesman and the pretender is, that the one sees into the future, while the other regards only the present; the one lives by the day, and acts on expediency; the other acts on enduring principles and for immortality. *Burke.*

How a minority,
Reaching majority,
Seizing authority,
Hates a minority.
                    L. H. Robbins.

Statesman, yet friend to truth! of soul sincere, in action faithful, and in honor clear, who broke no promise, served no private end, who gain'd no title, and who lost no friend; ennobled by himself, by all approved, praised, wept, and honored. *Pope.*

The three great ends for a statesman are: security to possessors, facility to acquirers, and liberty and hope to the people. *Coleridge.*

* * *

Scholars

The criterion of a scholar's utility is the number and value of the truths he has circulated, and the minds he has awakened. *Coleridge.*

One wise man's verdict outweighs all the fools'. *Browning.*

When a king asked Euclid whether he could not explain his art to him in a more compendious manner, he was answered that there was no royal way to geometry. Other things may be seized by might, or purchased with money, but knowledge is to be gained only by study, and study to be prosecuted only in retirement. *Johnson.*

A man doesn't begin to attain wisdom until he recognizes that he is no longer indispensable. *Admiral Byrd.*

The scholar who cherishes the love of comfort is not fit to be deemed a scholar. *Confucius.*

Mankind have a great aversion to intellectual labor, but, even supposing knowledge to be easily attainable, more people would be content to be ignorant than would take even a little trouble to acquire it. *Johnson.*

If common sense has not the brilliancy of the sun, it has the fixity of the stars. *Caballero.*

The more we study the more we discover our ignorance. *Shelley.*

Defer not till tomorrow to be wise,
Tomorrow's sun to thee may never rise.

Congreve.

Impatience of study is the mental disease of the present generation. *Johnson.*

Knowledge is proud that he has learn'd so much;
Wisdom is humble that he knows no more.

Cowper.

When God lets loose a great thinker on this planet, then all things are at risk. There is not a piece of science, but its flank may be turned tomorrow; nor any literary reputation, nor the so-called eternal names of fame, that may not be revised and condemned. *Emerson.*

If a man empties his purse into his head, no one can take it from him. *Franklin.*

Wisdom is never dear, provided the article be genuine. *Horace Greeley.*

He bids fair to grow wise who has discovered that he is not so. *Publilius Syrus.*

Intellect is invisible to the man who has none. *Schopenhauer.*

Many persons might have attained to wisdom had they not assumed that they already possessed it. *Seneca.*

Common sense is the knack of seeing things as they are, and doing things as they ought to be done. *C. E. Stowe.*

*   *   *

Scientists

The highest reach of human science is the recognition of human ignorance. *Sir W. Hamilton.*

Science is nothing but perception. *Plato.*

Science ever has been, and ever must be, the safeguard of religion. *Sir David Brewster.*

Don't hesitate to be as revolutionary as science. Don't hesitate to be as reactionary as the multiplication table. *Calvin Coolidge.*

I will frankly tell you that my experience in prolonged scientific investigations convinces me that a belief in God—a God who is behind and within the chaos of vanishing points of human knowledge —adds a wonderful stimulus to the man who attempts to penetrate into the regions of the unknown. *Agassiz.*

> Nature and Nature's laws lay hid in night
> God said, let Newton be,—and all was light.
> > *Pope on Newton.*

The person who thinks there can be any real conflict between science and religion must be either very young in science or very ignorant in religion. *Prof. Henry.*

Every great scientific truth goes through three stages. First, people say it conflicts with the Bible. Next they say it had been discovered before. Lastly, they say they always believed it. *Agassiz.*

The study of science teaches young men to think, while study of the classics teaches them to express thought. *J. S. Mill.*

* * *

Speeches and Speechmaking

Speech is a faculty given to man to conceal his thoughts. *Talleyrand.*

According to Solomon, life and death are in the power of the tongue; and as Euripides truly affirmeth, every unbridled tongue in the end shall find itself unfortunate; in all that ever I observed I ever found that men's fortunes are oftener made by their tongues than by their virtues, and more men's fortunes overthrown thereby, also, than by their vices. *Sir Walter Raleigh.*

Take care of the sense and the sounds will take care of themselves. *Lewis Carroll.*

Speeches cannot be made long enough for the speakers, nor short enough for the hearers. *Perry.*

There is no eloquence without a man behind it. *Emerson.*

What a long time you take to say nothing, Cinna! *Martial.*

It is usually said by grammarians, that the use of language is to express our wants and desires; but men who know the world hold that he who best knows how to keep his necessities private, is the most likely person to have them redressed; and that the true use of speech is not so much to express our wants as to conceal them. *Goldsmith.*

There is a wide difference between speaking to deceive, and being silent to be impenetrable. *Voltaire.*

Never is the deep, strong voice of man, or the low, sweet voice of woman, finer than in the earnest but mellow tones of familiar speech, richer than the richest music, which are a delight while they are heard, which linger still upon the ear in softened echoes, and which, when they have ceased, come, long after, back to memory, like the murmurs of a distant hymn. *Henry Giles.*

As the man, so is his speech. *Proverb.*

Charm us, orator, till the lion look no larger than the cat. *Tennyson.*

Why do you wrap up your neck in a woolen muffler when you are going to recite? The muffler would be more suitable for our ears. *Martial.*

First think, and then speak. *Proverb.*

The common fluency of speech in many men, and most women, is owing to a scarcity of matter and a scarcity of words; for whoever is a master of language and has a mind full of ideas, will be apt in speaking to hesitate upon the choice of both; whereas common speakers have only one set of ideas, and one set of words to clothe them in; and these are always ready at the mouth; so people come faster out of a church when it is almost empty, than when a crowd is at the door. *Swift.*

I don't know whether Phoebus fled from the dinner-table of Thyestes: at any rate, Ligurinus, we flee from yours. Splendid, indeed, it is, and magnificently supplied with good things, but when you recite you spoil it all. I don't want you to set before me a turbot or a two-pound mullet: I don't want your mushrooms or your oysters. I want you to keep your mouth shut! *Martial.*

One may think what he dare not speak. *Proverb.*

Rhetoric is nothing but reason well dressed, and argument put in order. *Jeremy Collier.*

Speak and speed: the close mouth catches no flies. *Proverb.*

It was justly said by Themistocles that speech is like tapestry unfolded, where the imagery appears distinct; but thoughts, like tapestry in the bale, where the figures are rolled up together. *Bacon.*

Sheridan once said of some speech, in his acute, sarcastic way, that "it contained a great deal both of what was new and what was true; but that what was new was not true, and what was true was not new." *Hazlitt.*

A good talker or writer is only a pitcher. Unless his audience catches him with heart and mind he's defeated. *Wilson Mizner.*

There are three things that ought to be considered before some things are spoken—the manner, the place, and the time. *Southey.*

Speaking without thinking is shooting without aiming. *Proverb.*

A printed speech is like a dried flower: the substance, indeed, is there, but the color is faded and the perfume gone. *Lorain.*

Young man, thy words are like the cypress, tall and large, but they bear no fruit. *Phocion.*

A sentence well couched takes both the sense and the understanding. I love not those cart-rope speeches that are longer than the memory of man can measure. *Feltham.*

A man's character is revealed by his speech. *Proverb.*

Never rise to speak till you have something to say; and when you have said it, cease. *Witherspoon.*

Gentlemen, you have just been listening to that Chinese sage, On Too Long. *Will Rogers.*

Speech both reveals and conceals the thoughts of men. *Proverb.*

Speech is silvern, silence is golden; speech is human, silence is divine. *German Proverb.*

As a vessel is known by the sound, whether it be cracked or not, so men are proved by their speeches whether they be wise or foolish. *Demosthenes.*

There are three things to aim at in public speaking; first to get into your subject, then to get your subject into yourself, and lastly, to get your subject into your hearers. *Gregg.*

The words of his mouth were smoother than butter, but war was in his heart: his words were softer than oil, yet were they drawn swords. *Psalms 55:21.*

Let any man speak long enough, he will get believers. *Stevenson.*

Speak but little and well if you would be esteemed a man of merit. *Trench.*

As it is the characteristic of great wits to say much in few words, so it is of small wits to talk much and say nothing. *la Rochefoucauld.*

There are braying men in the world as well as braying asses; for, what's loud and senseless talking and swearing, any other than braying. *l'Estrange.*

He who speaks, sows; who listens, reaps. *Proverb.*

It is of eloquence as of a flame; it requires matter to feed it, and motion to excite it; and it brightens as it burns. *Tacitus.*

A wise man reflects before he speaks; a fool speaks, and then reflects on what he has uttered. *Delile.*

A word fitly spoken is like apples of gold in pictures of silver. *Proverbs 25:11.*

Nothing produces such an effect as a good platitude. *Oscar Wilde.*

As empty vessels make the loudest sound, so they that have least wit are the greatest babblers. *Plato.*

The talkative listen to no one, for they are ever speaking. And the first evil that attends those who know not how to be silent is that they hear nothing. *Plutarch.*

Many a man's tongue shakes out his master's undoing.

*　　*　　*

What a spendthrift he is of his tongue.

Shakespeare.

> What is an epigram? a dwarfish whole,
> Its body brevity, and wit its soul.
> *Coleridge.*

We often say things because we can say them well, rather than because they are sound and reasonable. *Landor.*

There are many who talk on from ignorance rather than from knowledge, and who find the former an inexhaustible fund of conversation. *Hazlitt.*

He is a good orator who convinces himself. *Proverb.*

If thy words be too luxuriant, confine them, lest they confine thee. He that thinks he can never speak enough, may easily speak too much. A full tongue and an empty brain are seldom parted. *Quarles.*

> An epigram is but a feeble thing
> With straw in tail, stuck there by way of sting.
> *Cowper.*

It has been said in praise of some men, that they could talk whole hours together upon anything; but it must be owned to the honor of the other sex, that there are many among them who can talk whole hours together upon nothing. *Addison.*

An orator's virtue is to speak the truth. *Proverb.*

... out of the abundance of the heart the mouth speaketh. *St. Matthew 12:34.*

Gratiano speaks an infinite deal of nothing; his reasons are as two grains of wheat hid in two bushels of chaff; you shall seek all day ere you find them, and when you have them they are not worth the search. *Shakespeare.*

Labor to show more wit in discourse than words, and not to pour out a flood of the one, when you can hardly wring out of your brains a drop of the other. *Spencer.*

Every absurdity has a champion to defend it, for error is always talkative. *Goldsmith.*

He draweth out the thread of his verbosity finer than the staple of his argument. *Shakespeare.*

No fool can be silent at a feast. *Solon.*

When I was a child I used to think it was the thunder that killed people; as I grew older I found it was only the lightning that struck, and the noise of thunder was only noise. *Anon.*

Free and fair discussion will ever be found the firmest friend to truth. *G. Campbell.*

It is an excellent rule to be observed in all discussions, that men should give soft words and hard arguments; that they should not so much strive to silence or vex, as to convince their opponents. *Wilkins.*

> Three things must epigrams, like bees, have all,
> A sting, and honey, and a body small.
>
> *Latin distich.*

He who knows only his own side of the case, knows little of that. *J. Stuart Mill.*

He that is not open to conviction, is not qualified for discussion. *Whately.*

Eloquence is the child of knowledge. *Proverb.*

An epigram is a gag that's played Carnegie Hall. *Oscar Levant.*

Whosoever is afraid of submitting any question, civil or religious, to the test of free discussion, is more in love with his own opinion than with truth. *T. Watson.*

True eloquence scorns eloquence. *Pascal.*

Men are never so likely to settle a question rightly, as when they discuss it freely. *Macaulay.*

> He misses what is meant by epigram
> Who thinks it only frivolous flim-flam.
> > *Martial.*

Reply with wit to gravity, and with gravity to wit. Make a full concession to your adversary; give him every credit for the arguments you know you can answer, and slur over those you feel you cannot. But above all, if he have the privilege of making his reply, take especial care that the strongest thing you have to urge be the last. *Colton.*

An epigram is a half truth so stated as to irritate the person who believes the other half. *Matthews.*

Do not use thyself to dispute against thine own judgment to show thy wit, lest it prepare thee to be indifferent about what is right; nor against another man to vex him, or for mere trial of skill, since to inform or be informed ought to be the end of all conferences.

* * *

Where judgment has wit to express it, there is the best orator. *Penn.*

Everyone is eloquent in his own cause. *Proverb.*

. . . He that hath ears to hear, let him hear. *St. Mark 4:9.*

He is the eloquent man who can treat subjects of an humble nature with delicacy, lofty things impressively, and moderate things temperately. *Cicero.*

It is the first rule in oratory that a man must appear such as he would persuade others to be; and that can be accomplished only by the force of his life. *Swift.*

He is eloquent enough for whom truth speaks. *Proverb.*

Every man should study conciseness in speaking; it is a sign of ignorance not to know that long speeches, though they may please the speaker, are the torture of the hearer. *Feltham.*

What too many orators want in depth, they give you in length. *Montesquieu.*

There is no power like that of true oratory. Caesar controlled men by exciting their fears; Cicero, by captivating their affections and swaying their passions. The influence of the one perished with its au-thor; that of the other continues to this day. *Henry Clay.*

In oratory, the greatest art is to conceal art. *Swift.*

An epigram often flashes light into regions where reason shines but dimly. *E. P. Whipple.*

An orator without judgment is a horse without a bridle. *Theophrastus.*

Orators are most vehement when they have the weakest cause, as men get on horseback when they cannot walk. *Cicero.*

The effective public speaker receives from his audience in vapor, what he pours back on them in a flood. *Gladstone.*

Eloquence is vehement simplicity. *Cecil.*

The language of the heart which comes from the heart and goes to the heart is always simple, graceful, and full of power, but no art of rhetoric can teach it. It is at once the easiest and most difficult lan-guage—difficult, since it needs a heart to speak it; easy, because its periods though rounded and full of harmony, are still unstudied. *Bovee.*

It is the heart which makes men eloquent. *Proverb.*

An orator or author is never successful till he has learned to make his words smaller than his ideas. *Emerson.*

In oratory, affectation must be avoided, it being better for man, by a native and clear eloquence to express himself, than by those words which may smell either of the lamp or the inkhorn. *Lord Herbert.*

Oratory, like the drama, abhors lengthiness; like the drama, it must keep doing. Beauties themselves, if they delay or distract the effect which should be produced on the audience, become blemishes. *Bulwer.*

The elegance of the style, and the turn of the periods make the chief impression upon the hearers. Most people have ears, but few have judgment; tickle those ears, and depend upon it, you will catch their judgments such as they are. *Chesterfield.*

Talk often, but never long. *Proverb.*

Oratory is the huffing and blustering spoiled child of a semibarbarous age. The press is the foe of rhetoric, but the friend of reason; and the art of declamation has been sinking in value from the moment that speakers were foolish enough to publish, and readers wise enough to read. *Colton.*

True eloquence consists in saying all that is proper, and nothing more. *la Rochefoucauld.*

Brevity is a great charm of eloquence. *Cicero.*

It is but a poor eloquence which only shows that the orator can talk. *Sir Joshua Reynolds.*

The truest eloquence is that which holds us too mute for applause. *Bulwer.*

Those who would make us feel, must feel themselves. *Churchill.*

No man ever did, or ever will become most truly eloquent without being a constant reader of the Bible, and an admirer of the purity and sublimity of its language. *Fisher Ames.*

Eloquence is in the assembly, not merely in the speaker. *William Pitt.*

Eloquence is logic on fire. *Lyman Beecher.*

Eloquence is the transference of thought and emotion from one heart to another, no matter how it is done. *John B. Gough.*

There is not less eloquence in the voice, the eye, the gesture, than in words. *la Rochefoucauld.*

If any thing I have ever said or written deserves the feeblest encomiums of my fellow countrymen, I have no hesitation in declaring that for their partiality I am indebted, solely indebted, to the daily and attentive perusal of the Sacred Scriptures, the source of all true poetry and eloquence, as well as of all good and all comfort. *Daniel Webster.*

Speech is the body, thought, the soul, and suitable action the life of eloquence. *C. Simmons.*

Talking and eloquence are not the same. To speak and to speak well are two things. A fool may talk, but a wise man speaks. *Ben Jonson.*

True eloquence does not consist in speech. It cannot be brought from far. Labor and learning may toil for it in vain. Words and phrases may be marshalled in every way, but they cannot compass it. It must consist in the man, in the subject, and in the occasion. *Daniel Webster.*

The manner of speaking is full as important as the matter, as more people have ears to be tickled than understanding to judge. *Chesterfield.*

The pleasure of eloquence is, in greatest part, owing often to the stimulus of the occasion which produces it—to the magic of sympathy which exalts the feeling of each, by radiating on him the feeling of all. *Emerson.*

Honesty is one part of eloquence. We persuade others by being in earnest ourselves. *Hazlitt.*

* * *

Success—Fame—Reputation

The man who succeeds above his fellows is the one who, early in life, clearly discerns his object, and towards that object habitually directs his powers. Even genius itself is but fine observation strengthened by fixity of purpose. Every man who observes vigilantly and resolves steadfastly grows unconsciously into genius. *Bulwer.*

Success is full of promise till men get it, and then it is as a last year's nest, from which the bird has flown. *H. W. Beecher.*

Every man who is high up loves to think that he has done it all himself; and the wife smiles, and lets it go at that. *J. M. Barrie.*

Success soon palls. The joyous time is when the breeze first strikes your sails, and the waters rustle under your bows. *Charles Buxton.*

The gent who wakes up and finds himself a success hasn't been asleep. *Wilson Mizner.*

To know a man, observe how he wins his object, rather than how he loses it; for when we fail, our pride supports; when we succeed, it betrays us. *Colton.*

Herein the only royal road to fame and fortune lies:
Put not your trust in vinegar—molasses catches flies!
Eugene Field.

He that has never known adversity, is but half acquainted with others, or with himself. Constant success shows us but one side of the world. For, as it surrounds us with friends, who will tell us only our merits, so it silences those enemies from whom alone we can learn our defects. *Colton.*

After a feller gits famous it don't take long fer some one t' bob up that used t'set by him at school. *Kin Hubbard.*

It is success that colors all in life: success makes fools admired, makes villains honest: all the proud virtue of this vaunting world fawns on successs and power, howe'er acquired. *Thomson.*

If fame is only to come after death, I am in no hurry for it. *Martial.*

Nothing succeeds so well as success. *Talleyrand.*

Glory arrives too late when it comes only to one's ashes. *Martial.*

Let them call it mischief; when it is past and prospered, it will be virtue. *Ben Jonson.*

How prudently we proud men compete for nameless graves, while now and then some starveling of Fate forgets himself into immortality. *Wendell Phillips.*

The way to fame is like the way to heaven, through much tribulation. *Sterne.*

Nor Fame I slight, nor for her favors call;
She comes unlooked for, if she comes at all.
Pope.

Of present fame think little, and of future less; the praises that we receive after we are buried, like the flowers that are strewed over our grave, may be gratifying to the living, but they are nothing to the dead; the dead are gone, either to a place where they hear them not, or where, if they do, they will despise them. *Colton.*

There is not in the world so toilsome a trade as the pursuit of fame: life concludes before you have so much as sketched your work. *Bruyère.*

He that pursues fame with just claims, trusts his happiness to the winds; but he that endeavors after it by false merit, has to fear, not only the violence of the storm, but the leaks of his vessel. *Johnson.*

The temple of fame stands upon the grave; the flame upon its altars is kindled from the ashes of the dead. *Hazlitt.*

Our admiration of a famous man lessens upon our nearer acquaintance with him; and we seldom hear of a celebrated person without a catalogue of some of his weaknesses and infirmities. *Addison.*

I am not covetous for gold; but if it be a sin to covet honor, I am the most offending soul alive. *Shakespeare.*

Fame is a flower upon a dead man's heart. *Motherwell.*

Milton neither aspired to present fame, nor even expected it. His high ambition was (to use his own words), "To leave something so written, to after ages, that they should not willingly let it die." And Cato finally observed, he would much rather posterity should ask why no statues were erected to him, than why they were. *Colton.*

He who would acquire fame must not show himself afraid of censure. The dread of censure is the death of genius. *Simms.*

Men's evil manners live in brass; their virtues we write in water. *Shakespeare.*

No true and permanent fame can be founded except in labors which promote the happiness of mankind. *Charles Sumner.*

A really great man is known by three signs—generosity in the design, humanity in the execution, moderation in success. *Bismarck.*

Great minds have purposes, others have wishes. *Washington Irving.*

A contemplation of God's works, a generous concern for the good of mankind, and the unfeigned exercise of humility—these only denominate men great and glorious. *Addison.*

Difficulty is a nurse of greatness—a harsh nurse, who rocks her foster children roughly, but rocks them into strength and athletic proportions. The mind, grappling with great aims and wrestling with mighty impediments, grows by a certain necessity to the stature of greatness. *Bryant.*

Great men are meteors designed to burn so that the earth may be lighted. *Napoleon.*

The superiority of some men is merely local. They are great because their associates are little. *Johnson.*

Not a day passes over the earth but men and women of no note do great deeds, speak great words, and suffer noble sorrows. Of these obscure heroes, philosophers, and martyrs the greater part will never be known till that hour when many that were great shall be small, and the small great. *Charles Reade.*

No man has come to true greatness who has not felt in some degree that his life belongs to his race, and that what God gives him he gives him for mankind. *Phillips Brooks.*

> Not that the heavens the little can make great,
> But many a man has lived an age too late.
> *R. H. Stoddard.*

Subtract from the great man all that he owes to opportunity, all that he owes to chance, and all that he has gained by the wisdom of his friends and the folly of his enemies, and the giant will often be seen to be a pigmy. *Colton.*

Great men never made bad use of their superiority; they see it, and feel it, and are not less modest. The more they have, the more they know their own deficiencies. *Rousseau.*

He who is great when he falls is great in his prostration, and is no more an object of contempt than when men tread on the ruins of sacred buildings, which men of piety venerate no less than if they stood. *Seneca.*

Times of general calamity and confusion have ever been productive of the greatest minds. The purest ore is produced from the hottest furnace, and the brightest thunderbolt is elicited from the darkest storm. *Colton.*

What millions died that Caesar might be great. *Campbell.*

High stations tumult, not bliss create. None think the great unhappy, but the great. *Young.*

Some are born great; some achieve greatness; and some have greatness thrust upon them. *Shakespeare.*

He who comes up to his own idea of greatness, must always have had a very low standard of it in his mind. *Ruskin.*

The man who does his work, any work, conscientiously, must always be in one sense a great man. *Mulock.*

Reputation is what men and women think of us; character is what God and angels know of us. *Paine.*

The solar system has no anxiety about its reputation. *Emerson.*

The way to gain a good reputation, is, to endeavor to be what you desire to appear. *Socrates.*

It is a sign that your reputation is small and sinking, if your own tongue must praise you. *Matthew Hale.*

Reputation, reputation, reputation! Oh, I have lost my reputation! I have lost the immortal part of myself; and what remains is bestial. *Shakespeare.*

Good will, like a good name, is got by many actions, and lost by one. *Jeffrey.*

One may be better than his reputation, but never better than his principles. *Latena.*

I would to God thou and I knew where a commodity of good names were to be bought. *Shakespeare.*

In all the affairs of this world, so much reputation is, in reality, so much power. *Tillotson.*

There are two modes of establishing our reputation: to be praised by honest men, and to be abused by rogues. It is best, however, to secure the former, because it will invariably be accompanied by the latter. *Colton.*

Reputation is sometimes as wide as the horizon, when character is but the point of a needle. Character is what one really is; reputation what others believe him to be. *H. W. Beecher.*

A man's reputation is not in his own keeping, but lies at the mercy of the profligacy of others. Calumny requires no proof. *Hazlitt.*

Reputation is an idle and most false imposition, oft got without merit, and lost without deserving. *Shakespeare.*

Associate with men of good quality, if you esteem your own reputation; it is better to be alone than in bad company. *Washington.*

*   *   *

Teachers

The true aim of every one who aspires to be a teacher should be, not to impart his own opinions, but to kindle minds. *F. W. Robertson.*

In the education of children there is nothing like alluring the interest and affection; otherwise you only make so many asses laden with books. *Montaigne.*

Whatever you would have your children become, strive to exhibit in your own lives and conversation. *Mrs. Sigourney.*

Teachers should be held in the highest honor. They are the allies of legislators; they have agency in the prevention of crime; they aid in regulating the atmosphere, whose incessant action and pressure cause the life-blood to circulate, and to return pure and healthful to the heart of the nation. *Mrs. Sigourney.*

> Charming women can true converts make,
> We love the precepts for the teacher's sake.
>
> *George Farquhar.*

The one exclusive sign of a thorough knowledge is the power of teaching. *Aristotle.*

K

Delightful task, to rear the tender thought; to teach the young idea how to shoot, to pour fresh instruction over the mind, to breathe the enlivening spirit, and to fix the generous purpose in the glowing heart. *Thomson.*

The teacher who is attempting to teach without inspiring the pupil with a desire to learn is hammering on cold iron. *H. Mann.*

Those who educate children well are more to be honored than even their parents, for these only give them life, those the art of living well. *Aristotle.*

Do not train boys to learning by force and harshness; but direct them to it by what amuses their minds, so that you may be the better able to discover with accuracy the peculiar bent of the genius of each. *Plato.*

The best teacher is the one who suggests rather than dogmatizes, and inspires his listener with the wish to teach himself. *Bulwer.*

The method of teaching which approaches most nearly to the method of investigation, is incomparably the best; since, not content with serving up a few barren and lifeless truths, it leads to the stock on which they grew. *Burke.*

If ever I am a teacher, it will be to learn more than to teach. *Mme. Deluzy.*

If, in instructing a child, you are vexed with it for want of adroitness, try, if you have never tried before, to write with your left hand, and then remember that a child is all left hand. *J. F. Boyse.*

Let our teaching be full of ideas. Hitherto it has been stuffed only with facts. *Anatole France.*

He that governs well, leads the blind; but he that teaches, gives him eyes; and it is glorious to be a sub-worker to grace, in freeing it from some of the inconveniences of original sin. *South.*

What sculpture is to a block of marble, education is to the human soul. The philosopher, the saint, the hero, the wise, and the good, or the great, very often lie hid and concealed in a plebeian, which a proper education might have disinterred and brought to light. *Addison.*

Education does not mean teaching people to know what they do not know; it means teaching them to behave as they do not behave. *Ruskin.*

Knowledge does not comprise all which is contained in the large term of education. The feelings are to be disciplined; the passions are to be restrained; true and worthy motives are to be inspired; a profound religious feeling is to be instilled, and pure morality inculcated under all circumstances. All this is comprised in education. *Daniel Webster.*

The object of teaching a child is to enable him to get along without his teacher. *Elbert Hubbard.*

He is to be educated not because he is to make shoes, nails, and pins, but because he is a man. *Channing.*

Education is only like good culture; it changes the size, but not the sort. *H. W. Beecher.*

A true education aims to implant a love of knowledge; an adherence to truth because it is truth; a reverence for man because he is a man; an enthusiasm for liberty; a spirit of candor, of breadth, of sympathy; and, above all, a supreme regard for duty. *H. L. Wayland.*

X Educate men without religion, and you make them but clever devils. *Wellington.*

Next in importance to freedom and justice is popular education, without which neither justice nor freedom can be permanently maintained. *Garfield.*

The teacher is one who makes two ideas grow where only one grew before. *Elbert Hubbard.*

The true object of education should be to train one to think clearly and act rightly. *H. J. Van Dyke.*

Education is a better safeguard of liberty than a standing army. If we retrench the wages of the schoolmaster, we must raise those of the recruiting sergeant. *Everett.*

An industrious and virtuous education of children is a better inheritance for them than a great estate. *Addison.*

The real object of education is to give children resources that will endure as long as life endures; habits that time will ameliorate, not destroy; occupations that will render sickness tolerable, solitude pleasant, age venerable, life more dignified and useful, and death less terrible. *Sydney Smith.*

He that has found a way to keep a child's spirit easy, active, and free, and yet at the same time to restrain him from many things he has a mind to, and to draw him to things that are uneasy to him, has, in my opinion, got the true secret of education. *Locke.*

Neither piety, virtue, nor liberty can long flourish in a community where the education of youth is neglected. *Cooper.*

The sure foundations of the State are laid in knowledge, not in ignorance; and every sneer at education, at culture, and at book-learning which is the recorded wisdom of the experience of mankind, is the demagogue's sneer at intelligent liberty, inviting national degeneracy and ruin. *G. W. Curtis.*

You demand universal suffrage—I demand universal education to go with it. *W. E. Forster.*

Public instruction should be the first object of government. *Napoleon.*

No woman is educated who is not equal to the successful management of a family. *Burnap.*

All who have meditated on the art of governing mankind have been convinced that the fate of empires depends on the education of youth. *Aristotle.*

Do not ask if a man has been through college; ask if a college has been through him—if he is a walking university. *E. H. Chapin.*

If we work upon marble, it will perish; if on brass, time will efface it; if we rear temples, they will crumble into dust; but if we work upon immortal minds, and imbue them with principles, with the just fear of God and love of our fellow men, we engrave on those tablets something that will brighten to all eternity. *Daniel Webster.*

It is on the sound education of the people that the security and destiny of every nation chiefly rest. *Kossuth.*

'Tis education forms the common mind; just as the twig is bent the tree is inclined. *Pope.*

Better untaught than ill taught. *Proverb.*

He that teaches himself has a fool for his master. *Proverb.*

He who can, does. He who cannot, teaches. *G. B. Shaw.*

We loved the doctrine for the teacher's sake. *Proverb.*

* * *

Travelers—Explorers

All travel has its advantages. If the traveller visits better countries, he may learn to improve his own; and if fortune carries him to worse, he may learn to enjoy his own. *Johnson.*

Usually speaking, the worst bred person in company is a young traveller just returned from abroad. *Swift.*

> How much a dunce that has been sent to roam
> Excels a dunce that has been kept at home!
> > *Cowper.*

The bee, though it finds every rose has a thorn, comes back loaded with honey from his rambles, and why should not other tourists do the same. *Halliburton.*

It is not worth while to go round the world to count the cats in Zanzibar. *Thoreau.*

The travelled mind is the catholic mind, educated out of exclusiveness and egotism. *A. B. Alcott.*

The vagabond, when rich, is called a tourist. *Paul Richard.*

If a goose flies across the sea, there comes back a quack-quack. *German Proverb.*

He who never leaves his own country is full of prejudices. *Goldoni.*

The world is a great book, of which they who never stir from home read only a page. *Augustine.*

See one mountain, one sea, one river—and see all. *Greek Proverb.*

*   *   *

Wedding Anniversaries

Marriage is of a date prior to sin itself—the only relic of paradise that is left us—a smile of God on the world's innocence, lingering and playing still upon it. It was first celebrated by God Himself: and thus religion blessed her two children, and led them forth into life to begin its wondrous history. They learned to love Him as the sealer and interpreter of their love to each other; and if they had continued in their uprightness, life would have been a permanent form of wedded worship, a sacred mystery of spiritual oneness and communion. *Horace Bushnell.*

To be man's tender mate was woman born, and in obeying Nature she best serves the purposes of heaven. *Schiller.*

One of the good things that come of a true marriage is, that there is one face on which changes come without your seeing them; or rather there is one face which you can still see the same, through all the shadows which years have gathered upon it. *G. Macdonald.*

Take the daughter of a good mother. *Fuller.*

I chose my wife, as she did her wedding gown, for qualities that would wear well. *Goldsmith.*

If it were not for the Presents, an Elopement would be Preferable. *George Ade.*

Marriage is not a union merely between two creatures—it is a union between two spirits; and the intention of that bond is to perfect the nature of both, by supplementing their deficiencies with the force of contrast, giving to each sex those excellencies in which it is naturally deficient; to the one, strength of character and firmness of moral will; to the other, sympathy, meekness, tenderness; and just so solemn and glorious as these ends are for which the union was intended, just so terrible are the consequences if it be perverted and abused; for there is no earthly relationship which has so much power to ennoble and to exalt. There are two rocks, in this world of ours, on which the soul must either anchor or be wrecked—the one is God, and the other is the sex opposite. *F. W. Robertson.*

Two persons who have chosen each other out of all the species, with the design to be each other's mutual comfort and entertainment, have, in that action, bound themselves to be good-humored, affable, discreet, forgiving, patient, and joyful, with respect to each other's frailties and perfections, to the end of their lives. *Addison.*

Take not too short a time, to make a world-wide bargain in. *Shakespeare.*

Married in haste, we repent at leisure. *Congreve.*

The Christian religion, by confining marriage to pairs, and rendering the relation indissoluble, has by these two things done more toward the peace, happiness, settlement, and civilization of the world, than by any other part in this whole scheme of divine wisdom. *Burke.*

It is always incomprehensible to a man that a woman should refuse an offer of marriage. *Austen.*

A great proportion of the wretchedness which has embittered married life, has originated in the negligence of trifles. Connubial happiness is a thing of too fine a texture to be handled roughly. It is a sensitive plant, which will not bear even the touch of unkindness; a delicate flower, which indifference will chill and suspicion blast. It must be watered by the showers of tender affection, expanded by the cheering glow of kindness, and guarded by the impregnable barrier of unshaken confidence. Thus matured, it will bloom with fragrance in every season of life, and sweeten even the loneliness of declining years. *Sprat.*

Deceive not thyself by over-expecting happiness in the married state. Look not therein for contentment greater than God will give, or a creature in this world can receive, namely, to be free from all inconveniences. Marriage is not like the hill of Olympus, wholly clear, without clouds. *Fuller.*

Marriage has many pains, but celibacy has few pleasures. *Johnson.*

Marriage has in it less of beauty, but more of safety, than the single life; it hath not more ease, but less danger; it is more merry and more sad; it is fuller of sorrows and fuller of joys; it lies under more burdens, but is supported by all the strengths of love and charity; and those burdens are delightful. Marriage is the mother of the world, and preserves kingdoms, and fills cities and churches, and heaven itself. *Jeremy Taylor.*

The institution of marriage keeps the moral world in being, and secures it from an untimely dissolution. Without it, natural affection and amiableness would not exist, domestic education would become extinct, industry and economy be unknown, and man would be left to the precarious existence of the savage. But for this institution, learning and refinement would expire, government sink into the gulf of anarchy; and religion, hunted from earth, would hasten back to her native heavens. *T. Dwight.*

Oh, friendly to the best pursuits of man, friendly to thought, to virtue, and to peace, domestic life in rural leisure passed! Few know thy value, and few taste thy sweets. *Cowper.*

In the opinion of the world marriage ends all, as it does in a comedy. The truth is precisely the reverse, it begins all. *Mme. Swetchine.*

When it shall please God to bring thee to man's estate, use great providence and circumspection in choosing thy wife. For from thence will spring all thy future good or evil; and it is an action of life, like unto a stratagem of war, wherein a man can err but once! *Sir P. Sidney.*

A married man falling into misfortune is more apt to retrieve his situation in the world than a single one, chiefly because his spirits are soothed and retrieved by domestic endearments, and his self-respect kept alive by finding that although all abroad be darkness and humiliation, yet there is a little world of love at home over which he is a monarch. *Jeremy Taylor.*

Save the love we pay to heaven, there is none purer, holier, than that a virtuous woman feels for him she would cleave to through life. Sisters part from sisters, brothers from brothers, children from their parents, but such a woman from the husband of her choice, never! *Knowles.*

God has set the type of marriage everywhere throughout the creation. Every creature seeks its perfection in another. The very heavens and earth picture it to us. *Luther.*

One should believe in marriage as in the immortality of the soul. *Balzac.*

O marriage! marriage! what a curse is thine, where hands alone consent, and hearts abhor! *A. Hill.*

But happy they, the happiest of their kind, whom gentle stars unite; and in one fate their hearts, their fortunes, and their beings blend! *Thomson.*

A good wife is like the ivy which beautifies the building to which it clings, twining its tendrils more lovingly as time converts the ancient edifice into a ruin. *Johnson.*

When a man and woman are married their romance ceases and their history commences. *Rochebrune.*

There is more of good nature than of good sense at the bottom of most marriages. *Thoreau.*

The honeymoon is not actually over until we cease to stifle our sighs and begin to stifle our yawns. *Rowland.*

In the career of female fame, there are few prizes to be obtained which can vie with the obscure state of a beloved wife, or a happy mother. *Jane Porter.*

Men should keep their eyes wide open before marriage, and half shut afterward. *Mme. Scuderi.*

The sanctity of marriage and the family relation makes the cornerstone of our American society and civilization. *Garfield.*

What greater thing is there for two human souls than to feel that they are joined for life—to strengthen each other in all labor, to rest on each other in all sorrow, to minister to each other in all pain, to be one with each other in silent, unspeakable memories at the moment of the last parting. *George Eliot.*

K*

The surest way to hit a woman's heart is to take aim kneeling. *Douglas Jerrold.*

> That man that hath a tongue, I say, is no man,
> If with his tongue he cannot win a woman.
>
> *Shakespeare.*

Courtship consists in a number of quiet attentions, not so pointed as to alarm, nor so vague as not to be understood. *Sterne.*

Respect is what we owe; love, what we give. *Philip J. Bailey.*

We are shaped and fashioned by what we love. *Goethe.*

The supreme happiness of life is the conviction of being loved for yourself, or, more correctly, being loved in spite of yourself. *Victor Hugo.*

Love is the most terrible, and also the most generous, of the passions; it is the only one which includes in its dreams the happiness of someone else. *Alphonse Karr.*

*   *   *

Youth

Young men have a passion for regarding their elders as senile. *Henry Adams.*

Youth is the gay and pleasant spring of life, when joy is stirring in the dancing blood, and nature calls us with a thousand songs to share her general feast. *Ridgeway.*

Youth is the period of building up in habits, and hopes, and faiths. Not an hour but is trembling with destinies; not a moment, once passed, of which the appointed work can ever be done again, or the neglected blow struck on the cold iron. *Ruskin.*

Youth is the opportunity to do something and to become somebody. *T. T. Munger.*

> In sorrow he learned this truth—
> One may return to the place of his birth,
> He cannot go back to his youth.
>
> *John Burroughs.*

Youth is the season of hope, enterprise, and energy, to a nation as well as an individual. *W. R. Williams.*

Youth, with swift feet, walks onward in the way; the land of joy lies all before his eyes. *Bulwer.*

The excesses of our youth are drafts upon our old age, payable with interest, about thirty years after date. *Colton.*

> Life is but thought; so think I will,
> That youth and I are house-mates still.
>
> Coleridge.

The majority of men employ the first portion of their life in making the other portion miserable. *La Bruyère.*

In the morning of our days, when the senses are unworn and tender, when the whole man is awake in every part, and the gloss of novelty is fresh upon all the objects that surround us, how lively at that time are our sensations, but how false and inaccurate the judgments we form of things! *Burke.*

As I approve of a youth that has something of the old man in him, so I am no less pleased with an old man that has something of the youth. He that follows this rule may be old in body, but can never be so in mind. *Cicero.*

Youth holds no society with grief. *Aristotle.*

Youth is a wonderful thing. What a crime to waste it on children. *G. B. Shaw.*

The youth gets together his materials to build a bridge to the moon, or, perchance, a palace or temple on the earth, and, at length, the middle-aged man concludes to build a woodshed with them. *Thoreau.*

Whilst the morning shines, gather the flowers. *Latin Proverb.*

Unless a tree has borne blossoms in spring, you will vainly look for fruit on it in autumn. *Hare.*

My salad days, when I was green in judgment. *Shakespeare.*

The fairest flower in the garden of creation is a young mind, offering and unfolding itself to the influence of divine wisdom, as the heliotrope turns its sweet blossoms to the sun. *J. E. Smith.*

The self-conceit of the young is the great source of those dangers to which they are exposed. *Blair.*

Which of us that is thirty years old has not had his Pompeii? Deep under ashes lies the life of youth—the careless sport, the pleasure and passion, the darling joy. *Thackeray.*

No young man believes he shall ever die. *Hazlitt.*

Girls we love for what they are; young men for what they promise to be. *Goethe.*

I have often thought what a melancholy wo... this would be without children, and what an inhuman world without the aged. *Coleridge.*

I love little children, and it is not a slight thing when they, who are fresh from God, love us. *Dickens.*

It is good to be children sometimes · better than at Christmas, when its mighty Four elf. *Dickens.*

Childhood h othed by no memories

into the arms of 'se. *Emerson.*

hild is about a

'oubert.

'der they

CHAPTER 9

HUMOROUS STORIES FOR ALL OCCASIONS

"HELLO, JOE"

"PERKINS, Parkins, Peckham, and Potts—good morning."

"I want to speak with Mr. Perkins."

"Who's calling, please?"

"Mr. Pincham, of Pincham, Pettam, Poppum, and Potter."

"Just one moment, please. I'll connect you with Mr. Perkins' office."

"Hello, Mr. Perkins' office."

"I want to speak to Mr. Perkins."

"Mr. Perkins? I'll see if he's in. Who's calling, please?"

"Mr. Pincham."

"Just one moment. Here's Mr. Perkins. Put Mr. Pincham on, please."

"Just one moment, please. I have Mr. Pincham right here. O.K. with Perkins, Parkins, Peckham, and Potts, Mr. Pincham. Go ahead."

" 'Lo, Joe? How's about lunch?"

"O.K."

A PROBLEM

"Now, what we gwine do 'bout dat billy goat in de crate, boss?" asked the colored employee at the express office. "He's done et whar he's gwine!"

NO MORE BRAGGING

"Is your son's college education of any real value?"

"Yes, indeed. It has cured his mother of bragging about him."

COMPETITION

A young doctor and a young dentist shared the services of a receptionist and both fell in love with her.

The dentist was called away on business, so he sent for the receptionist and said: "I am going to be away for ten days. You will find a little present in your room."

She went in and found ten apples.

SALESMANSHIP

The life-insurance agent called upon a big businessman at the close of a busy day. When the agent had been admitted, the big fellow said:

"You ought to feel honored, highly honored, young man. Do you know that today I refused to see several insurance agents?"

"I know," said the agent. "I'm them."

PLENTY BIG ENOUGH

Friend: "That wasn't a very big account of your daughter's wedding in the paper this morning."

Father (sadly): "No, the big account was sent to me."

PAID IN FULL

A man received a big check for services rendered, and discovered that it was one penny short. A stickler for detail, he insisted that the difference be paid—and in due course received another check for the single penny. He presented it for payment at his bank.

The teller examined it closely and then asked, "How would you like this, sir? Heads or tails?"

GOOD PAY

Johnny, ten years old, applied for a job as grocery boy for the summer. The grocer wanted a serious-minded youth, so he put Johnny to a little test.

"Well, my boy, what would you do with a million dollars?" he asked.

"Oh, gee, I don't know—I wasn't expecting so much at the start."

SATISFIED

Personnel Director: "Have you any reference?"

Applicant: "Sure, here's the letter: 'To Whom it may concern. John Jones worked for us one week and we're satisfied.' "

OPENED BY MISTAKE

Wife: "Let me see that letter you've just opened. I can see from the handwriting it's from a woman and you turned pale when you read it."

Husband: "You can have it. It's from your milliner."

ORDEAL

Two Irishmen met. Said the first, "How are you, Mike?"

"Terrible, terrible!" replied the other. "It is shtarvation that is staring me in the face."

"Is that so," said the other. "It couldn't be very pleasant for aither of ye, I'm shure!"

HOLD IT, PLEASE

Photographer: "Please smile and watch for the little birdie."

Modern Youngster: "Oh, drop that 'little birdie' stuff! Get out your light meter and make some tests, adjust your lighting properly, and set your lens correctly so you won't ruin a sensitized plate."

GOOD PRECEDENT

Mrs. (belligerently): "Do you think I'm going to wear this old squirrel coat all my life?"

Mr. (brightly): "Why not, dear? The squirrels do."

NEXT CASE

Judge: "Have you ever been up before me?"
Accused: "I don't know, Judge. What time do you get up?"

OPPORTUNIST

"As soon as I realized it was a crooked business, I got out of it."
"How much?"

NOT HIS TERRITORY

Diner (beckoning waiter): "Is it raining outside?"
Waiter: "Sorry, sir, but this is not my table."

HE WAS ELIGIBLE

"I told the club they were a set of blind, stupid, obstinate, unmitigated asses."

"And what did they do?"

"They made me an honorary member."

EYE FOR AN EYE

Four young men visiting the Orient before the war, considering themselves exceedingly clever, had a Chinese servant upon whom they played all sorts of pranks. One night they nailed his shoes to the floor. But there was not a word of complaint nor sign of retaliation. He brought them their coffee as usual, smiling as he came.

The next day they put sand in the Chinese bed. But when he brought them their coffee, there was no resentment in his attitude, and he smiled as usual.

So the young men decided they would play no more tricks on a good fellow like that, and they told him so.

"No more nailee shoes to floor?" asked the Chinese.

"No."

"No more putee sand in bed?"

"No."

"Very well," he agreed, with a genuine Chinese smile. "Then no more putee mud in coffee."

THAT REMINDS ME

A traveler just home from abroad was describing an earthquake. "Most amazing thing I ever saw," he said dramatically. "The hotel rocked. Cups and saucers were flying all over the room, and—"

His meek-looking companion turned suddenly white. "Great Scott!" he cried. "That reminds me. I forgot to post a letter my wife gave me two days ago."

INFLATION

Lady: "How much are those tomatoes?"

Grocer: "Thirty-five a pound, ma'am."

Lady: "Did you raise them yourself?"

Grocer: "Yes, they were thirty cents a pound yesterday."

COULD USE THEM!

"The new baby has its father's nose and its mother's eyes."

"Yes, and if Grandpop doesn't stop leaning over the crib, it's going to have his teeth."

INCOMPETENT

Senator George McLean of Connecticut was Chairman of the Banking and Currency Committee. He was frankly disappointed and disgusted when President Harding sent forth the nomination of an old crony—rather than a well-qualified banker—for a high position on the Federal Reserve Board.

"What do you think of this nomination?" an inquiring Washington correspondent asked him.

"Why, I think it is a darn outrage," the crusty New Englander replied. "Moreover, every Senator on the Hill feels the same way about it."

"If that is the case," the correspondent said, "why don't you Senators rear up on your hind legs and refuse to confirm him?"

"My God, young man," Senator McLean replied, "we can't refuse to confirm a man merely because he is incompetent!" *Finance.*

YOU'RE TELLING ME!

On Christmas Eve, Jones was discovered by Brown trying to shove a horse onto his doorstep.

"Give a hand, old man," he pleaded. Brown, wondering, did so. They pushed the horse into the hall.

"Now just let's get him up the stairs." So they pushed and shoved.

"Now into the bathroom," said Jones.

When they had got the horse safely in, Jones closed the door softly.

"Why? Why? why?" asked Brown.

"I'll tell you," said Jones. "I've got a brother-in-law who lives with us and knows everything. But when he goes up to bathe to-

morrow, he'll shout down: 'Hey, there's a horse in the bathroom';
and for the first time I'll be able to shout back: 'You're tellin' me.' "

TO THE HEAD OF THE CLASS

Teacher: "Bobby, what is an oyster?"
Bobby: "It's a fish built like a nut."

PIPE DOWN

Professor Albert Einstein, in the course of a newspaper interview,
offered his idea of success in life in the following formula: "If a is
success in life, I should say that the formula is a equals x plus y plus
z, x being work and y being play."

"And what is z?" asked the reporter.

"That," replied the great scientist, with a laugh, "is keeping your
mouth shut."

TRUTH

Foreman: "How long have you been working here?"
Apprentice: "Ever since you came in the door."

A LARGE GROUP

A man was looking for a good church to attend and happened
into a small one in which the congregation was reading with the
minister. They were saying: "We have left undone those things we
ought to have done, and we have done those things which we ought
not to have done."

The man dropped into a seat and sighed with relief as he said to
himself: "Thank goodness, I've found my crowd at last."

FORE AND FOUR

Jones is devoted to golf and his wife is equally fond of auction
sales. They both talk in their sleep. The other night the people in
the next apartment heard him shout, "Fore!" and immediately his
wife yelled, "Four and a quarter!"

A SHOCKING STORY

A certain village paper had not been able to print any sensational
news for weeks, when during an electrical storm a live wire fell

across Main Street. Everyone feared to go near it. The city editor sent out two reporters. One to touch the wire and the other to write the story.

HIS EQUAL

Husband: "I passed Joe on the street yesterday and he refused to recognize me. Thinks I'm not his equal, I guess."

Wife: "You certainly are his equal! He's nothing but a bluffing, conceited idiot!"

YOU KNOW THE ANSWER

A man said he feared he would be of no use in the world because he had only one talent.

"Oh, don't let that discourage you," said his pastor. "What is your talent?"

"The talent of criticism," was the answer.

"Well," replied the pastor, "I advise you to do with it what the man of one talent in the parable did with his."

BINGO!

In his announcement one Sunday morning the minister regretted that money was not coming in quickly enough—but he was no pessimist.

"We have tried," he said, "to raise the necessary money in the usual manner. We have tried honestly. Now we are going to see what a bazaar can do."

SLIGHT UNDERSTATEMENT

Said the Florida man, picking up a watermelon: "Is this the largest grapefruit you can grow in these parts?"

"Stop!" said the Californian. "You're crushing that raisin."

COURTESY

The Quaker had heard a strange noise in the night and, waking, found that a burglar was busy ransacking the living room.

Eliphalet took up his fowling piece, or, as it is called nowadays, shotgun, and addressed the startled intruder: "Friend, I would do thee no harm for this vile world, and all that is in it—but thee stands where I am about to shoot!"

The burglar decamped.

PERFECT UNDERSTANDING

"Who's calling?" was the answer to the telephone.

"Watt."

"What is your name, please?"

"Watt's my name."

"That's what I asked you. What's your name?"

"That's what I told you. Watt's my name."

A long pause, and then, from Watt, "Is this James Brown?"

"No, this is Knott."

"Please tell me your name."

"Will Knott."

Whereupon they both hung up.

GOOD MEMORY

"So you really think your memory is improving under treatment. You remember things now?"

"Well, not exactly, but I have progressed so far that I can frequently remember I have forgotten something, if I could only remember what it is."

FOREIGN MISSIONS

Gothamite: "I'm from New York. I suppose you do not know where New York is?"

Salt Lake Citizen: "Oh, yes, I do. Our Sunday school has a missionary there."

BE CALM

A passenger in an airplane was far up in the sky when the pilot began to laugh hysterically.

Passenger: "What's the joke?"

Pilot: "I'm thinking of what they'll say at the asylum when they find out I have escaped."

SELF-INDICTED

Missus (at height of quarrel): "They say marriage makes people look alike and now I even talk like you."

Mister: "Oh, for goodness sake don't talk like a fool."

DID SHE SEE THEM!

He had never been outside the United States, and neither had she, but both were recounting their experiences abroad.

"And Asia. Ah, wonderful Asia. Never shall I forget Turkey, India—all of them. And most of all China, the celestial kingdom. How I loved it!"

"And the pagodas—did you see them?"

She held her ground.

"Did I see them?" She powdered her nose. "My dear, I had dinner with them."

STATION ANNOUNCEMENT

Uncle (to six-year-old after church service): "And how did you like it, dear?"

"Six-Year-Old: "I liked the music, but the commercial was too long."

THAT EXPLAINS EVERYTHING

An ardent golfer was visiting a friend and playing golf at his friend's club. On the first tee, he took his stance, gave a wild swing, and missed completely. "Gosh," he said to his opponent, "it's a good thing I found out early in the game that this course is at least two inches lower than the one I usually play on."

TOO LATE

A professor at medical school asked a student how much of a certain drug should be administered to a patient and the young man replied, "Five grains."

A minute later he raised his hand. "Professor," he said, "I would like to change my answer to that question."

The professor looked at his watch and replied, "Never mind, young man, your patient has been dead for 40 seconds."

HE DID

Salesman: "I've been trying all week to see you; may I have an appointment?"

Big Businessman: "Make a date with my secretary."

Salesman: "I did, and we had a grand time, but I still want to see you."

SPEAKING FRANKLY

Novice, at Bridge Party: "You're an expert at bridge, Mr. Jones. How would you have played that last hand of mine?"

Mr. Jones: "Under an assumed name."

WHAT A VOICE

Singer: "How do you like my voice?"

Accompanist: "Lady, I've played the white keys. I've played the black keys. But you're the first one I ever saw that could sing in the cracks."

CORN-FED TURKEY

"Sam," said the colonel to his negro cook, "I'm having special company on Thursday and I want your best turkey dinner. Now, none of your wild fowl. Get me a domestic, corn-fed turkey. Do you understand?"

"Yah, suh; yah, suh," replied Sam.

Came the festive affair. Placed before the colonel was a beautiful turkey. He was pleased until he made a first cut. Then he frowned. Then a second cut. He held his knife and called his cook from the kitchen.

"Sam, didn't I tell you I wanted a domestic, corn-fed bird?"

"Yah, suh ; yah, suh—dat am a domestic, corn-fed bird."

"Well, then," said the colonel, "how about this buckshot?"

"Well, suh," said Sam, shuffling from one foot to the other, "yuh see, suh, dat shot war meant fer me!"

TO THE POINT

An English cub reporter, reprimanded for relating too many details, and warned to be brief, turned in the following:

"A shooting affair occurred last night. Sir Dwight Hopeless, a guest at Lady Penmore's ball, complained of feeling ill, took his hat, his coat, his departure, no notice of friends, a taxi, a pistol from his pocket, and finally his life. Nice chap. Regrets and all that sort of thing."

HE HAD SEEN THEM

An artist painting in the country had a farmer spectator.

"Ah," said the artist, "perhaps you too are a lover of the beauties of nature. Have you seen the golden fingers of dawn spreading across the eastern sky, the red-stained, sulphurous islets floating in the lake of fire in the west, the ragged clouds at midnight, blotting out the shuddering moon?"

"Nope," said the farmer, "not lately. I've been on the wagon for over a year."

TOO NOISY

The three men who were cronies became convinced the world was making too many demands on their time and energy, so they packed up, gave up their jobs, and went to a cabin in the North Woods. At the end of the first year, one remarked, "This quiet is enjoyable."

A year later the second remarked, "Yes."

At the end of the next year the third replied disgustedly, "If you two are going to keep on chattering, I'm going home."

SPEED

Two men were flying East in a passenger plane, making the first air trip of their lives. The plane touched down at St. Louis and a little red truck sped out to its side to refuel it. The plane landed again at Cleveland and again a little red truck dashed up to it. The third stop was Albany and the same thing happened. One man looked at his watch and turned to his companion.

"This plane," he said, "makes wonderful time."

"Yes," said the other, "and that little red truck ain't doin' so bad either."

SMART TRADER

"You got a good-looking hat, Bill."

"Yeah! Bought it five years ago, had it cleaned three times, changed it twice in restaurants—and it's still good as new."

WE DON'T BLAME HIM

A Philadelphian committed suicide and left the following note:

"I married a widow with a grown daughter. My father fell in love with my stepdaughter and married her—thus becoming my son-in-law, and my stepdaughter became my mother because she was my father's wife.

"My wife gave birth to a son, who was, of course, my father's brother-in-law and also my uncle for he was the brother of my stepmother.

"My father's wife became the mother of a son, who was, of course, my brother, and also my grandchild for he was the son of my daughter.

"Accordingly, my wife was my grandmother because she was my father's mother—I was my wife's husband and grandchild at the same time—and, as the husband of a person's grandmother is his grandfather, I am my own grandfather!"

WONDERFUL MAN

The newlyweds were honeymooning at the seashore. As they walked arm in arm along the beach, the young groom looked poetically out to sea and eloquently cried out: "Roll on, thou deep and dark blue ocean—roll!" His bride gazed at the water a moment, then in hushed tones gasped, "Oh, Fred, you wonderful man! It's doing it."

HARD WORKER

Foreman: "Hey, you! How come you're only carrying one sack? All the others are carrying two."

Worker: "Gee whiz, boss, guess the other guys are too lazy to make two trips like I do."

REAL ENTERTAINMENT

A salesman was passing through a small town and had several hours to while away. Seeing one of the natives, he inquired: "Any picture-show in town, my friend?"

"Nope, not one, stranger," was the answer.

"Any poolroom or bowling alley?"

"None of them, either," came the reply.

"What form of amusement have you here?" asked the salesman.

"Waal, come on down to the drugstore. Thar's a freshman home from the university."

WE HAD THE SAME TROUBLE

A little man walked to the box-office, bought a ticket, and went in. A few minutes later he returned, bought another ticket, and again went inside. Three times the same thing happened. By the fourth time the girl in the box office was completely perplexed and asked: "Why do you keep buying tickets to go into the theater?"

"It's not my fault," replied the little man. "They keep tearing them up every time I go inside."

WHO SAID THAT?

The army recently inducted a recruit of more than average literary education. On his first day at camp he was utterly exhausted after several hours of drilling.

"At ease," finally ordered the officer.

"How wonderful is death," muttered the recruit.

The officer turned instantly. "Who said that?" he demanded.

The culprit smiled weakly and replied: "Shelley, I believe, sir."

TRUTHFUL

Fisherman: "It was that long . . . Never saw such a fish in my life."

Friend: "That, I can believe."

NO SPLURGING

Extract from a noncommissioned officer's letter to his wife: "I have now been made a corporal, which is my first step up in the army's ladder of success. However, for the time being, please speak to the neighbors as usual and don't under any circumstances move to a larger house or buy a piano."

THERE'S ONE BORN EVERY MINUTE

P. T. Barnum, the great showman, once received a letter from a Vermonter offering him a cherry-colored cat for $600. Always on the lookout for a novelty for his show, Barnum sent the $600— after getting the man's solemn word that the creature was cherry colored. A crate arrived. Barnum opened it and a black cat jumped out. Around its neck was a ribbon and from the ribbon hung a note which read:

"Up in Vermont our cherries are black."

TO WHOM IT MAY CONCERN

A couple of colored boys were crouched in a shell hole while a barrage whanged away over their heads. "Looka' here, Rastus," said one. "Ain't you skeert?"

"Not me," boasted the other. "Ain't no shell gonna come along got my name on it."

"Me neither," says the first fellow. "I ain't worried about my name on no shell. What I *am* worried about is, maybe there's one marked 'To whom it may concern.' "

TOO TOUGH

"Say, waiter, is this an incubator chicken? It tastes like it."

"I don't know, sir."

"It must be. Any chicken that has had a mother could never get as tough as this one."

COMPLETELY LOST

First Husband: "My wife finds my money wherever I hide it."

Second Husband: "My wife never finds mine. I put it in the basket with my undarned socks."

HE HOT-FOOTED IT

First Farmer: "I see, by the paper, your boy at Iowa is a very fast runner. It says he 'fairly burned up' the track during the race yesterday. I suppose you were there, and saw him do it."

Second Farmer: "I was there all right, but got there too late for to see the race. However, I did see the track, and there was nothing but cinders."

MINDING HIS BUSINESS

First Traveler: "I see you have your arm in a sling. Broken?"

Second Traveler: "Yes, sir."

First: "Accident?"

Second: "No I tried to pat myself on the back."

First: "What for?"

Second: "For minding my own business."

INFORMATION PLEASE

Lady of the House: "Why don't you go to work? Don't you know that a rolling stone gathers no moss?"

Tramp: "Madam, not to evade your question at all, but merely to obtain information, may I ask what practical utility moss is to a man like me?"

YOU CAN SAY THAT AGAIN

Farmer (after the city boy had milked his first cow): "Well, you learned something new today."

City Boy: "Yes, I learned that the man who says a cow gives milk is a liar."

ARTICULATE

A silk-hosiery manufacturer and an aluminum-household-utensil manufacturer sat next to each other at the club. Both remained quiet for many minutes gazing with worried and beaten expressions into space. Finally, one of them gave vent to a long-drawn-out sigh. The other looked around sympathetically and said: "You're telling me."

PRACTICE MAY MAKE PERFECT

Husband: "I am going to discharge our chauffeur. Four times recently he almost killed me."

Wife: "Darling, give him another chance."

BACKWARD IN HER HOMEWORK

Visitor: "I must congratulate you on your daughter's brilliant paper on The Influence of Science on the Principles of Government."

Father: "Yes, and now I hope she will begin to study the influence of the vacuum cleaner on the carpet."

YOU SAID IT

"Women are not very strong physically."

"Perhaps not, but they can put the cap on a fruit jar so that it takes a man twenty minutes to take it off."

AGREEABLE

George: "I know my wife fooled me when we were engaged."

Robert: "Why, what do you mean?"

George: "Well, when I asked her to marry me, she said she was agreeable."

THEY'RE EASY TO GET

Young Wife: "What is this ticket, darling?"

Hubby: "Only a pawn ticket."

Young Wife: "Why didn't you get two, then we could both go?"

NOTICE IN ADVANCE

Prospective Father-in-law: "Young man, can you support a family?"

Bridegroom-to-be: "Well, no, sir. I was just planning to support your daughter. The rest of you will just have to shift for yourselves."

MISSED SOMETHING

Boss: "You should have been here at nine o'clock."

New Stenographer: "Why? What happened?"

SO WE'VE FOUND

"What do you find best for cleaning windows?"

"I have tried lots of things, but I find my husband best."

PEACE

Two women in a railway car argued about the window and at last called the porter as referee.

"If this window is open," one declared, "I shall catch cold and will die."

"If the window is shut," the other announced, "I shall certainly suffocate."

The two glared at each other. The porter was at a loss, but he welcomed the words of a man with a red nose who sat near. Said he:

"First open the window. That will kill one. Next, shut it. That will kill the other. Then we can have peace."

EXPERIENCE

"I guess my father must have been a pretty mischievous boy," said one youngster.

"Why?" inquired the other.

"Because he knows exactly what questions to ask when he wants to know what I have been doing."

WATER POWER

A delegate at a state convention had listened to a very long speech and as he saw the speaker reach for a glass of water he said to his neighbor, "That's the first windmill I have ever seen which ran by water."

NONSUPPORT

Dorothy Parker was bored by a talkative actress who hadn't had a part for years. "I simply can't think of leaving the theater," the woman gurgled. "I'm wedded to it."

"Then," retorted Miss Parker, "why not sue it for nonsupport?"

NO TROUBLE

In a gay mood, a man telephoned a friend at two o'clock in the morning. "I do hope I haven't disturbed you," he said cheerily.

"Oh, no," the friend replied. "I had to get up to answer the telephone anyway."

THEY DO

Wife: "I think married men should wear something to show they're married."

Husband: "I do—this shiny suit."

CORRECT

The school teacher was taking her first golfing lesson. "Is the word spelled p-u-t or p-u-t-t?" she asked the instructor.

"P-u-t-t is correct," he replied. "Put means to place a thing where you want it. Putt means merely a vain attempt to do the same thing."

TRUTH IN ADVERTISING

Californian: "Now in my state we can grow a tree that size in about a year. How long did it take you to grow that one?"

Floridian: "Can't say for sure, but it wasn't there yesterday."

HONESTY

Rastus (throwing down four aces): "Dar, guess I wins dis time, all right."

Sambo (angrily): "You play dis game honest; play it honest! I knows what cards I dealt you!"

EXPERIENCE

Husband: "You're terribly extravagant. If anythir g should happen to me, you would probably have to beg."

Wife: "I'd get by. Look at all the experience I've had."

MODESTY

She: "Handsome men are always conceited."
He: "Not always. I'm not."

JUST A PAL

"He said you weren't fit to sleep with the pigs."
"And I suppose you pulled the old gag and said that I was."
"No, I stuck up for the pigs."

BUSY

"Grandma, do you have to take all those different kinds of pills every day?"

"Yes, Betty. Yellow ones for my liver, pink ones for my stomach, black ones for my heart, orange ones for my nerves."

"Well, Grandma, what are the red ones for—to direct traffic?"

NOTICE TO THE TREASURY

Brown: "So you took a five-hundred-dollar exemption on your income tax for the new bride?"

White: "Yes—and where you fill in your dependents I wrote 'Watch this space!'"

LOOKING AHEAD

Each time I pass a church,
I always pay a visit;
So when at last I'm carried in,
The Lord won't say, "Who is it?"

SMALL BUSINESS

Judge: "Now, John, did you have an assistant when you committed that burglary?"

John: "Naw, sir, boss. I never makes enough to hire a helper."

TYRO

Two negro soldiers were on a transport going overseas. Standing on the deck they gazed out across the vast expanse of water.

"That's the mos' water I've eber seen in all my life," said one. "Did yo' eber see so much water?"

Said his companion: "Yo' ain't seen nothin' yet. That's jus' the top ob it."

THE FIRST 100 YEARS ARE THE HARDEST

A curious tourist in the Ozarks inquired of an aged man sunning himself in front of a general store: "Just how old are you?"

Aged Man: "I'm jest a hundred."

Tourist: "Well, I doubt that you'll see another hundred."

Aged Man (dryly): "I ain't so sure about that. I'm stronger now than when I started my first hundred years."

AMATEUR GARDENER

New Suburban Gardener: "I don't seem able to tell my garden plants from weeds. How do you distinguish between them?"

Old Suburban Gardener: "The only sure way is pull 'em out. If they come up again, they're weeds."

CONSIDERATE

Prof.: "If there are any dumbbells in the room, please stand up."

A long pause, then a lone freshman stood up.

Prof.: "What! Do you consider yourself a dumbbell?"

Freshman: "Well, not exactly that, sir, but I hate to see you standing all alone."

TACT ALSO

"Pa," said Henry, looking from the book he was reading, "what is meant by 'diplomatic phraseology'?"

"Well," replied Pa, "if you were to say to a homely girl, 'Your face would stop a clock,' that would be stupidity, but if you said to her, 'When I look into your eyes, time stands still,' that would be diplomatic phraseology!"

BAD EXAMPLE

"Say, Pop, did you go to Sunday school when you were a little boy?"

"Yes, son—regularly."

"I'll bet it won't do me any good, either."

WE KNOW THE RAILROAD

A minister, traveling on one of those way-trains that stop at every station on the side line, was reading his Bible.

"Find anything about the railroad in that book?" asked the conductor, as he reached for the minister's ticket.

"Yes," replied the minister. "In the very first chapter it says that the Lord made every creeping thing."

AN ECONOMIST

"I'm glad you're so impressed, dear, by all these explanations I have been giving you about banking and economics," remarked the young husband.

"Yes, darling. It seems wonderful that anybody could know as much as you do about money without having any."

MISTAKEN IDENTITY

"Did my wife speak at the meeting yesterday?"

"I don't know your wife, but there was a tall, thin lady who rose and said she could not find words to express her feelings."

"That wasn't my wife."

HE KNEW

Lady (to tramp): "You would stand a better chance of getting a job if you would shave, cut your hair, and clean yourself up."

Tramp, to lady: "Yes'm. I found that out."

LIFE

If a man runs after money, he's a materialist. If he keeps it, he's a capitalist. If he spends it, he's a playboy. If he doesn't get it, he lacks ambition. If he gets it without working, he's a parasite. If he gets it after a life of hard labor, he's a fool who got nothing out of life.

SLOW THINKER

"I hadn't been talking to the fellow for more than five minutes when he called me a fool."

"What caused the delay?"

HE SITS LOOSE

An old darky down South was ninety-odd years of age and still in good health. Someone asked him how he kept so well at his time of life.

"Well, Captain Tom," he said, "when I works, I works hard, but when I sits, I sits loose."

L

WISH TO BE ANONYMOUS

Some time ago at a state democratic convention, where the noted newspaperman, William Allen White, was among the scribes reporting the news, the presiding democratic chairman said: "I fail to see any clergyman here, so I shall call on Mr. William Allen White to open the convention with a prayer."

White, who was a staunch republican, arose and said: "You will have to excuse me. I am not up on public praying, and the fact of the matter is, I prefer that the Lord doesn't know that I am here."

SETTLING DOWN

Professor: "I won't begin today's lecture until the room settles down."

Voice from the Rear: "Go home and sleep it off, old man."

CAUTIOUS

Rastus: "Where you goin', boy?"

Sambo: "I'se down to git myself some tuberculosis stamps."

Rastus: "What is dey? I ain't never heard tell of 'em."

Sambo: "Every year I gits myself fifty cents' worth of dem tuberculosis stamps and sticks dem on mah chest and I ain't never had tuberculosis yet."

MISTAKEN

A young woman boarded a crowded bus. A tired little man got up and gave her his seat. There was a moment of silence.

"I beg your pardon?" said the tired little man.

"I didn't say anything," rejoined the young woman.

"I'm sorry," said the little man. "I thought you said, 'Thank you.' "

MORE VICE PRESIDENTS

Office Boy: "I think I know what's wrong with this country."

Bank Executive: "What's that, son?"

Office Boy: "We are trying to run this country with only one vice-president."

DISCRIMINATION

"I hear you have broken your engagement to Joe because your feelings toward him aren't the same. Are you going to return his ring?"

"Oh, no. My feelings toward the ring are the same as ever."

WORRIES

Two old Scotsmen were sitting in the park talking and puffing away on their pipes.

"There's not so much pleasure in smokin', Sandy," said Mac.

"And why not, mon?" asked Sandy.

"Weel," replied Mac, "ye see, if ye're smokin' yer own t'bacca ye're thinkin' of the terrible expense, and if ye're smokin' some ither body's, yer pipe's rammed sae tight it winna draw."

YOU'RE IN THE ARMY NOW

The energetic sergeant was lecturing the new recruits:

"Here it is Monday morning and tomorrow will be Tuesday and the next day Wednesday—half the week gone and you guys don't know anything yet. Snap to!"

MODERN YOUTH

Grandfather: "Isn't it time for a little boy to go to bed?"

Freddy (eight years old): "I do not know, grandfather. And it doesn't interest me, as I have no children."

ITEMIZED ACCOUNT

A colored man, doing a hauling job, was told that he couldn't get his money until he submitted a statement. After much meditation he evolved the following bill:

"Three comes and three goes, at four bits a went, $3."

ACQUITTED

A seemingly stupid young fellow was being bullied in cross-examination. "Do you ever work?" demanded the attorney.

"Not much," the witness agreed.

"Have you ever earned as much as ten dollars in one week?"

"Ten dollars? Yeah. A couple of times."

"Is your father regularly employed?"

"Nope."

"Isn't it true that he's a worthless good-for-nothing, too?"

"I don't know about that," said the witness. "But you might ask him. He's sittin' there on the jury."

THIRTY DAYS

Judge: "Was the rock as large as my fist?"

Defendant: "Yassah, Jedge, it was dat big and maybe a little bigger."

Judge: "Was it as big as my two fists?"

Defendant: "Yassuh, Jedge, I 'spect it was bigger dan dat."

Judge: "Was it as large as my head?"

Defendant: "Jedge, it was as long, but I don't think it was as thick."

WHAT'S THE ANSWER?

A woman when launching her first ship was a little nervous. She turned to the shipyard manager, standing beside her, and asked: "How hard do I have to hit it to knock it into the water?"

BUYER OR SELLER

"You can take it as an elementary conception that when an article is sold it goes to the buyer," said Mr. Winter in the economics class.

"With the exception of coal," chirped the bright third-former.

"And why coal?" asked Mr. Winter.

"When that's bought, it goes to the cellar."

MANNERS

Herbert had been taught to rise when his mother came into a room, and to remain thus until she was seated or had left.

One day he had a friend with him when his mother arrived. He stood up, but his friend did not move, so Herbert asked him to do so.

A few minutes later his mother entered again, and the same procedure was gone through. When Herbert's mother entered for the third time, her son rose and the young guest asked, "I say, does your mother think she's the national anthem?"

SILLY

A man received a letter the contents of which irritated him very much. He rushed over to a telegraph office and wrote out the following wire, requesting the operator to rush it to the writer of the letter: "Piffle. Piffle. Piffle. Piffle. Piffle. Piffle. Piffle. Piffle. Piffle." The operator said, "You know you can send ten words as cheaply as nine. You can send another word without extra charge."

The man replied, "Well, I can't think of another word." She suggested, "You might add another 'Piffle.'"

He thought about it for a moment and then said, "Well, that would sound silly."

DIFFERENT

"I knew an artist who painted a cobweb so realistically that the maid spent several hours trying to get it down from the ceiling."

"I just don't believe it."

"Why not? Artists have been known to do such things."

"Yes, but not maids."

HE LEARNT THEM

"Well, dear, and what did Mamma's little baby learn in school today?"

"I learnt two kids not to call me 'Mamma's little baby.'"

IN BOTH SENSES

Joseph Chitty, the famous English judge, was one day listening to a particularly uninteresting case. It dealt with household goods and agricultural implements. After talking about the implements until the court was nearly asleep, the lawyer remarked: "And now, my lord, I will address myself to the furniture."

"You have been doing that for an hour already," replied the learned judge.

REFRESHED

A young author was introduced to a movie critic in the large city. The writer's first picture had just been shown on Broadway, and he immediately asked the critic what his opinion was.

"It was refreshing," returned the critic. "Very refreshing."

"Say, that's swell," beamed the young author. "Did you really find it so refreshing?"

"Absolutely," was the reply. "I felt like a new man when I woke up!"

DIFFERENT ENVIRONMENT

Vacationist: "Any big men born here?"

Native: "Nope. Not very progressive 'round here; best we kin do is babies. Diff'rent in the city, I s'pose."

TOO MUCH CHARACTER

"Did you do what I said an' ask the bank manager for a loan on the strength of your character?"

"Yes, an' he refused it on the strength of his."

SEEING DOUBLE

Second (to boxer): "Well, old man, I'm afraid you're licked now."

Boxer (gazing dizzily across to the opposite corner): "Yeah, I should have got him in the first round when he was alone."

LIKES HIS JOB

"It's not the work I enjoy," said the taxicab driver, "it's the people I run into."

STEWARDS

Dr. Ralph W. Sockman, pastor of Christ Church, New York City, tells the following interesting story:

We Americans, you know, when we start to think back to our basic philosophy of life come back to that foundation that is basically religious. Whatever you may say about the founders of this country, they had one overwhelming belief. They believed in the sovereignty of God. Rather whimsical proof of that came to my attention, perhaps to yours, out of a New Orleans law office. It seems that a New York law firm was trying to clear the title to a piece of property in New Orleans and it got the title back to 1803. That didn't satisfy the New York lawyer so he asked the New Orleans attorney to have the title cleared further back. The New Orleans attorney wrote him this letter: "Please be advised that in the year 1803 the United States of America acquired title to the Territory of Louisiana from the Republic of France by purchase, the Republic of France having first acq..:ed title from the government of Spain by conquest, the government of Spain having originally acquired title by virtue of the discovery of Christopher Columbus, a Genoese sailor who, before setting out on his voyage of discovery, received the support of Queen Isabella of Spain, Queen Isabella having first secured the sanction of his Holiness, the Pope. The Pope is the Vicar of Jesus Christ; Jesus is the Son of God; God made Louisiana." I suppose that lawyer got it back about where it belongs. When we cut down through all these titles of property, all these labels of government, we come back to the basic proposition that everything we have came from God and we are stewards of it.

NEXT TIME SHE WILL STAND

Two glamour girls boarded a crowded streetcar, and one of them whispered to the other: "Watch me get a seat from a male passenger."

Pushing her way through the straphangers she turned her charms upon a gentleman who looked embarrassable. "My dear Mr. Brown," she gushed loudly, "fancy meeting you on the streetcar. Am I glad to see you! My, but I'm tired!"

The sedate gentleman looked up at the girl, whom he had never before seen, and as he rose said pleasantly, "Sit down, Bertha, my girl. It isn't often that I see you out on washday. No wonder you're tired. By the way, don't deliver the washing till Wednesday. My wife is going to the district attorney's office to see whether she can get your husband out of jail!"

DAFFYNITION

Bachelor—A man who has been crossed in love. A married man is one who has been double-crossed.

ACCEPTANCE SPEECH

Best Acceptance Speech—Upon receiving a beautiful silver gift a famous baseball player picked it up and simply said, "Shore is pretty," and sat down.

HE FOLLOWED INSTRUCTIONS

Then there's the rookie who took the sergeant's advice and put on a clean pair of socks every day. A week passed by. "Where are your shoes?" snarled the sergeant. "I can't get them on over seven pairs of socks," replied the rookie. *Camp Blanding (Fla.) Para Blasts.*

SPEED

A famous minstrel man has related this story of a conversation he overheard in Fort Worth some years ago. Two Negro men were discussing the subject of speed.

Said one of the darkies: "You claims you is fast! You says you's so fast folks calls you Speedy! Jest how fast is you, boy?"

"I'll tell you how fast I is," replied the other. "In my room dere's jes' an electric light, and it's twenty feet from ma baid. Come night time, I kin walk over to dat 'lectric light, turn it out, git into baid and be all covered up befo' de room gits dark."

CLOSE SCHEDULE

A Northern passenger on a small Mississippi River steamboat in the deep South was considerably perturbed when he heard the captain say his craft would be delayed some four or five hours, pending arrival of some expected cargo. He sought out the officer and expressed his regret that the craft would be late in arriving at New Orleans.

"Late?" said the captain. "Why I reckon we'll get in 'bout on time."

"But I just heard you say we'd be delayed here for four or five hours."

"Shucks," said the placid riverman, "we don't run on a schedule as close as all that."

EDUCATION

"A young lady who used to live next door to us," writes the editor of *The Postage Stamp*, "is out in Montana helping to instruct the Indians in grammar. We've heard from her recently, and she was pretty discouraged up until the other day. The only really loyal students she has are Mr. and Mrs. Bear-Don't-Walk. The others are continually bolting classes. She didn't think she was getting any place even with the dogged Bear-Don't-Walks, until she learned that this family had just applied to the Indian Agent to change its name to Bear-Doesn't-Walk."

ORDER IN THE COURT

The *Houston (Texas) Press* style book admonishes reporters against the use of clichés and bromides. Among the examples is the word "bailiff."

"Don't write 'bailiff of the court.' What else can there be a bailiff of?"

"Hay," an office wag scrawled in with pencil. *Editor & Publisher.*

HIS PROBLEM

"My advice to you Mr. Brown, is to go through the movements of driving without using the ball," said the golf instructor.

"My dear fellow," answered Mr. Brown, "that's precisely the trouble I'm trying to overcome!"

SPORTING CHANCE

As a hunter, Irvin S. Cobb, the famous author, was not exactly a Daniel Boone.

One day Mr. Cobb went duck hunting. His guide rowed him to a likely spot and soon a flock of ducks settled on the water at a most convenient distance.

Cobb aimed his gun.

"You mustn't do that, Mr. Cobb," warned the guide.

"Do what?" said the mighty hunter.

"Shoot when the ducks are on the water. You must wait until they rise."

"Why?"

"You must give them a sporting chance."

"Sporting chance," laughed Cobb. "They always get a sporting chance when *I* shoot!"

THE EASY WAY

Dorothy: "I have a very literary boy friend. He recommended Einstein's *The Theory of Relativity* as a most interesting book."

Lou: "Excellent! And have you read it yet?"

Dorothy: "No, I'm waiting for it to come out in the movies, first." *Pathfinder.*

GOLDWYNIANA

Film Producer Samuel Goldwyn usually succeeds in having his own way. Some time ago he and another producer got into an argument over the services of a well-known writer.

Goldwyn insisted that the writer belonged to him. The other claimed the scenarist. Finally, after hours of debate, the rival producer suggested that they submit the dispute to arbitration.

"All right," said Goldwyn. "I'll agree to arbitration. Nobody can say I'm not fair. But remember—no matter what the outcome he goes to work for me!" *Milwaukee Journal.*

IT WOULD HAVE BEEN SMARTER

The gentleman left his country club slightly worse for wear. Turning into the main highway in his car he decided in his alcoholic daze that the safest procedure was to keep his eyes glued on the car ahead and follow it closely.

He did this for some time, and he was just congratulating himself when the car ahead suddenly stopped and he crashed into it.

The irate driver of the first car stuck his head out of his window and bellowed, "What's the big idea?"

"What's the big idea?" the other retorted, "why didn't you stick out your hand?"

The first driver's eyes opened wide with astonishment. "I didn't think I had to do that in my own garage," he yelped.

GUESSED WRONG

Judge: "I have been informed that you are six months behind in your alimony, Rastus. What have you to say?"

Rastus: "Ah knows it, Judge, but I jes' couldn't help it. Mah second wife ain't nowhere near as good a worker as Ah expected her to be!"

YOU COULDN'T FOOL HIM

Store Manager: "What's your name?"

Applicant: "Scott."

Manager: "And your first name?"

Applicant: "Walter."

Manager (smiling): "That's a pretty well known name."

Applicant (proudly): "It ought to be. I've been delivering groceries around here for two years now."

HE KNEW WHAT HE LIKED

A man sat down at a lunch counter and ordered four poached eggs and chips, a dozen oysters, and a grilled steak. After wading through these he finished off with four doughnuts and two cups of coffee.

When the waiter had finished serving, he remarked: "You must enjoy your meals."

"Far from it," replied the diner. "As a matter of fact, I hate 'em—but I'm nuts about bicarbonate of soda."

MISTAKEN IDENTITY

First Father: "What, your son is an undertaker? I thought you said your son was a doctor?"

Second Father: "No, I said he followed the medical profession."

SMILE WHEN YOU SAY THAT

. . . Are you sure you had a muffler? . . . Those tables are reserved. . . . The apple pie is all gone. . . . I must have made a mistake in my addition. . . . Please read the guarantee more carefully. . . . I think you can get good tickets from the speculator down the street. . . . Let me see your tickets, please, a mistake has been made. . . . This space is reserved for guests. . . . Our contract is clear on that point. . . . Will you please spell your name again? . . . We are not responsible for hats and overcoats. . . . Who is this speaking, please? . . . Mr. Jones is in a conference this afternoon. . . .

HERITAGE

Father: "Don't you think our son gets his intelligence from me?"
Mother: "He must—I've still got mine."

SCHOOL TEACHER

A salesman stood in the hotel lobby reading a letter from his wife.

"Hang it," he exclaimed, "this is what I get for marrying a school teacher."

"What's the matter?" asked his friend.

"Here's what my wife has just written me: 'Dear Jack: I notice that you have written me "Dearest Lucy." Now, either your grammar is bad, or else you are not a good husband. If I am the only Lucy you have, the "Dearest" is not correct; and if you have more than one Lucy, you've got something to explain when you get home.' "

A BEAR FOR PUNISHMENT

Father: "Yes, son, I'm a self-made man."

Son: "Dad, that's what I like about you. You take the blame for everything."

HARDY GURKHAS

Two Gurkha soldiers, who had volunteered for service with India's sky troops, asked an N.C.O.:

"From what height are we supposed to jump?"

"Five hundred feet," was the reply.

"Nothing doing," they said; "it's too high. Can't we try from three hundred feet?"

The N.C.O. explained that from such a low height there was a danger of the parachutes not opening in time, and the Gurkhas broke into smiles.

"Oh, that's different," they said. "We get parachutes, do we?"

THANKS

Man (to his wife): "Do you know, dear, that the biggest idiot always marries the prettiest woman?"

Wife: "It is high time for you to hand me a compliment, but I must say you did it very nicely."

BOTH RIGHT

Husband: "Darling, did you ever stop to realize that if you knew how to cook we'd be able to save some money?"

Wife: "Yes, and if you knew how to save money we could keep a cook."

A REFORMER

Lilly: "Do you think Lucy will make Jim a good wife?"

Billy: "I don't know, but she'll make him a good husband if she gets the chance."

SMART LAD

"And what," asked the teacher, "do two ducks and a cow remind you of?"

"Quackers and milk," said the little boy.

AH'LL SAY

"Doctah," said the wife of one of his patients, "Ah come to see if Rastus can have a slice of ham wid dat mustard plaster dat you told me to fix for him, 'count of it's a powerful strong prescription to take alone."

BROOKLYNESE

Brooklyn Teacher: "What is a stoic?"

Brooklyn Youth: "De boid that brings de babies."

EASY PAYMENTS

Anent the case of borrowing and repaying money on the installment plan, there is the story about two Negroes, who stood in the alley at Birmingham listening to a terrible commotion going on in one of the shanties, on the porch of which hung the distinctive and truly Southern sign "Sleepers Wanted."

From the outside, the slamming and banging of furniture plainly could be heard and there was an occasional shout, above the hubbub.

Another colored man came along and inquired: "What's all the ruckus about?" "Oh, that's just the white gennelmun come to collect one of them easy payments," was the response. *Finance.*

DIFFICULT TO GET IN

Into swanky St. Thomas Church walked a colored man. After due inquiry, and some difficulty, he located the rector and said: "Sah, I'd like to join dis church."

The rector was in a dilemma. "My good man," he said, "where do you live?" "I live in Harlem," was the reply. "Then don't you think it would be wise to join a church in your own neighborhood?"

"Yes, sah, but I desires to join dis church."

The rector pondered. "My man," said he, "suppose you go home and pray over this important step."

The man agreed. The next day he appeared. "Rectah," he said, "I went home and done what you tole me. When I axed Him how could I get into St. Thomas' Church he say: 'Rastus, whaffo yo ax me how? Why, man fo ten yeahs Ah been tryin' to get in dat church myself.' "

WORKING HIS WAY

A haughty senior girl sniffed disdainfully as a tiny freshman cut in. "And just why did you have to cut in while I was dancing with a four-letter man?" she inquired nastily.

"I'm sorry, ma'am," said the frosh, "but I'm working my way through college, and your partner was waving a five-dollar bill at me."

PREPARED

Old Gentleman: "You're an honest lad, but it was a ten-dollar bill I dropped, not ten ones."

Youngster: "I know, mister, but the last time I found a bill the man didn't have any change."

NOT EASY

"When I went to work for you, didn't you say something about my getting a raise?"

"I did say that you would if you did your work well."

"I knew there was a catch in it somewhere."

HE KNEW HOSPITALS

Jimmy, 6, youngest of eleven children, was taken to the hospital to see his father who was quite ill. Jimmy was quiet, almost reverent, until time came for him to leave. Then he tiptoed up to the bedside and whispered in his father's ear:

"Kin I see the baby now?"

RIGHT

Auntie: "And what will you do, my little darling, when you grow up to be a great big girl?"

Child: "Reduce."

YES, WE HAVE NONE

Clerk: "No, madam, we haven't had any for a long time."

Manager (overhearing): "Oh, yes; we have it madam. I will send to the warehouse and have some brought in for you." (Aside to clerk): "Never refuse anything. Send out for it."

As the lady went out laughing, the manager demanded: "What did she say?"

Clerk: "She said we haven't had any rain lately."

SPEAK UP

Judge: "Are you the defendant in this case?"

Darkey: "No, suh. I'se got a lawyer to do my defendin'. I'se de gent'man what stole the chickens."

REAL MATHEMATICIAN

Constable (to professor who had been run down): "Did you chance to notice the number of the car, sir?"

Professor: "Well, not exactly, but I remember noticing that if it was doubled and then multiplied by itself, the square root of the product was the original number with the integers reversed."

ANOTHER VIEWPOINT

Rastus: "Have you ever thought what you would do if you had Henry Ford's income?"

Sambo: "No, but I have often wondered what he would do if he had mine."

G. I. BRIDE

John A. Straley tells the story about the two Irishmen, who were standing in front of the kangaroo's cage in the Bronx zoo.

"Bejabers, Pat," Mike said, as he burst into tears. "Can yez read that there sign on the beast's cage?"

"Oi can thot," Pat replied. "It says 'A native of Australia.' But why are yez cryin?"

"You know my brother is with the American army in Australia," Mike sobbed. 'We jist got a cable from him in Sydney, saying he's married one av thim." *Finance.*

EMPTY HANDED

Inviting a friend to his wedding anniversary the man explained: "We're on the seventh, Apartment D; just touch the button with your elbow."

"And why should I use my elbow?"

"Well, for heaven's sake. You're not coming empty handed, are you?"

SCOTCHMAN

Undertaker: "Are you one of the mourners?"
Scotchman: "I am, sir. The corpse owed me ten dollars."

CAN YOU SPARE A DIME?

"Buddy, couldja spare a dime?"

"No, but come along and I will buy your breakfast."

"Man, I've et three breakfasts now trying to get a dime!"

YES, DEAR—NO, DEAR

First Sergeant: "Stand up straight, throw your shoulders back and button up your coat."

Married Recruit (absent-mindedly): "Yes, dear."

CURIOSITY

Curious Lady: "Little boy, how is it that your mother's name is Jones and yours is Smith?"

Boy: "She got married again and I didn't."

HE SHOULD KNOW

Professor: "Here you see the skull of a chimpanzee, a very rare specimen. There are only two in the country—one is in the national museum and I have the other."

HE WON'T EAT IT EITHER

Disgusted Diner: "You can't expect me to eat this stuff! Call the manager."

Waiter: "It's no use; he won't eat it either."

HE REALLY BUGLED

Two Negro soldiers were discussing the relative merits of their company buglers. Said one, "When dat boy of ouahs plays roll call, it sounds 'zactly like the Boston Symphony playin' *De Rosary.*"

The second colored boy snorted.

"Brothah, you ain't got no bugler a-tall. When Snowball Jones wraps his lips aroun' dat bugle of his, an' plays mess call, I looks down at mah beans, an' I sez: 'Strawberries, behave. You is kickin' de whipped cream out of de plate.' "

HE DID ALL RIGHT

William H. Madden, raconteur of Irish stories, relates the tale of Mike O'Brien who had made his fortune in the construction business, despite the fact that Mike had never learned to read nor write. As was Mike's habit on a Sunday, he got out his boat and went fishing. During the afternoon, a storm swept over the lake, the boat overturned and poor Mike was drowned. One of Mike's friends came over to express his regrets to the widow.

"I hope, Mrs. O'Brien, that Mike left you well off."

"Indeed, he did," Mrs. O'Brien replied. "He left me forty-five thousand dollars in cash."

"Forty-five thousand!" his friend cried in astonishment. "Sure and he did all right by you."

"Didn't he do all right," said Mrs. O'Brien, "for a man who couldn't read, write nor swim." *Finance*.

HE CAUGHT BIG FISH

When President Cleveland's second child was born, the doctor asked the proud father to bring him a scale so that he could weigh the new offspring. Cleveland looked all over the house but could not find one. Finally he recalled that he had a scale in the cellar, which he used to weigh the fish he caught on his numerous trips. He fetched it, and when they placed the child upon it, they discovered that the new baby weighed 25 pounds.

FIFTY-FIFTY

Her Father: "Young man, how in the world do you expect to support my daughter when I can hardly manage it myself?"

Her Boy Friend: "Well, what would be the matter with our going fifty-fifty on it?"

THAT'S DIFFERENT

Mother: "Mrs. Smith says that one-half the world doesn't know how the other half lives."

Father: "Well, she shouldn't blame herself, dear; it isn't her fault."

TWO-THIRDS FOR THE DOCTOR

Admiral Dewey, hero of the Battle of Manila Bay, enjoyed splendid health. Once when he was complimented on his superb physique, he smiled and said, "I attribute my good condition to plenty of exercise and no banquets. One-third of what we eat, you know, enables us to live."

"In that case," he was asked, "what becomes of the other two-thirds?"

"Oh," replied the doughty admiral, "that enables the doctor to live."

REAL ECONOMY

"Why are you home so late, dear?"

"Well, I just missed the street car at one corner. Then I went around the corner to catch the bus, but I missed that, too. So I ran all the way home behind the street car, and saved the nickel fare."

"Why didn't you run behind the bus, and save a dime?"

MODERN

"I am Brave Eagle," said the Indian chieftain, introducing himself to the paleface visitor. "This is my son, Fighting Bird."

"And here," he added, "is my grandson, DC-4."

THE MISSING TALENT

A certain Negro preacher in Georgia failed to satisfy his flock and a committee from the congregation waited on him to request his resignation.

"Look here!" exclaimed the rejected shepherd indignantly. "What's de trouble wid mah preachin'? Don't I argufy?"

"You sho does, eldah," agreed the spokesman.

"Don't I 'sputify concerning de Scriptures?"

"You suttingly does."

"Den whut's wrong?" inquired the parson in profound bewilderment.

"Well, eldah," was the reply, "hit's dis way. You argufies and you 'sputifies, but you don't show wherein."

SURE TEST

Jackson and his wife were doing a little fly hunting about the house.

"How many have you caught?" she asked after a while.

"Six," replied her husband. "Three males and three females."

"How absurd!" his wife sniffed. "How could you tell if they were males or females?"

"Easy, my dear," he retorted. "Three were on the apple pie and three were on the mirror."

BLUFF

Two trucks met on a country road just wide enough for one. Truck driver No. 1, a scrawny, frail little man, leaned out of his cab.

"Turn out, you," he shouted. "If ya don't, I'll do to you what I did to the last guy who wouldn't turn out for me."

Two hundred pound, muscular driver No. 2, not caring for trouble, pulled out. As the other truck rumbled by, he yelled: "What'd ya do to that other guy?"

"Turned out for him," said No. 1.

OLD STORY TO MARRIED MEN

"Dear," the little woman reported, "a man came yesterday gathering old clothes."

"Did you give him anything?" the husband inquired.

"Yes, Henry," she said. "I gave him that ten-year-old suit of yours and that dress I bought last month."

MOUNTAIN CLIMBING

On week-end leave, a soldier attended a movie at one of the Broadway houses. He was escorted by an usher who led him skyward on ramp after ramp to the floor level of the top balcony, where he stopped and pointed upward into the grayness. "You'll find a seat up there somewhere. This is as far as I go. Above this level, my nose bleeds."

WRONG DIRECTION

Farmer: "You must be brave to come down in a hundred-mile gale like this in a parachute."

Soldier: "I didn't come down like this in a chute. I went up in a tent."

MISTAKEN IDENTITY

Mrs. Clancy was returning from shopping in no pleasant humor. As she approached the door, she saw Mrs. Murphy, who occupied the street floor, sitting at her window.

"I say, Mrs. Murphy," she called out in deep sarcasm, "why don't ye take your ugly mug out of the window an' put your pet monkey in its place? That'd give the neighbors a change they'd like."

"Well now," Mrs. Murphy retorted, "it was only this mornin' that I did that very thing, an' the policeman came along an' when he saw the monkey he bowed and shmiled an' said, 'Why, Mrs. Clancy, when did ye move downstairs?'"

FORTUNATE BREAK

Father: "Who broke that chair in the parlor last night?"

Daughter: "It just collapsed all of a sudden, Pop. But neither of us was hurt."

MODERN FAMILIES

Two baby sitters were discussing their infant charges. "Are you going to the dance tomorrow night?" one asked the other.

"I'm afraid not," she replied.

"What!" exclaimed the first. "I thought you were so fond of dancing?"

"I'd love to go," explained the conscientious sitter, "but to tell you the truth, I'm afraid to leave the baby with its mother!"

GOOD DESCRIPTION

Little Mary was walking in the garden. She happened to see a peacock, a bird she had never seen before. After gazing in silent admiration, she quickly ran into the house and cried out: "Oh, granny, come and see! One of your chickens is in bloom!"

THE TRUTH, THE WHOLE TRUTH

A relief worker drove four miles into the country to take supplies to a deserving farmer. Before she left, she checked up on a rumor that had come to the welfare office: "We are told that you have been seen driving a car. How about it? You know help isn't given to people who own cars."

Promptly the farmer replied: "No, lady, I hain't no car. I drive one once in a while when it is loaned to me."

"Who owns the car?" asked the worker.

"My brother-in-law's sister," he replied. "Sometimes she lets me drive it."

The explanation was satisfactory and the lady drove away. When she had gone the farmer chuckled: "She shore never figured out that my brother-in-law's sister is my wife."

MISTAKEN IDENTITY

"Why did the foreman fire you?"

"Well, the foreman is the man who stands around and watches others work."

"Yes. But why did he fire you?"

"He got jealous of me. A lot of the fellows thought I was the foreman!"

A LITTLE LATER

"Sam, how long does you get in the jug for shootin' yo' wife?"

"Two weeks."

"Only two weeks for killin' yo' wife?"

"Yeah. Then I gets hung."

THE BETTER PART

Once Clarence Darrow was visiting Brand Whitlock, then Mayor of Toledo, when an admirer of the great lawyer burst into the office and asked Whitlock to introduce him.

"Ah, Mr. Darrow," gushed the intruder, "you have suffered a great deal in your life for being misunderstood, haven't you?"

Darrow smiled wryly and replied, "Yes, my friend, but I haven't suffered half as much as I would have if I had been understood."

BRITISH VERSION

At a party in London an American from the West was asked by a lovely English girl what part of the states he was from.

"Idaho," he told her.

"Isn't that interesting," she said. "You know, over here, we pronounce that Ohio."

ALMOST HEARD IT

Amos (after a narrow escape at a railroad crossing): "How come you blow yo' hawn? You oughta know it wouldn't do you no good."

Sambo: "Boy, dat wa'n't my hawn. Dat was Gabriel's."

A BARGAIN

Some years ago a clothier in Paris had 49 coats he could not sell. He explained his predicament to a business acquaintance. "I have marked the overcoats down fifty per cent," he said, "and still they will not buy. What shall I do?"

"I will give you a list of provincial merchants," said the other. "Send seven overcoats to each, but send them an invoice for six only. They will think it is a mistake and will take advantage of it."

A week later the overcoat man rushed into his friend's store in a great rage. "Fine advice you gave me," he shouted. "Each one to whom I sent the seven coats, and invoiced only six, returned the six mentioned in the invoice and kept the extra one."

WHO AM I?

Of all nuisances, the one who runs up to you, grasps your hand, and says, "You don't know me, do you?" is the worst.

Such a person once confronted William Howard Taft as he stood talking with a friend in Washington. He walked up and said, "How do you do, Mr. Taft; I'll bet you don't know me." Taft replied, "You win," and turned his broad back and walked away.

WORST JOKE

Student: "Could one refer to the Venus de Milo as the girl who got the breaks?"

English Librarian: "Why not, may I awsk? It's an 'armless joke."

VITAMINS

Little Betty concluded her evening prayer: "Lord, please, if you don't mind, from now on put the vitamins we need in pies, cakes and ice cream cones instead of spinach and cod liver oil."

HOW ABOUT FOG LIGHTS?

Cowboy: "What kind of a saddle do you want—one with or without a horn?"

Dude: "Without a horn, I guess. There doesn't seem to be much traffic on these prairies."

NO BARGAIN

A farmer was trying to sell a broken-winded horse to the army, and was trotting him around for inspection. He stroked the animal's back and said to the army buyer, "Hasn't he got a lovely coat?"

The army man had noticed that the horse was touched in the wind, and answered, "Sure, his coat's all right, but I don't like his pants."

THE TRUTH

The celebrated pianist, Leopold Godowsky, was once importuned by a father to pass judgment on his daughter's ability as a pianist. Godowsky, who had worked patiently but without success with the young woman through several lessons, sought to evade a direct reply. But the father was not to be put aside, and wrote demanding an utterly frank statement.

Godowsky laughed, reached for a piece of paper, and wrote: "Your daughter is not without lack of talent, and she manages to play the simplest pieces with the greatest difficulty."

DIFFICULT CHOICE

One day in the White House President Coolidge was sitting with some of his political cronies, when some reference was made to the blunt style of oratory affected by Senator Jim Watson, of Indiana.

One of those present said: "Last week I heard Jim Watson speak before a group of constituents, and he said, 'Now I have given you all the facts, and you can vote for me or go to the devil.'"

Mr. Coolidge, who had been silently regarding the tips of his shoes, raised his eyes to the little group and with no particular emphasis remarked, "It was a difficult alternative."

SUCCESS

"If you get up earlier in the morning than your neighbor," said the town philosopher, "and work harder, and scheme more, and stick to your job more closely, and stay up later planning how to make more money than your neighbor, and burn the midnight oil more, planning how to get ahead of him while he's snoozing, not only will you leave more money when you die than he will, but you'll leave it much sooner."

HEAD OF THE CLASS

"How did Junior make out in his latest exams?"

"Oh, he's doing much better. He was almost on the top of the list of those who failed."

DIPLOMAT

Father: "I hope you appreciate, young man, that in marrying my daughter you are getting a big-hearted, generous girl."

Suitor: "I do, sir. And I trust she has acquired those fine qualities from her father."

RISKY UNDERTAKING

Bugler: "I'm entering the contest for the best bugler in camp. How do you think I'll come out?"

Corporal: "On a stretcher, probably."

TAKING NO RISK

Bill was just out of college, and got a job on the local staff of a newspaper. He listened intently to the city editor's instructions:

"Never write anything as a fact unless you are absolutely sure about it, or you'll get the paper in wrong. If you're not sure of an item being a fact use the words, 'alleged,' 'reputed,' 'claimed,' 'rumored,' or 'it was said.' "

Bill kept repeating this instruction in his mind as he went on his first assignment, and this is the first story he turned in:

"It is rumored that a party was given yesterday by a number of reputed ladies. Mrs. Smith, it was said, was hostess, and the guests, it is alleged, with the exception of Mrs. Jones, who says she is fresh from Wheeling, were all local people. Mrs. Smith claims to be the wife of Joe Smith, rumored to be the president of an alleged bank."

FOLLOWED INSTRUCTIONS

"Where have you been, Johnnie?"

"Playing ball, Mother."

"I told you to beat the rug, didn't I?"

"No, ma'am, you told me to hang the rug on the line and then beat it."

OLD STORY BUT STILL GOOD

He had opened a fish market and ordered a new sign painted, of which he was very proud. It read, "Fresh Fish For Sale Here."

"What did you put the word 'fresh' in for?" said his first customer. "You wouldn't sell them if they weren't fresh, would you?"

He painted out the word, leaving just "Fish For Sale Here."

"Why do you say 'here'?" asked his second customer. "You're not selling them anywhere else, are you?"

So he rubbed out the word "here."

"Why use 'for sale'?" asked the next customer. "You wouldn't have fish here unless they were for sale."

So he rubbed out everything but the word "Fish," remarking: "Well, nobody can find fault with that sign now, anyway."

A moment later another customer came in.

"I don't see what's the use of having that sign 'Fish' up there," said he, "when you can smell them a block away."

And that's how he went out of business.

YES OR NO

Lawyer: "Now, sir, did you, or did you not, on the date in question, or at any other time, previously or subsequently say or even intimate to the defendant or anyone else, alone or with anyone, whether a friend or a mere acquaintance, or in fact, a stranger, that the statement imputed to you, whether just or unjust, and denied by the plaintiff, was a matter of no moment or otherwise? Answer me, yes or no."

Witness: "Yes or no what?"

OBSERVATION

Three-year-old Willie had taken his mother's powder puff and was making himself up, as he'd seen her do. His five-year-old sister came in, looked at him a moment, then took the puff from Willie's hand. "Only ladies use powder; gentlemen wash themselves."

NORTH AND SOUTH

"What is the Mason-Dixon line?"

"It's the division between 'you all' and 'youse guys'!"

NO BIDS

First Shopper: "You seem to be busy."

Second Shopper: "Yes, I'm trying to get something for my husband."

First Shopper: "Have you had any offers yet?"

FAST THINKERS

Passenger: "Conductor, that fellow sitting opposite me is a lunatic. He claims he is George Washington."

Conductor: "Be calm, lady; I'll take care of the matter." (shouting) "Next station, Mount Vernon!"

VOICE OF EXPERIENCE

Wife: "I think I hear burglars. Are you awake?"
Husband: "No!"

PSYCHOLOGY

A psychologist says that any girl can marry any man she wants, if she repeats often enough to him these four words: "You are so wonderful!"

GO AHEAD

A junk shop near a railroad crossing carries a sign with this hint to motorists: "Go ahead; take a chance. We'll buy the car."

MARK TWAIN

A man once challenged Mark Twain to cite some passage from the Scriptures expressly forbidding polygamy.

"Certainly," replied the humorist. " 'No man can serve two masters.' "

DIGGING

When Rex Beach appeared as guest of honor at a writers' club he declined to make a speech, but agreed to answer any question asked by the club members.

"Tell me, Mr. Beach," said one young lady, "to what one thing do you attribute your success?"

The famous author considered the question briefly, and then replied: "I can best answer that by telling the story of a Swede in Alaska. He was owner of several rich mines, and all his friends wondered how he had managed to become so successful. One night one of their number asked him.

" 'Ay never tolt anybody before,' he replied, 'but Ay will tell you. Ay yust kept diggin' holes.' "

DISCREET

The celebrated actor, Maclyn Arbuckle, was once a lawyer in a wild section of Texas, where the morning greeting was not "Fine morning, isn't it?" but "Wonder who gets it today."

Arbuckle was deeply inquisitive about the bad men of the section, and finally mustered up courage to corner the worst of their number and put him to a test.

"What would you do, Mr. Simmons," he timorously inquired, "if somebody called you a liar?"

Simmons scowled. "By word of mouth?"

"Yes," replied Arbuckle.

Simmons took out his Colt and regarded it lovingly. Then he looked at his questioner with a most terrifying expression.

"How big a man?" he inquired.

SIGNS

Mother: "What makes you think your young man has matrimonial intentions?"

Daughter: "Well, when we were looking at Easter hats he tried to convince me I look better in a two ninety-eight model than one that cost fifteen dollars."

NEVER TOLD HIM

Desperately in need of 50 cents, a husband finally got up enough courage to open his pay envelope before taking it to his wife. He hurried back to the cashier who had given him the envelope.

"You've given me ten dollars too much," he stammered.

The cashier counted the bills and coins, then replied impatiently: "It's quite correct. I suppose you've forgotten that you got a ten-dollar raise last month."

He placed his hand across his eyes, shrank into his collar and said faintly: "My wife never told me."

HOME ECONOMICS

A Youngstown (O.) reporter had been fussing about the butter situation during the war, and finally decided to make some himself. He got a half pint of cream and went to work, shaking it seven and a half minutes in a jar. This was only the beginning. He gathered up the little ball of butter, "washed" it in ice water, salted it and looked upon it with love. It was pale. So he added some food coloring.

He also got some on his white shirt, ruining the shirt. Figuring his time, wear and tear on the shirt and other things, he had an eighth of a pound of butter which figures out at about $16.50 a pound. So he went out and bought a pound of oleo. *Editor & Publisher.*

NOT SO HARD

A group of businessmen were discussing a certain tightfisted banker. Every man present had suffered some unpleasant experience at the hands of this banker, and all save one offered fervent testimony concerning his unremitting toughness and hardheartedness.

"Haven't you something to say against that scamp?" the silent member was asked.

"No," was the reply. "I don't think he's so tough."

"He turned you down on a loan, didn't he?"

"Yes," replied the quiet one, "but he hesitated before he refused."

SECOND THE MOTION

It was the weekly meeting of a Negro club. At the end of the usual business, a loud voice yelled from the back of the hall: "Mistah Chayman, Ah makes a motion dat Sam Jackson am a low-down, sneaking mis'rable chicken thief."

Down in front a little fellow leaped to his feet.

"Who makes dat motion dat Ah'm a low-down, sneakin', mis'rable chicken thief?"

A huge sour-faced Negro arose.

"Ah makes dat motion," he said.

"Mister Chayman," said Sam quickly, "Ah seconds dat motion."

RIGHT NUMBER

Customer: "Are these half dozen rings all you have in stock? Why, you have a whole trayful of engagement rings over there!"

Jeweler: "Yes, sir. But it'll take that whole trayful of engagement rings to work off those half dozen wedding rings!"

PLEASURE

A man going down the street met a friend he had not seen for some time. During the course of the conversation his friend seemed to be in pain. When asked what the trouble was he replied that his feet hurt because his shoes were too short. When asked why he did not get larger shoes, he replied that his wife was sick, his son was in jail, his daughter married a ne'er-do-well, he had lost all he had in a bad business venture and the only pleasure he got from life was to take these tight shoes off when he got home in the evening.

OPPOSITES

"They say people with opposite characteristics make the happiest marriages."

"Yes. That's why I'm looking for a girl with money."

WE'VE EATEN THAT SANDWICH

"This inn is historic. Almost everything here has its legend."

"Let's get them to tell us about this curious old ham sandwich. I'm sure it must have a quaint story attached."

HAIRCUT

A professor was once accosted by a dirty little bootblack. "Shine, sir?" he asked.

The professor was disgusted by the dirt on the lad's face. "I don't want a shine, my lad," he said, "but if you will go and wash your face I'll give you a dime."

"Right, guv'nor," replied the boy, as he made his way to a neighboring fountain. Soon he returned, looking much cleaner.

"Well, my boy," said the professor, "you have earned your dime; here it is."

"I don't want your dime, guv'nor," replied the boy. "You hang on to it and git your hair cut."

FOIR AWAY

There was a young girl in the choir
Whose voice went up hoir and hoir

Till one Sunday night
It went out of sight
And they found it next day in the spoir.

THE STARTING POINT

Ramsay MacDonald, former Prime Minister of England, was discussing the possibility of lasting peace with another government official. The latter, an expert in foreign affairs, was unimpressed by the Prime Minister's idealistic viewpoint.

"The desire for peace does not necessarily insure it," he remarked somewhat cynically.

"Quite true," admitted Mr. MacDonald. "Neither does the desire for food satisfy your hunger, but at least it gets you started toward a restaurant."

WORST MORON STORY

The moron dove into the swimming-pool exclaiming, "Gee, I wish it was Wednesday."

"How come?" asked a bystander.

" 'Cause," said the moron, picking himself up, "they put water in the pool then."

OUT SHE GOES

A deaf woman entered a church with an ear trumpet. Soon after she had seated herself, an usher tiptoed over and whispered, "One toot, and out you go."

WE'VE BEEN THERE

Brown: "Did you fish with flies?"

Gray (back from camping holiday): "Fish with them? We fished with them, camped with them, ate with them, slept with them!"

KNEW ALL THE ANSWERS

Caller: "Is the boss in?"

New Office Boy: "Are you a salesman, bill collector, or a friend of his?"

"All three."

"He's in a business conference. He's out of town. Step in and see him."

NOT TOO PROMISING

Eugene Field was sometimes a little forgetful of his debts. During his columnist days in Chicago, he was sought out by a visiting New York friend, from whom he had borrowed $25 some months before.

"Gene," the friend said, "I think you ought to clear up that old debt." And Field replied, "You're absolutely right; I'll do something about it tomorrow."

The next day, Field's column included mention of his friend's visit to Chicago. Then it revealed:

"He is in town to look after one of his permanent investments."

A REVISED MEMORY

A Northern tourist was visiting the little cabin of an ancient darkey known as Uncle Mose, who lived in a small Virginia town, and who often entertained visitors with stories of the "War Between the States."

"I understand you remember seeing Lincoln," the visitor remarked.

Uncle Mose looked sheepish. "No, suh," he replied. "Ah used to 'member seeing Massa Linkum, but since Ah j'ined de church Ah doan' 'member seein' him no mo'."

SAYS BETTY CO-ED

The coach was all wrong about our team not having a good line— I've been out with them all.

DOMESTIC SCENE

"Oh, Henry. You're just awful, and I'm sick of you. You sit there reading your old newspaper, not paying any attention to me. You don't love me any more."

"Nonsense, Isabel. I love you more than ever. I worship the ground you walk on. Your every wish is my command. I thrill at your proximity. Now for Pete's sake shut up and let me read the funnies."

MONEY TALKS

The story is told that Winston Churchill hailed a cab in West End and told the cabbie to drive him to BBC, where he was scheduled to make a speech to the world.

"Sorry, sir," said the driver. "Ye'll have to get yourself another cab. I can't go that far."

Mr. Churchill was somewhat surprised, and asked the cabbie why his field of operations was so limited.

"It hain't ordinarily, sir," apologized the driver, "but ye see, sir, Mr. Churchill is broadcasting in an hour, and I wants to get 'ome to 'ear 'im."

Mr. Churchill was so well pleased that he pulled out a pound note and handed it to the driver, who took one quick look at it and said: "Hop in, sir. To the devil with Mr. Churchill."

ONE POINT OF VIEW

Life is cruel to men. When they are born, their mothers get the compliments and flowers. When they are married, their brides get the presents and publicity. And when they die, their wives get the insurance and winters in Florida.

OCCASIONAL SHOWERS

"Daddy, don't they ever give showers for the groom?"

"No, son. There will be storms enough for him after the bride begins to reign."

NO INTEREST

"What did the audience do when you told them you had never paid a dollar for a vote?" inquired the first politician.

"Some of them cheered, but the majority seemed to lose interest," replied the other.

PERFECT ILLUSTRATION

Dean: "What is density?"

Hansen: "I can't define it, but I can give an illustration."

Dean: "The illustration is good. Sit down."

M

NEW IDEA

Husband (the ingenious type): "I've invented a new type of woman's handbag, dear."

Wife (skeptically): "What's new about it?"

Husband: "The zipper's at the bottom. Isn't that where everything usually is when you want it?"

TRY, TRY AGAIN

"Mamma, what's a second-story man?"

"Your father is one, dear. If I don't believe his first story, he always has another one ready."

NICE TRICK

The corporal was preparing to fingerprint a recruit.

"Wash your hands," he said.

"Both of them?" asked the recruit.

After a moment's hesitation, the corporal said: "No, just one. I want to see you do it."

STILL A GOOD STORY

A Methodist Negro exhorter shouted: "Come en jine de army of de Lawd!"

"Ise don jined," replied one of the congregation.

"Whar'd you jine?" asked the exhorter.

"I jined de Baptist Church."

"Why, chile," said the exhorter, "you ain't in de army; you's in de navy."

SMART GIRL

Employer to newly hired steno: "Now I hope you thoroughly understand the importance of punctuation?"

Steno: "Oh, yes, indeed. I always get to work on time."

QUARANTINE

Old Lady: "Little boy, why aren't you in school instead of at this movie?"

Little Boy: "Well, you see, lady, I've got the measles."

IMPRESSIONS

A colored porter in a hotel was asked why rich men usually gave smaller tips than poor men.

"Well, suh," the porter answered, "the rich man don't want nobody t'know he's rich, and the po' man don't want nobody t'know he's po'."

IT WORKS

"Sambo, how do you do your work so good and do it so fast?"

"Well, boss, Ah sticks de match ob enthusiasm to de fuse of energy an' jes' nacherly explodes, Ah does."

CARELESS SPEECH

Minister: "Well, Mose, how is your better half this morning?"

Mose: "She am done bettah, suh. But pahson, yo' is sho' careless wif yo' fractions."

TALL AND SHORT

Detective: "You're looking for your cashier? Is he tall or short?"

Banker: "Both."

IT'S ESSENTIAL

A small boy at the zoo asked why the giraffe had such a long neck.

"Well, you see," said the keeper gravely, "the giraffe's head is so far removed from his body that a long neck is absolutely necessary."

PRONUNCIATION

First Freshman: "I hear you got thrown out of school for calling the dean a fish."

Second Frosh: "I didn't call him a fish. I just said, 'That's our dean,' real fast."

IDEA

A Midwest manufacturer sent his son through his plant to improve efficiency and find ways to cut down portal-to-portal liability. After lengthy study, the son returned. "The plant is in pretty good shape," he declared. "My only suggestion is that you bank the curve near the timeclock."

HIS SELECTION

Son: "Can I have any kind of sea food I like?"

Mother: "Yes, dear. What shall I order for you?"

Son: "Salt-water taffy."

AT SEA

Two men, slightly inebriated, boarded a two-decker bus. There was a naval officer behind them. Tom went upstairs, leaving Bill to pay the fares. Bill turned to the officer and offered to pay two fares.

"My good man," said the scandalized officer, "I'm a naval officer, not a conductor."

"Hey, Tom," he shouted, "come on down. We're on a battleship."

CONTENTED COMPOSER

Beneath the gruff exterior of the great Johannes Brahms lurked a vast good humor that delighted his friends.

One day in his later years the composer encountered a friend whom he had not seen for several months, and confided in him: "While you were away I started many things, serenades, part songs and so on, but nothing would work out well. Then I thought: I am too old. I have worked long and diligently and have achieved enough. Here I have before me a carefree old age and can enjoy it in peace. I resolved to compose no more."

Brahms' friend regarded him with alarm and incredulity. "Compose no more!" he exclaimed.

The great composer smiled and added: "And that made me so happy, so contented, so delighted that all at once the writing began to go."

MODERN WAGE EARNER ON VACATION

He writes a picture postcard home: "Having a wonderful time and a half."

MUST YOU GO?

There was once a young man who told his girl friend he'd never seen such dreamy eyes before. To which she replied, "You have never stayed so late before."

KENTUCKY HILLS

An old man in the Kentucky hills was giving his summary of the atom bomb. "This here town will be the fust one that will be bombed one evening."

"Hardly," objected a visitor. "This town is a long way from the coast."

"Sure it'll be bombed," persisted the prophet. "It's the county seat, ain't it?"

GUILTY

Judge: "Who was driving when you collided with that car?"
Drunk (triumphantly): "None of us. We were all in the back seat."

OFTEN TRUE

Toastmaster: "What is the hardest part of your work as a lecturer?"
Lecturer: "As a rule the hardest part of my work is waking up the audience after the man that introduces me has concluded his remarks."

LOUDER, PLEASE

Voice over Telephone: "Tommie Hagan will not be in school today."
Teacher: "Who is this speaking, please?"
Voice: "This is my father speaking."

TIME TO LEAVE

She: "My father takes things apart to see why they don't go."
He: "So what?"
She: "So you'd better go."

THRIFT

She: "I can't make them out. They have no car, no piano, no radio, and she hasn't any jewelry, no furs."
"He: "They probably have some money."

EXPENSIVE TASTES

A mountaineer coming to town saw for the first time a bunch of bananas.

"Want to try one?" asked a friend.

"No, I reckon not," said the man of the mountains. "I've got so many tastes now I can't satisfy, I don't reckon I'll take on more."

RESPONSIBLE

Employer: "For this job, we need a responsible man."

Applicant: "I'm your man. In all my other jobs when anything went wrong, I was always held responsible."

IT MAKES A DIFFERENCE

Mister (exuberantly): "A man is never older than he feels. Now this morning I feel as fresh as a two-year-old."

Missus (sweetly): "Horse or egg?"

KEEP IT QUIET

Farmer: "Let me tell you, my friend, that horse knows as much as I do."

Friend: "Well, don't tell anybody else; you might want to sell him some day."

WHAT EVERY RENTER HOPES FOR

Customer: "Young man, what do I get for my money if I rent this apartment?"

Salesman: "You get a home, on which we pay your taxes, your insurance, your water bill, buy your coal, fire your furnace and hot-water heater, furnish your window shades, gas stove, electric refrigerator, do your decorating and repairing, cut your grass, sweep your walks, clean your hall, pay the light bill for your garage, empty your garbage, fight your battles with the neighbors . . . and you ask me what do you get for your money!"

Customer: "Pardon me for being so stupid—where do I sign?"

NOT A BAD IDEA

Daughter: "Yes, I've graduated, but now I must inform myself in psychology, philology, bibli—"

Practical Mother: "Stop! I have arranged for you a thorough course in roastology, bakeology, stitcholoy, darnology, patchology, and general domestic hustleology."

KEEP THE CHANGE

A customer went into an expensive food store and asked the price of a peach.

"Fifteen cents," said the clerk.

The customer handed him 25 cents.

"Keep the change," he said. "I stepped on a grape as I came in."

DAMAGED

A man in a restaurant was having trouble cutting his steak. No matter how much he jabbed at it, he got no results. Finally he called the waiter. "You'll have to take this back and bring me another."

"Sorry, sir," said the waiter after closely examining the steak. "I can't take it back. You've bent it."

SHE WAS A STAR PUPIL

A high school girl seated next to a famous astronomer at a dinner party struck up a conversation asking, "What do you do in life?"

He replied, "I study astronomy."

"Dear me," said the young miss, "I finished astronomy last year."

EXPECTING TOO MUCH

"Doctor," inquired the anxious patient, "will the anesthetic make me sick?"

"No, I think not."

"Well, how long will it be before I know anything?"

"My dear sir," responded the exasperated medico, "aren't you expecting almost too much from the anesthetic?"

DEFINITION

Teacher: "What is the difference between caution and cowardice?"

Pupil: "Caution is when you're afraid and cowardice is when the other fellow's afraid."

AMPLE EVIDENCE

At the age of 16 the late Supreme Court Justice Louis Brandeis went to Europe with his parents, and while there attended school in Dresden.

Before admitting the prize student from Kentucky, the headmaster of the school demanded certificates of birth and vaccination. Young Brandeis did not have the certificates, but he did have a ready tongue.

"Why do you need the certificates?" he asked.

"As proof, of course," said the headmaster.

"To prove that I was vaccinated you have only to look at my arm," replied Brandeis, "and the fact that I am here to show you the arm should be ample proof that I was born."

He was admitted. *Milwaukee Journal.*

HE UNDERSTOOD

A man was giving some advice to his son. At the end of a rather stern lecture, he said: "Now, my boy, you understand perfectly what I mean?"

"Yes," replied the boy, "what it boils down to is this: If I do well it's because of heredity, and if I fail it's my own fault."

DIFFICULT CHOICE

Lulu: "Last night my date asked me to marry him and make him happy."

Sue: "Which did you decide to do?"

HARD WORK

Sandy was paying $7.50 weekly for board and lodging. One day his landlady said: "Sandy, I'm afraid I'll have to charge you $1 a week more, you are such a good eater."

"For goodness' sake," cried Sandy, "dinna do that. I'm killing myself already trying to eat $7.50 worth."

NO HELP

The great ocean liner rolled and pitched.

"Henry," faltered the young bride, "do you still love me?"

"More than ever, darling," was Henry's fervent answer.

Then there was an eloquent silence.

"Henry," she gasped, turning her pale, ghastly face away, "I thought that would make me feel better, but it doesn't."

DIFFICULT PROBLEM

A farmer was losing his temper trying to drive two mules into a field, when the parson came by.

"You are just the man I want to see," said the farmer. "Tell me, how did Noah get these into the ark?"

CHAUNCEY DEPEW

Once upon a time the mayor of a large city introduced Chauncey Depew by suggesting that he was like an automatic machine—"you put in a dinner and up comes a speech."

When Mr. Depew gained his feet, he suggested that the difference between his after-dinner speaking and the chairman's was that his honor the mayor "puts in a speech and up comes your dinner."

WE'RE REVISED TOO

"I'm a self-made man."

"You're lucky. I'm the revised work of a wife and three daughters."

APPEARANCE

"I need a holiday," said the cashier. "I'm not looking my best."

"Nonsense," said the boss.

"No, it isn't nonsense; the men are beginning to count their change."

THERE WAS A REASON

"But how on earth did you come to get so completely intoxicated?" asked the magistrate.

"I got in bad company, your honor. You see, there were four of us. I had a bottle of whisky—and the other three don't touch the stuff."

OBSERVATION

"Sir," stormed the defense lawyer, "you have admitted you were seated on the right side of the passenger coach where you couldn't see

M

an extra track. Will you please explain to this jury how you can swear the line was double-tracked?"

"Well," meekly answered the witness, "I could look across the aisle and through the coach windows. I saw a train whiz by occasionally, and took it that there was either a track under it or else this railroad had some mighty good railroaders."

SNEEZE

I sneezed a sneeze into the air,
It fell to ground I knew not where
But hard and cold were the looks of those
In whose vicinity I snooze.

Commerce.

GLAD TO REFUND

A farmer had just made a purchase of a bushel of grass seed.
"Is this seed guaranteed?"
"Guarantee the seed?" the merchant replied. "I should say so. If that seed doesn't grow, bring it back, and we'll refund you your money."

THE HAMMER

It's the only knocker in the world that does any good.
It keeps its head.
It doesn't fly off the handle.
It keeps pounding away.
It finds the point, then drives it home.
It looks at the other side, too, and thus often clinches the matter.
It makes mistakes, but when it does, it starts all over.

TRUTH

Wife: "I've been asked for a reference for our last maid, and I don't know exactly what to say. If I told the truth, I'd say she was lazy, unpunctual, and impertinent. Can you think of anything favorable we could say?"
Husband: "You might say she's got a good appetite and sleeps well."

ALL GRANDPARENTS WILL UNDERSTAND

Mother (on 'phone): "Daughter, dear, could Papa and I leave your kiddies with you and Bob tonight? We're invited out for the evening."

HE KNEW BETTER

They were out at sea—the ship was rolling and rocking something awful. One passenger got sick, and soon he was leaning over the rail. The Captain came along and said: "Sorry, you cannot be sick here."

The passenger regarded the Captain a moment and said, "Watch."

WINNING FRIENDS

Motor Cop: "Hey, you! Didn't you hear me say 'Pull over'?"

Driver: "Why I thought you said, 'Good afternoon, Senator.' "

Motor Cop (smiling): "Isn't it a warm day today, Senator?"

CHANGE THIS STORY AS YOU WISH

An advertisement appeared in the want ad columns reading as follows: "Wanted—Yale man or equivalent for position with a corporation." Someone asked a Harvard man what was meant by the words "or equivalent," and he said, "The equivalent would be two Princeton men or a Harvard man part time."

PREPARED

Youth: "There's a very important question I've been wanting to ask you for days and days."

Girl: "Go right ahead. I've had the answer ready for months and months."

SCARED

An Irishman was telling a friend of his narrow escape in France.

"The bullet went in me chest and came out me back," he said.

"But," protested his friend, "it would have gone through your neart and killed you."

"Me heart was in me mouth at the time."

SAD WORLD

A shipwrecked sailor spent five years on a desert island. One day he was overjoyed to see a ship drop anchor in the bay. A small boat came ashore and an officer handed the sailor a bunch of newspapers.

"The captain suggests," he told the sailor, "that you read what's going on in the world and then let us know if you want to be rescued."

GO EASY

Mother: "Have you scolded Willie about the low marks on his report card?"

Father: "No. Every time I do he reminds me that he's an exemption on my income tax."

DESCRIPTION

"If you're looking for my husband, he's gone fishing. Just walk down to the bridge until you find a pole with a worm on each end."

EDITOR'S SON

An editor had cause to admonish his son because of the lad's reluctance to attend school. "You must go every day and learn to be a great scholar," said the fond father, "otherwise you can never be an editor, you know. What would you do, for instance, if your magazine came out full of mistakes?"

"Father," was the reply, "I'd blame the printer."

And the father wept with joy, because he knew he had a successor for the editorial chair. *Commerce.*

SO SAY WE ALL

Wife: "There's an old-clothes man at the door."

Husband: "Tell him I can't afford to buy any."

WEIGHTY MATTER

In a small town where two brothers are engaged in the retail coal business a religious revival was held and one of the brothers got converted. He tried to persuade his partner to join the church. One day he asked: "Why can't you join the church like I did?"

"It's a fine thing for you to belong to the church," replied the other, "but if I join the church who'll weigh the coal?"

POOR LOCATION

On a little service station away out on the edge of a western desert there hangs a shingle bearing this strange legend: "Don't ask us for information. If we knew anything, we wouldn't be here."

FOOD FOR THOUGHT

A young matron entered a grocery in one of our large cities. The counters were filled with gorgeous fruits and vegetables of every kind.

"How much are your watermelons?" she asked the grocer.

"Two dollars each," he replied.

"And your peaches?"

"Seventy-five cents a basket."

"And how much are those lovely cherries?"

"Eighty cents a pound."

The inquiring customer turned slowly away, saying: "Isn't it a shame to put them out here where people can see them!"

HONEYMOON

Employee: "Please, sir, I'd like next week off if it's convenient."

Boss: "What's up?"

Employee: "My girl's going on her honeymoon and I'd like to go with her."

HE KNEW

The preacher was visiting a home and wanted to read a chapter from the Bible. The husband said to his little son:

"Bobby, go and get the Bible—you know, the big book we read so much."

So in a little while Bobby came in carrying the mail-order catalogue.

SALESMAN

A man went into a restaurant located near a depot. It was early in the morning. He sat down at one of the tables and near him sat a group of boys. A newsboy came in and yelled, "Paper! Paper!" One

of the boys said, "We can't read and we don't enjoy the pictures."
To which the newsboy replied, "Well, then, smell it. It's about half
baloney anyway."

ADVERTISING PAYS

From an English grave marker: "Sacred to the memory of Jonathan
Thompson, a pious Christian and affectionate husband. His disconso-
late widow continues his grocery business at the old stand on Main
Street and best prices in town."

This from a Maryland cemetery: "Here lies Jane Smith, wife of
Thomas Smith, marble cutter. This monument erected by her husband.
... Monuments of this same style are $250."   *The Presbyterian.*

TACT

An Army sergeant had made an outstanding reputation for himself
lecturing to enlisted men and non-commissioned officers on a certain
subject. His captain called him in and said he had done such a splendid job they were going to ask him to lecture to a special group.

When he walked into the lecture room to appear before this group,
he noticed there was not a man in the room who did not outrank him,
and it was the biggest collection of brass hats he had ever seen.

In a moment of embarrassment, while he tried to think of an appropriate beginning, he said modestly, "There are thousands of men
in the army who know this subject much better than I do." He hesitated for a moment, and knew that was the wrong thing to say, because, after all, he had been selected because of his particular ability.
Then he blurted out, "But I don't see any of them in this room."

THE AWAKENING

Tom J. McKearnan, head of the famous Moffett Studios in Chicago, tells another of those ubiquitous bride and bridegroom stories.

The first evening, after the newlyweds came back from their honeymoon, the husband came home to find his bride studiously going
through his bank books.

"Why darling," he cried, "this leads me to believe you might have
married me for my money."

"Don't be silly," the bride retorted. "I worship the very ground you walk on—and any other property you may acquire in the meantime." *Finance*.

CRAMMING

Two little girls were discussing their families. "Why does your grandmother read the Bible so much?" asked one.

"I think," said the other little girl, "that she is cramming for her finals." *Capper's Weekly*.

HE ANSWERED

Professor: "Why don't you answer me?"

Student: "I did, professor. I shook my head."

Professor: "But you don't expect me to hear it rattle way up here, do you?"

CONVINCING

Prosecutor: "Now tell the court how you came to take the car."

Defendant: "Well, the car was parked in front of the cemetery. So naturally I thought the owner was dead."

INFLATION

Judge: "Why did you steal that fifty thousand dollars?"

Accused (plaintively): "I was hungry."

GOOD REASON

He: "I wonder why a girl can't catch a ball like a man?"

She: "Oh, a man is so much bigger and easier to catch."

THINGS HAPPENED

"How was the wedding?" asked the preacher's wife.

"It was fine until I asked the bride if she would 'obey' and she said, 'Do you think I'm crazy?' The groom was in sort of a daze and mumbled, 'I do.' That's when things really began to happen," replied the preacher.

NO USE STUDYING?

The teacher was talking about the law of gravity. "Sir Isaac Newton," she explained, "was looking at an apple tree and an apple fell to the ground. And from that he discovered gravitation. Wasn't that marvelous?"

"Yes," answered a boy in the last row scornfully, "but if he had been settin' lookin' at books, he wouldn't have discovered nothin'."

NOT REAL

Saleslady: "Isn't it a sweet doll? Lay it down and it closes its eyes and goes to sleep just like a real baby."

Mother: "Hmm, I can see you don't know real babies."

WHY THE DELAY?

A merchant took out a fire-insurance policy and the same day his store burned to the ground. The insurance company suspected fraud, but couldn't prove anything. It had to content itself with writing the following letter:

"Dear Sir: You took out an insurance policy at 10 A.M. and your fire did not break out until 3:30 P.M. Will you kindly explain the delay?"

APPEARANCE

"I notice you put your biggest apples on top. Why?" asked the cynical customer.

"For the same reason you comb your longest hairs over your bald spot," replied the grocer grimly.

AN IDEA

Mrs.: "Did you tell her that what I told you was in strict confidence?"

Miss: "Certainly not. I didn't want her to think it was important enough for her to repeat."

HE'LL BE SORRY

Judge (in dentist's chair): "Do you swear to pull the tooth, the whole tooth and nothing but the tooth?"

EXPENSIVE INFORMATION

"Daddy, if you will give me a dime, I'll tell you what the ice man said to mamma."

"O.K., here's your dime."

"He said, 'Do you want any ice today, lady?' "

TOO CRUEL

"You naughty thing!" cried a little girl who saw a cat carrying a kitten by the nape of its neck. "You are not fit to be a mother! You're hardly fit to be a father."

IT SEEMED LIKE YESTERDAY

A Scot who had worn the same hat for 25 years decided with heavy heart to buy a new one. Going into the only shop in the neighborhood he said: "Well, here I am again."

NATURALLY

Teacher: "Can any bright pupil tell me why a man's hair turns gray quicker than his mustache?"

Pupil: "Sure, teacher. It's 'cause his hair has a twenty-year start on his mustache."

TOO CLOSE

"How close did it come to you?" asked the farmer, driving up to the tree where his hired man had taken shelter from an electrical storm. "Well," stammered the hired man, still excited, "I don't know, but my pipe wasn't lit before."

POLITENESS

Customer: "Why is it I never get what I ask for here?"

Waiter: "Perhaps, madam, we are too polite."

ANXIOUS

A blushing young woman handed the telegraph clerk a telegram containing only a name, address and one word—"yes."

Wishing to be helpful, the clerk said: "You know, you can send nine more words for the same price."

"I know I can," replied the young woman, "but don't you think I'd look too eager if I said it ten times?"

FUNDAMENTALS

"You're the biggest dumbbell I've ever had the misfortune to employ in my coal yard! I can't teach you a thing."

"Well," said Mike, "I've larnt wan thing since I've been with you."

"Yes? And what's that?" asked the employer.

"That sixteen hundred pounds make a ton."

He kept his job.

THEY WEAR WELL

Billie proudly announced to his teacher: "We've got a new baby and it cost $100."

"Goodness," the teacher replied. "Isn't that a lot of money for a tiny baby?"

"Yes, but think how long they last!"

BETTER OR WORSE

Business was a bit dull in town, so the carpet-sweeper salesman thought he'd try a rural neighborhood. When he began his sales talk the hillbilly interrupted with, "Don't waste your breath. I got a carpet sweeper."

The salesman was ready for his reply. "Good," he said. "Then I can make you a generous allowance on your old sweeper in part payment on a splendid new model."

The hillbilly seemed tempted, then shook his head. "No," he said, "I can't make that kind of a deal. After all, I took her for better or wuss."

A SECOND THOUGHT

Junk Man: "Any beer bottles today, lady?"

Lady: "Do I look as though I drank beer, sir!"

Junk Man: "Any vinegar bottles today, lady?"

HE WASN'T SELLING THEM

A house-hunter got off a train at a suburban station, and said to a boy standing near: "I'm looking for Mr. Brown's new block of brick houses. How far are they from here?"

"Twenty minutes' walk," said the boy.

"Twenty minutes!" exclaimed the prospective buyer. "Nonsense, the advertisement said five."

"Well," replied the boy, "you kin believe me or the advertisement, whichever you want. But I ain't trying to make no sale."

FORGETFUL

Private Jackson was on the carpet for the third time in as many days. The captain was very stern. "Did you call the sergeant a liar?" he demanded.

"I did, sir," admitted Jackson.

"And a louse?"

"Yes, sir."

"And did you also say he was a cock-eyed, knock-kneed, dirty-tongued stooge?"

Jackson hesitated, then said regretfully, "No, sir. I forgot that."

SMILE WHEN YOU SAY THAT

Hubby: "Darling, what's wrong? Why the bandage on your eye?"
Wife: "Don't be funny. This is my new hat."

THE REAL TEST

"Was your uncle sensible until the last?"
"I won't know until his will is read tomorrow."

BIASED

"Why don't you like girls?"
"They're too biased."
"Biased?"
"Yeh—buy us this, buy us that, until I'm broke."

AN EARLY SETTLER

Bystander: "I observe that you treat that gentleman respectfully."
Grocer: "Yes, he's one of our early settlers."
Bystander: "Early settler! Why, he can't be more than thirty years old."

Grocer: "That may be true, but he pays his bills on the first of every month."

A HARD LIFE

The Navy cook had just prepared orders of fried eggs for a mob of sailors. Wearied by his efforts, he sat down, yawned, lit a black cigar and wrote a letter to his sweetheart.

"Darling," he began, "for the past three hours shells have been bursting all around me."

ENOUGH

Little Johnny was telling his mother about the day in school. "Mother," he said, "today our teacher asked me whether I had any brothers or sisters, and I told her I was the only child."

"And what did she say?" asked his mother.

"She said, 'Thank goodness!' "

JUROR EXCUSED

A juryman asked the court to be excused, declaring: "I owe a man twenty-five dollars that I borrowed, and as he is leaving town today for some years I want to catch him before he gets to the train and pay him the money."

"You are excused," the judge announced in a cold voice. "I don't want anybody on the jury who can lie like you."

SOLD OUT

As the train pulled into the station, a traveler on the platform called to a boy and tossed him a coin. "Son," he said, "here's fifty cents. Get me a sandwich and get one for yourself."

Just as the train was pulling out, the boy returned to the platform where the passenger was waiting. "Here's your quarter, mister," he shouted. "They only had one sandwich."

TIRED

A farmer drove into town to visit his doctor. "Doc," he said, "the first time you're out our way I wish you'd stop in and see my wife." "Is she sick?" "Not exactly." "What's the trouble, then?" "Well, yesterday morning she got up at the regular time, about four o'clock, milked the cows, got breakfast for the hands, done her housework, churned, and along about ten o'clock at night she said she felt a bit tired. I expect she needs a tonic or something."

TO THE POINT

The cub reporter was told to cut his story to bare essentials. Following his orders he did so and produced one the next day:

"J. Smith looked up the elevator shaft to see if the car was on its way down. It was. Age 45."

HARD TO RECOGNIZE

"Is this the laundry?" the irritated customer shouted into the telephone. "Well, you sent me a batch of very old handkerchiefs instead of my shirt."

"Them ain't handkerchiefs," replied the laundry, "that's your shirt."

NO STOPPING

An ambitious young man asked a great merchant to reveal the secret of his success. "There is no secret," said the merchant. "Just jump at your opportunity."

"But," said the young man, "how can I tell when my opportunity is coming?"

"You can't," said the merchant. "You just have to keep jumping."

INSCRIBED

Little Herbert had bought Grandma a book for Christmas and wanted to write a suitable inscription on the flyleaf. He racked his brain, until suddenly he remembered that his father had a book with an inscription of which he was very proud. So Herbie decided to copy it.

You can imagine Grandma's surprise on Christmas morning when she opened her gift, a *Bible,* and found neatly inscribed the following phrase: "To Grandma, with the compliments of the Author."

HELPFUL SUGGESTION

"How did you lose your job at the dress shop, my dear?"

"Just because of something I said. After I had tried twenty dresses on a woman, she said, 'I think I'd look nicer in something flowing,' so I asked her why she didn't jump in the river."

NEVER FAILED

Passenger: "You'll bring me down safely, won't you?"

Pilot: "I've never left anyone up there yet."

SMART DOCTOR

Woman: "Doctor, is it true that sleeping outdoors will cure insomnia?"

Doctor: "Perfectly true. But sleeping indoors will do the same thing."

FOREVER

"Eternity is so vast—who can comprehend it?" said the speaker.

"Perhaps," said the little man in the back row, "you never bought anything on the monthly payment plan."

WHAT'S WRONG WITH HOLLYWOOD

A Hollywood film actress was applying for a passport.

"Unmarried?" asked the clerk.

"Occasionally," replied the actress.

SMART GUY

A wise guy stepping up to a bus as it stopped the other morning said to the driver: "Well, Noah, you've got here. Is the Ark full?"

The motorman answered back: "Nope, we need one more monkey. Come on in."

TO THE HEAD OF THE CLASS

Harold had taken his first dancing lesson. When he returned home his mother asked him how he liked it. "Why mother, it's easy," said Harold. "All you do is turn around and keep wiping your feet."

EXPERIENCE

In a college town a student called at a boarding house to ask about rooms.

"What do you charge for your rooms?" he asked.

"Five dollars up," was the reply.

"But I'm a student," he said, thinking the price a little high.

"That being the case, the price is $5 down," replied the landlady, who had had experience.

SAVES TIME

Older Woman: "I have my husband trained so he eats out of my hand."

Young Bride: "Saves a lot of dishwashing, doesn't it?"

HE WILL LEARN

"How come you didn't turn out?" demanded the sergeant. "Didn't you hear the bugle blow reveille?"

"Honest, Sergeant, I'm afraid I'm going to be a flop as a soldier. I don't know one tune from another."

REASONABLE

Bridge Player: "Does your husband complain about getting his dinner so late?"

Other Bridge Player: "Oh, no. He just complains about having to get it."

SOUNDS LOGICAL

Pat, a truck driver, stopped suddenly on the highway. The car behind crashed into the truck and its owner sued the Irishman.

"Why didn't you hold out your hand?" the judge asked Pat.

"Well," he said indignantly, "if he couldn't see the truck, how in hivin's name could he see my hand?"

LINE IS BUSY

Bill: "I haven't spoken to my wife in weeks!"

Sam: "Whassa matter? Mad at her?"

Bill: "Nope. I'm afraid to interrupt her!"

FATHER KNEW

Her Father: "What? She's consented to marry you? Young man, you're the second-happiest man in the world."

PATIENCE

Husband: "You will never succeed in making that dog obey you."

Wife: "Nonsense. It is only a matter of patience. I had a lot of trouble with you at first."

WORRYING

"You sho' does look worried."

"Boy, I'se booked up solid on worrying. I'se got so many worries on my mind that if sumpin' happens to me today, Ah won't get time to worry about it foh two weeks."

SIMPLE

First Aid Instructor: "How would you rescue a man from drowning?"

Eager Pupil: "That's easy. First you take the man out of the water, and then you take the water out of the man."

FIFTY-FIFTY

One of the boys who just got back from a southern trip tells how he heard a couple of colored fellows talking about a divorce one of them had just received.

"An' what about dat house you an' your woman got?" asked the friend of the lately liberated chap. "What you do wid dat, huh?"

"We splits it up—fifty-fifty."

"Divides yo' house? How you do dat?"

"Fifty-fifty. Ah takes de outside, she takes de inside."

HE FIXED IT

Husband: "When anything goes wrong around our house, I just get busy and fix it."

Wife: "Yeah? Since you fixed the clock, the cuckoo backs out and asks: 'What time is it?' "

TROUBLE SLEEPING

During a conversation with an old friend he hadn't seen for some time, a Florida farmer asked how he had been sleeping.

"I sleep good nights," he said, "and I sleep pretty good mornings, but afternoons I just seem to twist and turn."

HIGH PRICE OF MEAT

Farmer: "You can't go wrong on this mare, sir. She's sound, gentle, a good worker and a fine saddle horse."

City Slicker: "What I want to know, is she tender?"

SINKS ON PURPOSE

A Negro was asked if he wouldn't like to volunteer for submarine duty.

To this the gangling, good-natured boy replied: "No, suh. I don't want to get on no ship that sinks on purpose."

INCOME TAX

Some day a tax return may contain only three questions:

How much money have you got?

Where is it?

How soon can you get at it?

BEST YEARS

They were having one of those dandy marital arguments and the little woman was getting to the tearful stage. "How can you talk to me like that," she wailed, "after I've given you the best years of my life?"

"Yeah?" returned the husband, unimpressed by her emotion. "And who made 'em the best years of your life?"

BOYHOOD DREAM

Lawyer: "As a boy I always wanted to be a pirate."

Businessman: "You're lucky—not everyone gets to realize his boyhood ambition."

STEALING

Husband: "If a man steals—no matter what—he will live to regret it."

Wife: "You used to steal kisses."

Husband: "Well, you heard what I said."

BOUGHT AND PAID FOR

Joan, 5, out to tea, was puzzled when she saw the family bow their heads for grace.

"What are you doing?" she said.

"Giving thanks for our daily bread," she was told. "Don't you give thanks at home, Joan?"

"No," said Joan, "we pay for our bread."

MISUNDERSTOOD

Customer: "Give me a pound of those grapes. My husband is fond of them. Do you know if they have been sprayed with any kind of poison?"

Clerk: "No, ma'am; you'll have to get that at the drugstore."

HIRED HIM

Among the questions asked in the examination of an applicant for a place on the Washington police force was this one: "What would you do to disperse a crowd quickly and quietly?"

The answer: "I'd pass the hat."

WRONG IDEA

She: "Did anyone ever tell you how wonderful you are?"

He: "No, I don't think anyone ever did."

She: "Then I'd like to know how and where you got the idea?"

WRONG BUSINESS

"I feel sure, my poor man," said the sympathetic old lady, visiting a state prison, "it was poverty that brought you to this."

"No, ma'am, quite the contrary," returned the prisoner. "I happened to be coining money."

SPECIAL SERVICE

"I ordered a dozen oranges, but you sent me only ten."

"Part of our special service, madam. Two were bad, so we threw them away for you."

COMPLETE INFORMATION

The junior member of a firm of lawyers went several hundred miles to consult a client. When he arrived, he found he had forgotten his client's name. He telegraphed his partner, "What is our client's name?"

The answer came: "Jones, Joseph H. Yours is Kent, Jasper T."

GUILTY

Conscientious Citizen: "I couldn't serve as a juror, Judge. One look at that fellow convinces me he's guilty."

Judge: "Quiet. That's the district attorney."

MARRIED LIFE

Young Actor: "I've got a job at last, father. It's a new play and I'm a man who has been married twenty years."

Father: "Splendid. That's a start anyway, my boy. Maybe some of these days they'll give you a 'speaking' part."

COLD

Two mountaineers were complaining about the cold. "Nearest I ever came to freezing," said one, "was when I was holding the lantern for my wife while she cut the kindling."

THERE IS A DIFFERENCE

Old Lady (afraid of passing her destination, poking the car conductor with her umbrella): "Is that the First National Bank?"

Conductor: "No, madam, them's my ribs."

HE HAD THE ANSWER

The teacher had forbidden the eating of candy and the chewing of gum during school time. One day she became suspicious of a lump in Jimmie's cheek.

"Jimmie, are you eating candy or are you chewing gum?" she asked. "No, ma'am," replied Jimmie. "I'm just soaking a prune to eat at recess."

AN OLD ONE BUT GOOD

A Harvard man enlisted in the United States Army as a private. He had been in service only a few weeks when his captain posted a notice on the bulletin board. The Harvard man read it and sniffed.

"It is pretty hard," he told another soldier, "to take orders from a man who knows no better than to end a sentence with a preposition."

The captain overheard him. Next day the bulletin carried this notice: "There is in this company a certain amount of insubordination up with which I shall not put."

GOOD OBSERVATION

A city boy and a country lad were walking down a street. Coming toward them was a product of the beauty parlor—permanent wave, scarlet fingernails, drugstore complexion and gaudy lipstick.

"Now what do you think of that?" asked the city boy.

The farm boy looked carefully and observed: "Speaking as a farmer, I should say that it must have been mighty poor soil to require so much top-dressing."

IN TEXAS

A Harvard professor, traveling deep in the heart of Texas, found himself seated next to a Texas cowboy and fell into conversation with him. The Texan confessed to 87 years of age, whereupon the professor said: "To what do you attribute your remarkable longevity?"

The Texan thought a moment and answered gravely: "Well, I never stole a horse and I never called a man a liar to his face."

SALESMAN

Customer: "You don't seem quick at figures, my boy."

Newsie: "I'm out of practice, sir. Most people say, 'Keep the change.'"

BASEBALL

A country girl attended her first ball game. After watching the entire game she met one of the players. In her sweet little way she asked, "Why does the fellow behind the plate wear the muzzle when it's the one with the big stick in his hand that does all the growling?"

PENNY AND DOLLAR

The dollar, with his nose turned up scornfully, said to the penny: "Why, I am worth one hundred of you." "Yes," said the penny, "but even at that I am a good deal better than you. I go to Sunday school and church, both. You don't show up at either one."

HANDLE WITH CARE

"Sorry to hear your engagement is broken off, old man."

"I'll get over it. But the worst blow was when she returned my ring marked 'Glass—Handle With Care.' "

BE CAREFUL!

Bill: "How do you like this rainy weather?"

Joe: "It's terrible."

Bill: "And how's your wife?"

Joe: "Oh, about the same."

AN EXAMPLE OF UNDERSTATEMENT

A Texas banker, in order to impress one of his friends in one of the Eastern banks with the magnitude of the Lone Star State, forwarded to him this classic:

Texas occupies all of the continent of North America except a small portion set aside for Canada, the United States and Mexico. Texas owns the north half of the Rio Grande, the only dusty river in the world, and the only one which is navigable by pedestrians.

Texas is so big that the people in Brownsville call the Fort Worth people Yankees and the citizens of El Paso sneer at the residents of Texarkana as being snobs of the effete East. It is 150 miles farther from El Paso to Texarkana than it is from Chicago to New York. The United States with Texas left out would look like a three-legged Boston terrier.

Unless your front gate is at least 18 miles from your front

door, you do not belong to society as constituted in Texas. Down at the King Ranch the gate is 150 miles from the front door. Other Texas landlords have whole mountain ranges and rivers on their ranches. One Texan has 40 miles of navigable river on his farm.

If the proportion of cultivated land in Texas were the same as that in Illinois, the value of Texas crops would equal that of the other 47 states combined. *Finance.*